perfect pairings

perfect pairings

A Master Sommelier's Practical Advice
for Partnering Wine with Food

EVAN GOLDSTEIN
With recipes by Joyce Goldstein
Photographs by Joyce Oudkerk Pool

University of California Press
Berkeley Los Angeles London

University of California Press, one of the most distinguished university presses in the United States, enriches lives around the world by advancing scholarship in the humanities, social sciences, and natural sciences. Its activities are supported by the UC Press Foundation and by philanthropic contributions from individuals and institutions. For more information, visit www.ucpress.edu.

University of California Press
Berkeley and Los Angeles, California

University of California Press, Ltd.
London, England

Design by Nola Burger
Photography by Joyce Oudkerk Pool
    with the assistance of Jami Witherspoon
Food styling by Pouké
    with the assistance of Jeffrey Larsen
Prop styling by Carol Hacker/Tableprop
Copyediting by Erika Büky and Laura Meyn
Indexing by Patricia Deminna

Text type: 10.25/14 Chaparral
Display type: Univers and Univers Ultra Condensed
Composition: Integrated Composition Systems
Printing and binding: Friesens

Library of Congress Cataloging-in-Publication Data
Goldstein, Evan.
    Perfect pairings : a master sommelier's practical advice for partnering wine with food / Evan Goldstein ; with recipes by Joyce Goldstein.
        p.   cm.
    Includes bibliographical references and index.
    ISBN 0-520-24377-3 (cloth : alk. paper)
    1. Cookery.   2. Wine and wine making.   I. Goldstein, Joyce Esersky.   II. Title.
TX714.G648 2006
641.2'2—dc22   2005025771

Manufactured in Canada

15   14   13   12   11   10   09   08   07   06
10   9   8   7   6   5   4   3   2   1

CONTENTS

RECIPES

Photos follow page 118

GEWÜRZTRAMINER

Cheese Fondue 111

Savory Meat Strudel 113

Salmon with Spiced Onions and Currants 115

Duck with Orange Sauce 117

VIOGNIER

Ginger and Orange Fried Chicken 124

Halibut with Orange and Mint Salsa Verde 126

Brazilian Fish and Shellfish Stew 128

Moroccan Lamb Tagine with Raisins, Almonds, and Honey 130

red wines

CABERNET SAUVIGNON

Steak au Poivre 140

Spanish Lamb Ragout with Roasted Sweet Peppers 142

Lamb Steaks with Greek-Inspired Tomato Sauce 144

Coffee- and Pepper-Rubbed Rib Roast 146

MERLOT

Roast Cornish Hens Stuffed with Pork and Prunes 153

Tuna with Rosemary and Citrus Tapenade 155

Catalan Bean and Sausage Stew with Mint 157

Mediterranean Vegetable Ragout on a Bed of Polenta 159

PINOT NOIR

Pork Loin Glazed with Pomegranate and Orange 168

Stuffed Roasted Squab 170

Salmon with Soy, Ginger, and Sake 172

Lamb Shish Kebabs 174

SANGIOVESE

Italian Meatball and Vegetable Soup 181

Roast Leg of Lamb with Olives and Orange 183

Osso Buco with Mushrooms and Tomatoes 185

Rustic Paella 187

SYRAH

Moroccan Lamb Barbecue 195

Duck with Sausage and Lentils 197

Pork Chili Verde 199

Korean Short Ribs 201

ZINFANDEL

Seared Tuna with Rosemary, Garlic, and Hot Pepper 209

Pasta with Artichokes, Pancetta, Mushrooms, and Peas 211

Brazilian Feijoada 214

Barbecued Chicken Sandwiches 216

dessert wines

Hazelnut Torte with Coffee Buttercream 232

Citrus Marmalade Tart 235

Lemony Ricotta Soufflé Cake with Raspberry Sauce 238

Caramel-Coated Cream Puffs 240

Coconut Panna Cotta with Mango Sauce 243

Tartufo Budino 245

ACKNOWLEDGMENTS

Most wine and food pairings are a confluence of diverse influences, and so is this book. During its creation, countless people have been inspirational and motivational, while others have been patient and tolerant. And many, truly those to whom I am most thankful, have been all those things.

I thank my wife, Barbara, for her unequivocal love and support, for her discriminating palate, and for reminding me with frequency that it's *only* fermented grape juice; my daughter, Elena, whose ability to discern today's apple juice from yesterday's at age three still dwarfs any of my gustatory accomplishments; and my son, Adam, whose love of food and request to attend cooking classes at age seven was heartwarming to his dad and a source of family pride.

I thank my mother, Joyce, without whose passion for food, wine, and all things of a sensual nature I'd likely still be trying to make it as a struggling rock-and-roll drummer, and whose recipes grace this book and make it far better than it would be without them; my sisters, Karen and Rachel, whose palates are better than mine; and my father, Marc, who, in spite of recognizing and appreciating gourmet cuisine, would be far happier with a grilled-cheese sandwich, made with real American cheese!

I express my profuse thanks to the team at the University of California Press: my editor, Blake Edgar, whose support and belief in this project made it happen; Nola Burger and Nicole Hayward for their design prowess; Dore Brown, Erika Büky, and Chalon Emmons for their perspective and assistance with the text; and Jenny Wapner and Matthew Winfield for keeping the engine humming.

I also thank my agents, Eric and Maureen Lasher, and my indispensable right hand during this project, Christie Dufault, who organized the tastings, kept copious notes on the hundreds of wines we tasted, provided balanced opinions, and kept the devil out of the details!

Appreciative gratitude goes out to all the producers, importers, and winemakers who shared their wines, souls, and personal artistry.

And finally there are my peers and friends, who collectively have influenced me more than they will ever know. Among them are Nunzio Alioto, Stephen Brauer, Sam Bronfman II, Val Brown, Fred Dame, Gilles Deschamps, Barbara Ensrud, Doug Frost, Joël Girodot, Diana Goldstein, Peter Granoff, Daniel Hallé, Mike Holden, Chet Hutchinson, Brian Julyan, Masa Kobayashi, Danny Kopelson, Nick Lander, Barbara Lang, Erika Lenkert, Bob Long, Chris Lynch, Karen MacNeil, Danny Meyer, Bill Newlands, Steve Olson, Ronn Owens, Kathleen and Michel Rege, Andrea Immer Robinson, Jancis Robinson, David Rosengarten, Leslie Sbrocco, Ab Simon, Harvey Steiman, Madeline Triffon, Paul Wagner, Alice Waters, Josh Wesson, Wilfred Wong, Mary Ann Worobiec-Bovio, Kevin Zraly, and the late, great Gerard Jaboulet.

INTRODUCTION

Numerous books on wine, and wine and food pairing, have been written over the years. And many stories have been told about the moonlike surface of Châteauneuf du Pape and that magical bottle of Rioja Gran Reserva that paired so seamlessly with an unbelievable meal at Restaurant XYZ. But while there is a lot of excellent writing about wine, food, and the synergy between them, much of it has actually missed most of "us."

"Us" I define as Joe and Mary America-at-Table: people who really enjoy wine, and wine with food, but don't have the inclination or the time to learn the language of wine specialists. They (or we) are people who simply want to celebrate the simple pleasures of tasty food, drink delicious wine, enjoy the company of family and friends sharing a meal, and have a way to think and talk about what "worked" in an enjoyable combination of wine and food.

Over the years I have found that most individuals do want some guidance and useful information and are curious about wine but don't want to have to take a class or pore over a reference book before going to their local wine store or supermarket to shop for food and drink. This group includes me. Having spent many of my formative years hanging out with friends and family and appreciating the pleasures that good, unpretentious wine and food can bring to the table, I can't spend too much time with people who are sooooo serious about wine and food that the planning of all their vacations is based on traipsing about wine regions and special restaurants. Nor do I buy into the belief that the enjoyment of wine depends on the exclusive consumption of wines scoring ninety points or above on somebody's scale or costing the equivalent of a second mortgage.

Much of the world's quality wine is being discussed and consumed in a vacuum. Horizontal tastings of Riesling across geography, verticals of Chateau Doesn't-That-Impress-You, and samplings of the latest and greatest release of Evan's "Acme Vineyard" Zinfandel are, for the most part, served, judged, and revered in isolation—in the complete absence of anything resembling food. And although the "wine and food thing" has been on the rise over the past few decades, and more and more people are expressing an interest in learning about it, most of them feel as if they are on the outside and do not really know where to begin.

That's where I hope this book can be of use. Over the last twenty-plus years and in varying professional capacities, I have taught well in excess of twenty-five thousand people about wine, food, and the enjoyment of both. Along the way I have discovered that people want to know what wines are "like" (dry or sweet, tannic or not tannic, what style they're made in, and so forth), how they taste, and, finally, what foods they pair best with. That's about as far as most of us want to take it. Some get deeper into the subject, but they are in the minority.

Intriguingly, however, even these relatively wine- and culinaria-obsessed folks confide that there is not much out there that covers the pairing of wine and food—why and how they work together. For those people, it is my intention to provide solid, nuanced information. In collaborating with the renowned chef Joyce Goldstein (aka Mom) in developing and exploring particular recipes tailored to different types of wine, my aim has been to create a forum in which both the wine buffs and the foodies feel comfortable and included in this book's broader audience. It's a risky but deliberate strategy.

Many authors make wine and food pairing much more complicated than it needs to be. I believe that if you have to think too deeply, it's simply not worth it. A better goal is to reach a personal comfort zone of wine and food in which you can decide effortlessly whether it's the wine or the food that will drive a particular dining experience. Whether you choose the wine first and pick compatible recipes, or choose your menu first and then the wine to accompany it, you will ultimately find pairing as intuitive and natural as breathing.

So read on—there's something here for everyone. For the novice or the more experienced wine lover, the professional wine and food geek, or the weekend "let's-try-this-wine-with-this-dish" warrior, *Perfect Pairings* can help.

And always remember, as we say at my house, if you don't like the wine you selected, you can always run downstairs or to the fridge and pick out something else!

HOW TO USE THIS BOOK

This book is designed to be a practical and easy-to-use guide for learning about wines and their styles and how to pair them with food. The flow is logical, beginning with an introduction on how to taste wines with thought and increasing discernment. The goal of this section is to provide you with some coaching and direction that will help you discover a thoughtful approach toward wine tasting and evaluation and develop a more confident palate.

Once we've established a wine comfort zone, the next section of the book explores cooking for and with wine and how recipes and ingredients can influence the choice of wine to accompany a meal. This section, which includes opinions, pointers, and discussion of a few wine-friendly foods and their tricks, seeks to (as the title of my son's first-grade reading development book eloquently put it) "explode the code." Here, that means addressing and at times challenging the orthodoxies of wine and food philosophy (for instance, the idea that you must *always* serve red wine with meat and white wine with fish).

The heart of the book is the separate chapters looking at twelve varietals (grape types), along with sparkling wines and dessert wines, each exploring the *where* (where the grapes are from and the wines are made), the *how* (how they are interpreted and produced to define their style), and the *what* (what they taste like). Finally, we consider what you need to bear in mind when cooking to accompany the specific styles of each wine.

Each varietal chapter concludes with a selection of recipes that have been created specially for this book to highlight particular interpretations and styles of the given wine. Each recipe is followed by comments from Joyce and me about the rationale behind the dish and its pairing with the wine. In the Chardonnay chapter, for example, I discuss four acknowledged and readily available styles of Chardonnay: oak-aged and influenced by malolactic fermentation, European and mineral-scented, explosive and tropical-fruit-packed, and aged/mature and nutty. We've developed dishes that highlight each of these styles. Every varietal chapter also includes a lexicon of tasting descriptors associated with that varietal and recommendations of producers who make wines that are representative of their regions and geographies in different price categories.

To round out the book, we present several menus that are mixed and matched from the book's recipes to create fun and educational dining events. *Perfect Pairings* is interspersed with tips, useful pointers, and a "cheat sheet" to reinforce and summarize key points. It concludes with a glossary of everyday wine terminology that will help you understand more about how wines are made and how they are described.

Throughout this book I encourage experimentation. Whether you choose to do informal wine tastings to learn about grapes, wines, styles, and geographies or to create delicious meals to further your learning and pleasure, it's all about fun, enjoyment, and what works best for you. Remember that, ultimately, what gives you the most happiness along the wine and food journey is all that matters.

So, let's move on to the basics of tasting.

TASTING AND ENJOYING WINE

Nobody is born with a wine palate. As nobody consumes Merlot as mother's milk, wine appreciation is completely learned. Learning to enjoy and to discriminate among wines is an acquired taste or skill and one for which everybody, regardless of level of perceived sophistication, is entitled to his or her own opinions.

Think about it. As my friend Steve Olson once put it, on the day you figure out you can spit out the strained spinach and have seconds on mashed bananas, taste opinions are born. Your point of view ultimately determines your wine preferences. I want to help you learn to feel comfortable saying, "Delicious!" or "Blech!" and to understand why you have the preferences that you do. Once you know something about a wine's background—the grape type, characteristic flavors, region of origin, production style, and so on—you'll know what to expect from your first sip.

The idea of wine evaluation is implicitly bizarre. No other consumer product causes such paralysis by analysis. Certainly we do not experience angst when shopping for soda, mineral water, shampoo, or chocolate-chip cookies! Although wine is no longer the exclusive domain of the so-called wine snobs, people are nevertheless intimidated by the variables and complexities of this magic beverage.

Learning wine appreciation is much like training for running a marathon: you have to temper your initial expectations. Wine lovers aren't born overnight but are formed with focused practice, best accompanied by the feedback, company, and direction of someone whose palate they trust and respect. Eventually you'll experience a moment when the lightbulb goes on. For me it was listening to dining-room babble while sipping a red Burgundy at Thanksgiving when I was about sixteen years old. The wine's complexity and layering of flavor all of a sudden made sense, and, as a reminder of that day, I still have the empty bottle, displayed with many others along the walls of my dining room.

Wine evaluation or tasting is a series of cross-references, with tastes framed against past experience. Once you've tried twenty or thirty Zinfandels, your palate will begin to recognize a basic varietal character linking those different bottles. With the recognition of that varietal "signature," you can taste each successive Zinfandel against that standard and give it the yea or nay vote.

It's always helpful and informative to taste more than one wine so that you can compare. How can we find out what we prefer if not through comparison? Tasting two or three wines side by side is a great way to learn.

SAMPLING WITH ALL YOUR SENSES

With a little discipline, you can enjoy tasting wine and learn quickly. If you don't employ a systematic approach, you'll lose the benefit of context and your growing personal experience and perception.

In wine evaluation, we make use of all the senses:

Sight: The appearance of a wine is often overlooked, but it's packed with information.

Smell: Most evaluation is done through aroma analysis.

Taste: It's overrated in the evaluation process but still essential.

Touch: Wine possesses tactile qualities, such as body and texture, that are critical to enjoyment and understanding.

Hearing, too, in the figurative sense—listening to what the wine has to say—is also an evaluative step!

SIGHT

The appearance of a wine provides information about the wine's quality and age. With experience you can sense, literally at a glance, how a wine was vinified (or made) and from what type of grape or grapes it was produced. Wines that have spent a long time aging in an oak barrel may look deeper and richer than those that have not. This contrast would be obvious in a side-by-side comparison of current releases of a barrel-fermented Chardonnay with one that was fermented in a stainless-steel vat. Wines of different grapes display different hues: a lightly pigmented, cherry-colored Pinot Noir contrasts dramatically with an inky black Zinfandel, for example.

Examine the wine against a neutral background. A sheet of white paper or a white shirtsleeve will do fine. Avoid tinted backgrounds that will distort the wine's appearance. Ample light is critical, and natural light is far better than incandescent. Tilt the glass away from you and look across the surface of the wine. Compare the color at the rim of the glass with the color in the center. The difference, referred to as *rim variation*, is more common in red wines than in whites.

ROSÉ AND BLUSH WINES

A rose is a rose, except when it's a . . . rosé! While rosé wines come in varied types, the best examples are made from red grapes. When pressed, all grapes run with clear juice; it is during the process of alcoholic fermentation that color is bled (the French call this process *saigner*) from the skins. The color of wine made from red grapes progresses from clear to blush to rosé to red. If the skins are removed when the liquid reaches a rosé color, the resulting wine will share characteristics with both reds and whites: mild red-wine flavors with a chillable white wine personality. Rosés should be served at a slightly warmer temperature than whites, however; an ideal temperature is around 55 degrees.

Dry rosés can be refreshing alternatives to light- or medium-bodied white wines. The grapes most commonly employed in dry rosés include Grenache, Carignan, Mourvedre, Cabernet Sauvignon, and Cabernet Franc. Pinot Noir lends itself to a lovely rosé still wine (often called *vin gris*), which can be quite enjoyable for warm-weather drinking. *Vin gris* and other dry blushes and rosés are delicious with fish, fowl, white meats, grains and pasta, and summer produce.

However, not all blush or rosé wines are dry. Off-dry examples such as white Zinfandel, blush Merlot, and Rosé d'Anjou (made from Cabernet Sauvignon and Cabernet Franc in the Loire Valley's Anjou region) can easily take the place of a Riesling or Chenin Blanc. These wines, which should be served somewhere between 45 and 50 degrees, are excellent with ketchup-slathered burgers, aromatic curries, spicy Asian fare, and sweet barbecue sauce. Production methods for off-dry rosés vary; many are mass produced, and grapes are blended to achieve the desired color and sweetness profile.

Generally, the more the layers of color change from the center of the glass to the edge, the older the wine is likely to be.

The wine at the center of the glass should look bright rather than milky, hazy, or anemic. Although unfined and unfiltered wines are fashionable today and can be dull in appearance, most wines will reflect light and display brilliance; these are signs of quality production. Wines shouldn't exhibit effervescence; the exceptions are sparkling wines (obviously), young whites that may retain a bit of youthful spritz, and specific interpretations of whites and even reds that, by design, may impart a prickle to the tongue. Identify the color of the wine with descriptors that are meaningful to *you*. One person's straw yellow is another's light sunflower. Does the color make contextual sense? Remember that red wines fade and lose color as they age, whereas white wines darken and intensify in hue. If a producer's new release of Cabernet Sauvignon is a faded mahogany brown, there's likely a problem. But if a friend at home pulls out a well-stored ten-year-old Chardonnay that still appears youthful in color, this, of course, is good!

Take note of the depth of color of the wine. Generally, wines that are deeper and more saturated in hue will have more muscle and oomph, while those less intense in color will be lighter and more elegant. Although color is no guarantee of quality, it will give you a sense of what to expect from the wine: a full or light body, powerful or delicate flavors.

Finally, swirl the wine to examine the so-called tears, or legs. Swirl the glass and note how liquid rivulets form and run down the inside of the glass from the apex of the "swirl line." The speed at which the tears form and run down the side of the glass can tell you something about the wine's personality and body, but, again, they are not an indication of quality. The rule of thumb is straightforward: the slower the formation and fall of the tears, the higher the alcoholic content or sugar in the wine. Thus richer, full-bodied wines tear more slowly than lighter wines; and, in general, warmer-climate wines (most reds, for example) will tear more slowly than cooler-climate wines (whites). The tears of sweet wines, with their higher sugar content, fall

WINE AGE AND COLOR

	WHITE	ROSÉ	RED
YOUNG	Water white Green/silver Straw	Pink Salmon Deep pink	Black Blue Purple
MIDLIFE	Yellow Yellow/gold Gold	Orange Copper Rose-gold	Red Garnet Red/brown/tawny
MATURE	Yellow-brown/gold-brown Caramel/toffee Brown	Tawny Light amber Brown	Mahogany Amber Brown

more slowly than most others. If you find in your initial swirl that the tears aren't forming, swirl several more times. As when you season a pan, you need to create a thin coating of wine on the glass for the tears to form.

SMELL

Most information about a wine is discerned in the nose, *not* in the mouth. Most of what we think of as taste is actually what we smell. When your nasal passages are congested with colds or allergies and you can barely breathe through your nose, you can barely taste anything at all. Fillet of sole tastes the same as chicken. It's essential to spend time sniffing and reflecting on the wine's aroma. Professionals will tell you that about 75 percent of their evaluation time is spent analyzing the aromas of a wine.

As with looking at wine, smelling it is a learned skill. Several short, sharp sniffs are more efficient than one big inhalation. The nose is a very sensitive instrument, one that fatigues quickly and should not be overworked. By swirling the wine in the glass, you increase the surface area and the wine's exposure to air and thus deepen the aromatic impact. I always recommend picking up the glass, smelling the wine statically, and then swirling it and going back for a second sniff. Cupping your hand over the glass will further amplify the aroma.

First make certain that the wine smells clean—free of faults. Wine should smell like wine, not vinegar, rotten eggs, or roadkill. If in doubt, ask for an opinion from someone else. Second, the description on the label should match what you get in the nose and subsequently the glass. If the label says it's a rich, smooth, and chocolaty Cabernet Sauvignon and what you smell is a bitter, sharp, and austere wine, something's wrong. The initial scents of wine are largely fruit-driven. Yes, wine sometimes actually smells like grapes, as a grapey Grenache-based wine or Gamay Beaujolais will do. Most, however, smell fruity but not grapey per se. That's to say we smell fruit other than grapes. For example, Chardonnay can put forth aromas of lemon, apple and even pineapple. This may sound surreal to the novice wine drinker (it's grape juice, right?), but if the aroma is not obvious and if a wine's not *speaking* to you, close your eyes and free-associate. Think of it as going to the science museum and trying to identify the aroma of the mystery vials laid out to explain our olfactory system. And remember, one person's lemon is another's grapefruit, so don't obsess about nailing the exact descriptors, because a given wine will have a wide variety of aromas.

Some wines will display earthiness, or what wine folks often refer to as *terroir*. It's an all-encompassing term that is commonly and erroneously referred to as the taste of the earth (or dirt). It's far more than that: *terroir* includes the effects of soil composition, drainage, slope, weather, and sun exposure, among other factors. *Terroir* is most commonly associated with traditionally produced Western European wines. A great German Riesling may hint at dry slate and petrol, or a classic red Barolo may remind you of black truffle and parched earth. These are not, of course, additives to the wines but rather characteristics that express themselves more noticeably in cool climates (such as central or northern France) than in warm ones (such as southern Australia or central California). Although the term has snob appeal, *terroir* is neither good nor bad. It simply is. You sense it as both aroma and taste. In wines where *terroir* is profound, the fruit is usually more subdued, and vice versa. Distinctive *terroir* aromas are generally obvious and become easier to discern with experience. Try a classically interpreted European wine alongside its American or Australian counterpart, and the difference becomes clear: for example, a French red Bordeaux's minerally *terroir* can be readily distinguished from a Napa Valley Cabernet Sauvignon's fruit-forward nature.

Many wines are aged in oak barrels (known as *barriques*), which can impart aromas and flavors. Most classic, small wine barrels are traditionally coopered by heating and bending the wooden staves over fire; the resulting charring of the staves affects the flavor of the wine. In whites, you may detect aromas of caramel, vanilla, toast, cinnamon, or other sweet spices. In reds, the nuances are more likely to be chocolate, smoke, toast, coffee, and, again, vanilla and sweet spices.

As you smell, you develop initial insights into the wine's personality. Tartness in wine (its acidity) can be estimated by salivation. If you are very sensitive to acidity, smelling a sharp white wine such as a young Pinot Grigio can make you salivate in the same way that placing a lemon slice directly under your nose will do. Nasally detected bitterness, especially in ample red wines, may indicate the presence of tannins, naturally occurring compounds in red wines that produce a gritty, chalky sensation, similar to the astringent effect of strong black tea. Alcohol, which may come off as a hot or slightly burning sensation in the top of the nose, can be evident and provides a clue as to the richness or body of the wine. Fuller-bodied wines are by definition higher in alcohol and may prickle your nose. Compare a sniff of wine with one of vodka, gin, or whiskey to get an exaggerated example of this burning sensation.

TASTE AND TOUCH

As you may have gathered by now, I believe that tasting (from an evaluative standpoint) is overrated. Once you've made comprehensive visual and olfactory assessments of the wine, the tasting serves merely to confirm your observations. Of course, there are certain attributes that can be evaluated best through tasting, but, by and large, appearance and aroma will give you a clear sense of the wine. For me, the primary reason for actual tasting is the enjoyment.

In tasting, the key is ensuring that you take in enough to evaluate. Many people sip wine like coffee, covering about 15 percent of their taste buds, and not thoroughly coating the mouth for maximum appreciation and evaluation. So sip amply! Some people like to slurp the wine; this, like swirling the wine in the glass, incorporates extra air into the wine. "Chewing" the wine to move it around in your mouth can also be helpful.

The ultimate yardstick in tasting is overall balance. Do all of the components come together seamlessly? Individual characteristics shouldn't stick out: too much oak, too much alcohol, sugar, or acidity.

Everything hinges on the acidity or tartness of the wine. Rate it on a one-to-ten scale. If flat water is a zero and liquid electricity is a ten, we're looking for a five to seven in the mouth, depending on the wine. A wine with an acidity of less than five will seem flabby or watery in the mouth. White wines, which generally come from cooler climates and have an acidity rating of five to nine, are usually sharper than reds, which need sun and warmer climates to ripen the grapes (and typically rate between five and seven). Next, note whether the wine is dry to the taste, off-dry (exhibiting a slight sweetness), or perceptibly sweet in style (like a dessert wine). Is that acidity level appropriate for the wine? Is a dry wine too sharp? Is a dessert wine cloyingly sweet? Either of those impressions could well be perceived in an out-of-balance wine: one is too acidic and the other not acidic enough.

A wine's body or texture is directly related to the amount of alcohol it contains. Lighter-bodied wines are less alcoholic (7 to 10 percent alcohol), while a fuller-bodied wine will have ample alcohol (13 to 16 percent). Again, is there enough acidity to balance the alcohol? Too little, and the wine will come off in your mouth as clunky and heavy, like a Christmas tree drooping under the weight of too many ornaments. Texture, too, is important. We can speak of a wine as having a silky or smooth mouthfeel (especially if it's been in oak and has slightly more alcohol), or being lean or austere, or somewhere in between.

The flavors will generally be consistent with what you picked up in your nose, though you may discover a few additional flavors in the mouth. Last, measure the finish or persistence of the wine. How long do the flavors linger in the mouth after you swallow? The longer the finish, the better the wine is said to be. Good wines have a ten- to thirty-second finish, the best wines linger even longer. Acidity is again critical, as it "pushes" through the finish as a big wave brings a bodysurfer in to shore. Wines that are deficient in acidity are often described as short or thin.

OVERALL EVALUATION

Once you have swirled, looked, sniffed, and tasted, you are in a position to make a judgment on the wine. It's empowering, as you become more experienced, to decide that a wine is bad or simply not to your taste. There are plenty of wonderful bottles out there that may not please *you*. By the same token, as you become more seasoned and comfortable with your palate and judgment, you become less dependent on the opinions of others. This should be your long-term goal, for wine, like art, is a personal taste. After all, you have the right to walk into the Louvre and give the Mona Lisa an 89- or even a 75-point score. Why not?

STORAGE, SERVING TEMPERATURE, AND GLASSWARE

A number of my winemaker friends lament that once their wine has left the winery, it may travel a rough road to the mouth of the consumer. Three things can compromise the quality of any wine after it has left the winery: storage, serving temperature, and choice of glassware.

STORAGE

Proper storage is essential for any wine, both for its long-term aging and its near-term enjoyment and pleasure. Try to store your wine in a place that is cool (55 to 60 degrees Fahrenheit), dark (free from any direct sunlight or regular incandescent light), free of vibration (no shaking on top of the refrigerator), and moderately humid (approximately 50 percent humidity). A classic wine cellar isn't obligatory; any cool, dark area of your home will do, as long as it is not subject to the extremes of temperature that can prematurely age any wine. More and more people are opting for readily available, self-contained home wine-storage units that allow you to control temperature and humidity.

SERVING TEMPERATURE

White wines are best served chilled but not glacially cold—which, alas, is often their fate. Although warm white wines certainly do little for one's enjoyment, no bottle should be showing icicles! The ideal range is somewhere between 45 and 57 degrees Fahrenheit. A slightly warmer temperature, closer to 60 degrees, is actually better for showing off more complex, dry whites, especially Chardonnay, whereas rosés and light- to medium-bodied aromatic whites, such as Riesling and Pinot Gris, should be served somewhere between 45 and 50 degrees, dessert wines around 41 to 46 degrees, and Champagne and sparkling wines at about 50 degrees.

Refrigerate white or sparkling wines just before you are ready to enjoy them. Wines left sitting in cold storage for more than a few days will taste noticeably duller than wines that have been just chilled; this is especially true of sparkling wines. If necessary, pull the wine out of the fridge and let it come back to room temperature before chilling it down again.

Red wines present themselves best when served at a cool cellar temperature, *not* room temperature. Served warm, red wines show poorly, with the fruit understated and the tannins and alcohol screaming. In fact, slight chilling (to between 53 and 57 degrees) works wonders for red wines with high concentrations of fruit and lower levels of tannins—wines like Pinot Noir, fruit-

CHOOSING WINES FOR LONG-TERM STORAGE

There's a wine adage that states that thirty minutes in the glass is worth six months in the bottle. So if a wine continues to improve as it sits in your glass, chances are it's worth cellaring. If it tastes still better a few hours later, you can safely invest in several bottles and forget about them in your cellar for a few years.

forward Merlot, some Sangioveses, and even a soft, juicy Cabernet Sauvignon. The ideal serving temperature varies with the weight and structure of the wine. If a full-bodied wine is served too cold, the tannins will accentuate the wine's bitterness, so more classic reds (like Cabernet Sauvignon, Zinfandel, and Syrah), ample in tannins, are best enjoyed between 56 and 65 degrees. Lighter- to medium-bodied wines should be served at the cooler end of the scale.

A word about decanting, or the process of pouring wine from the bottle into a larger, carafe-like vessel. We decant wines for one of two primary reasons:

- *To leave behind the sedimentary deposit that builds up in most full-bodied red wines after five to eight years.* If you are decanting for this reason, do so in front of a light source, such as a candle or small flashlight. As you pour the wine from the bottle into the decanter or carafe, stop pouring when the sediment begins to be visible at the neck of the bottle.
- *To aerate a young wine.* This is the more frequent rationale for decanting red wines, and it can enhance your enjoyment of any young, full-flavored red (or even white) wine. In this case a rough decanting (no worries about sediment), just glugging it into a carafe, suffices.

If decanting makes sense for the wine you are serving, ensure you do it far enough ahead of time to enjoy its benefits, generally fifteen to thirty minutes prior to drinking.

GLASSWARE

The average person doesn't need and can't store ninety different types of glasses matched to each and every kind of wine. But the style of glassware does affect the enjoyment of wine, and, if you can, you should have a small assortment: white wine glasses, different glasses for older and younger reds, and smaller glasses for dessert wine. If you are truly pressed for space, choose one very good all-purpose glass: it should have a reasonably long stem, a bowl of about five to six fingers' height and tapering toward the rim (which should be sheer rather than beaded), and a capacity of eleven to fifteen ounces. If you can, select a ten- to fifteen-ounce all-purpose glass for whites and a high-quality glass with a capacity of fifteen to twenty-three ounces for reds. Champagne flutes are a great addition: choose glasses that are tall, with a slightly tapered sheer rim and a capacity of six to nine ounces. If you can add glasses for dessert wines, choose a smaller all-purpose glass with a tapered, sheer rim and a capacity of approximately eight ounces. Lead

THE 20/20 RULE

Always practice what my friend Leslie Sbrocco calls the 20/20 rule. Pull any young white wine that you intend to drink out of the fridge twenty minutes before you pop the cork, and pull the cork out of any young red wine at least twenty minutes before you intend to consume it. For older wines, wait until closer to serving time.

crystal is lovely, of course, but if that's too expensive or too fragile for your style, choose blown glass in preference to molded glass. Reputable and widely available, Riedel, Spiegelau, and Schott-Zwiesel glasses come in a range of styles.

The condition of the glassware is also critical, as nothing spoils a wine more than a dirty glass or one coated with soap film. Glassware should be spotlessly clean; hand polishing with a clean, dry cloth adds a sparkle. (I am reminded of a fellow who once noted that all of his wines had a lemony aroma and discovered that his housekeeper had polished all his glassware with Lemon Pledge!)

Now you are equipped to enjoy a glass of wine and head to the stove!

CREATING PAIRINGS THAT WORK

The practice of pairing wine and food has been around for a long time. For many Europeans, for people who have grown up in households where wine is a part of daily life, and for folks who have spent time eating their way across France, Italy, Spain, and other gastronomically rich corners of the world, the notion of pairing wine and food is a happy and familiar one.

But for wine and food lovers in the United States, learning what goes with what has often been a roller-coaster ride. Knowing little about pairing wine and food, we first explored (and were handcuffed by) the European and classically grounded "old rules" of color coding: red wine with red meat, and white wines with fish and poultry. While there's some inherent value to those time-honored rules, they leave little to the imagination and discourage the freedom of mixing and matching. Once this became apparent, many Americans embraced culinary anarchy, with people deciding they could serve whatever wine with whatever food they wanted. This extreme encouraged an experimental spirit but led to more misses than hits. And when a memorable match occurred, the diner didn't know why it worked. I favor a middle course between those diametrically opposed approaches, because, as with most things in life, the truth seems to lie somewhere in between. I am both a firm advocate of the classics and a devout believer in shaking things up (and violating taboos) for the right reasons!

First and foremost, wine and food appreciation and enjoyment are personal. No two mouths react the same way to tastes. If somebody were to ask, "What's your most memorable wine and food experience?" at a dinner party (which, by the way, is fun to do), the responses would be all over the place. Most would be simple, formed more by memorable events and settings and good company than by the intricacies of the pairings themselves. Indeed, most people do not, thank goodness, spend their time overanalyzing wine and food and trying to pair, for example, the lemongrass and light green-olive flavors of XYZ Sauvignon Blanc with the tossed spring greens dressed with a lemongrass, citrus, and cold-pressed olive oil vinaigrette flecked with pieces of . . . green olive! This connect-the-dots approach to flavor, espoused by many epicurean magazines, even more winemakers, and a few too many chefs, is unnecessary and intimidating.

So what's really happening when you serve a particular wine with a particular food? Once the emotion and the heart are removed from our thinking, the more objective rationale lies in our intrinsic ability to ascertain characteristics that are "measured" in the mouth. Most of these quantifiable characteristics are referred to as *primary tastes*. But to understand taste, it is crucial to grasp the significant difference between taste and flavor. Though I get into this in more detail below, tastes are, simply stated, quantifiable—the sourness of a lemon, the sweetness of honey, the bitterness of dark chocolate, or the saltiness of a fresh oyster. All these tastes can be measured on a scale from low to high. On the other hand, the countless flavors—strawberry, butterscotch, steak—are personal, subjective, and impossible to measure.

If you move in circles that include wine aficionados, you are likely familiar with those who wax poetic about the pear and apple qualities of a Chardonnay, the apricot and nectarine flavors of a Riesling, or the black pepper and smoked-meat character in a glass of Syrah. We know there are not, in fact, essences of the above or any flavors added to wines. However, many people can, with experience, detect these suggestions of flavor, which are essentially reinforced aromas of the wine that is being enjoyed. Smell and taste are inextricably linked, as colds and allergies so frequently remind us. The ability to smell is essential to sensual appreciation of both wine and food. Without smell, your ability to appreciate the difference between pork and veal is significantly diminished, just as the ability to identify blackberry versus blueberry in a Merlot is moot. As we will see later in the discussions of individual varietal wines, the lexicon of flavors creates an exciting vocabulary for talking about all grapes. But although the glossary of adjectives for wine and food is full of flavors, these terms have very little to do with determining what will make a great pairing. Yes, it's true that a wine that displays a minty personality can pair well with mint as an ingredient in a dish. However, the echo factor doesn't ensure a perfect match.

Only one of the two stars, either the wine or the dish, can effectively take center stage. If you want to show off a special bottle of wine, the food selection should play a supporting role. If you want to showcase a spectacular recipe, it's best to choose a lower-key wine. Much like two people in a conversation, in the wine and food partnership one must listen while the other speaks, or the result is a muddle.

Finally, wines change when served with food. Whatever your perception of a wine's flavor and personality when you taste it on its own, the wine won't be the same when tasted with a meal. Oddly, the most critically acclaimed wines are typically rated and scored alongside other wines of a similar genre but rarely actually tasted with food. Critics may say that sensational XYZ wine "goes well with pasta," but in all likelihood this is no more than an educated guess. These wines may show gorgeously as solo performers, but when served with dinner they can seem different, or even downright unpleasant.

Armed with a context for our thinking and with the traditional epicurean paradigms questioned, let's agree that there are other quantifiable factors and rationales that bring wine and food together. The common wisdom is that wines and foods, like people, pair well with those that resemble them. Some successful wine and food pairings are grounded in shared characteristics. An off-dry Riesling served alongside a pork tenderloin with an apricot chutney illustrates this type of pairing: the sweetness of the chutney complements the slight sweetness of the wine. Other matches succeed through the truism that opposites attract. As with people, wines and foods can harmonize successfully despite seeming disparate at first glance. Ever wonder why a crisp glass of Sauvignon Blanc goes sublimely with a plate of raw oysters? Think of what a squeeze of lemon would do—cut through the oystery taste of the oyster. The wine acts the same way by countering the saline character of the oyster and refreshing the palate.

This "opposites attract" theory was cutting-edge, even radical, in the 1980s. Today, it's accepted and taught by many wine and food experts. At the root of this thinking is the principle that wines and foods share certain basic tastes. Tastes are not flavors. Tastes are simple, the core ones being sweet, sour, salty, and bitter. All are present to some degree in food, and different dishes reveal various combinations of them. For example, some cuisines are founded on plays of salt and sweet, such as a Thai chicken satay with peanut sauce, or salt-brined or dry-rubbed pork shoulder smoked slowly and served with a sweet, tangy barbecue sauce. Wine is also a play of basic tastes, of which three (sweet, sour, and bitter) are the building blocks that define a wine's profile and reveal how (and with what) it would be best served. This combination of tastes holds what I call the keys to wine and food matching. There are six of them for wine and three for food.

THE KEYS TO UNDERSTANDING WINE

KEY 1. ACIDITY

If you're betting on one horse, choose this one. It's the most important factor in pairing wine with food. There are several ways in which acidity, the sourness or tartness factor, figures in wine.

Acidity is the ultimate contrast to an array of dishes.

If you are seeking to "cut" a dish that is rich, salty, oily, fatty or mildly spicy, serving the dish alongside a tart-tasting wine will be effective and refreshing. Think of what I call the "lemon-wedge rule": just as a squeeze of lemon juice will accent or "cut" a rich or salty dish (tempering the brininess of seafood, for example), an acidic wine will do the same. Foods served with cream- or butter-based sauces, oily or strong-tasting fish or shellfish, mildly piquant dishes, and virtually all deep-fried foods are prime candidates.

Acidic wines are the best wines to pair with tart foods.

Tart dishes, such as a green salad dressed with a vinaigrette, and sharp ingredients, such as capers, leeks, and tomatoes, harmonize best with wines of similar sharpness. A wine that is less tart than the dish it is accompanying will be thinned out and may come off quite unpleasantly. When serving wine with a sharp dish or ingredients, you would be hard-pressed to find a wine that is too tart! Examples of wines that can be too puckery on their own but sing with food include Pinot Blanc, cool-climate Chardonnay or Sauvignon Blanc, and some brut Champagnes.

Acidity brings out the integrity of good, simple ingredients.

I like to think of the acid in wines as the gastronomic equivalent of the yellow highlighter pen. The quick swoosh of the highlighter makes the words on a page stand out. A wine's acidity can mimic this phenomenon with food by bringing out the essence of an ingredient's flavor. The summer's first sweet corn or vine-ripened heirloom tomatoes, freshly cracked boiled crab or lobster, and farm-fresh mozzarella cheese all take on another dimension when paired simply with a sharp, uncomplicated wine to make their vibrant and delicious flavor "pop."

Acidity allows a tart wine, which may seem too sharp for sipping on its own, to work perfectly in conjunction with food. To some it is counterintuitive to think that a sour, unpleasant bottle can turn into liquid magic at the table—but sometimes life is stranger than fiction.

By the way, low-acid wines are more difficult to match with food. It's best to serve them with milder ingredients that contain a touch of sharpness (such as a squeeze of lemon). A flat Pinot Grigio or Chardonnay may perk up if paired with an otherwise mild fish mousse served with a wedge of lemon and a tangy jicama salad. With some experimentation and exploration, the role of acidity, and its importance, will become increasingly clear to you.

KEY 2. SWEETNESS

Wines can be sweet in varying degrees. Unctuous dessert wines have specific serving guidelines, which I cover in the dessert wine section. Wines can also be off-dry (a little sweet) or semi-dry (medium sweet). We often find a little sweetness in Rieslings, Chenin Blancs, lighter-style Muscats, and some styles of sparkling wine.

Sweetness is a great counterbalance to moderate levels of spicy heat.

Many Asian preparations, such as spicy Korean barbecued chicken or the archetypal Chinese twice-cooked pork, need not be paired exclusively with beer! Here, moderate amounts of sweetness in the wine provide a nice foil for the heat and tame its ferocity, even alleviating the burning sensation caused by the peppers.

Sweetness in the wine can complement a slight sweetness in food.
Offering an off-dry Chenin Blanc with a fillet of grouper, served with a fresh mango salsa, would be a good example of this observation. Others would include pairing sweet wines with dishes accompanied by chutney or sauces made with fresh or reconstituted dried fruit (such as raisins, apricots, and cherries). The fruit flavors resonate well with most off-dry wines.

Sweetness can be an effective contrast to salt.
This is the rationale behind the long-established matches of French Sauternes with salty Roquefort (and similar blue cheeses) and port with English Stilton. However, this genre of pairing requires some experimenting, as not all of these marriages are happy ones.

Sweetness can take the edge off foods that are too tart.
This type of contrast requires precise balance, or the food can make the wine come across as sour. Many Asian appetizers with vinaigrettes, at once tart and sweet, pair seamlessly with off-dry wines. The ever-popular green papaya salad, found in the cuisines of Thailand, Vietnam, and Myanmar, is a classic example.

Dessert-style or extremely sweet wines must be sweeter than the dessert itself.
The wisdom of this rule is evident to anybody who has ever attended a wedding and experienced the unfortunate pairing of expensive dry brut Champagne with cake covered in gloppy, white buttercream frosting. Dom Perignon suddenly tastes like lemony seltzer water. At a minimum, the levels of sweetness in the wine and the dessert should match. With wedding cake, serving a sweeter bubbly (such as the seemingly misnamed but sweeter extra dry or demi-sec styles) would be a much better call, as the sweetness of the wine and the cake are better matched. Fruit-based desserts are more compatible tablemates for dessert wines; avoid thick, sweet buttercreams and ganache with bubblies!

KEY 3. SALTINESS
As with your own health, salt in wine and food pairings is important and necessary in small quantities. Just as doctors would encourage us to pay close attention to sodium intake, so at table you need to be aware of the salt content of dishes and how it will affect wine selection. For maximum enjoyment with wine, salt should be reduced, rather than amplified, in perception, so I offer the following opinions:

Saltiness is lessened by wine's acidity.
Again, whites and sparkling wines, as a rule, are inherently sharper and therefore generally fare better with salty dishes than most red wines. For example, the zesty bite of acidity from a glass of young Pinot Grigio is a refreshing foil to deep-fried calamari or salt-crusted baked fish.

Salt perception is exaggerated by tannin.

Tannin is the substance that creates a chalky taste and sandpapery texture in red wines (see key 4 below). This is an important consideration when serving a salty dish. Tannin will often accentuate an excess of salt, resulting in a match with as much charm as sucking on a salt lick, especially when you're serving a rich red wine, ample in tannin (bitterness).

Alcohol is accentuated by salt.

An abundance of salt in food will make wines seem "hotter" (more alcoholic) than they are. This is extremely important to know, because you want the wine to harmonize with the dish, not come across like a shot of vodka. High levels of spice and heat (from jalapeño, cayenne, and so on) will also make wine come across as quite hot. Drinking full-bodied wine with Texas five-alarm chili almost always leads to heartburn!

Salty dishes can be counterbalanced by off-dry or sweet wines.

Saltiness and sweetness are often magic together. Though people don't think of them that way, salty/sweet combinations are time-honored and well loved. Snickers bars, Reese's peanut butter cups, and cookie-dough ice cream are extreme cases of this phenomenon, but it's equally present in savory Thai fish cakes with their accompanying sweet/hot sauce, the contrast of country ham and sweet mustard, and a salty fast-food hamburger with sweet ketchup and relish.

If, despite the cautions above, a wine and food combination comes off as being flat, try a sprinkle from the salt shaker. Occasionally, adding salt to the dish can miraculously revive the wine's presence.

KEY 4. TANNIN

In wine, tannin can be associated with a bitter taste and a somewhat gritty texture. This is the same astringency (from tannic acid) encountered in tea that has been steeped too long. Tannins in wine come from two sources: fruit tannins generated from the skins of grapes, especially in big, generous red wines, and wood tannins from the oak barrels in which the wine is aged.

Longer maceration of wine with its skins amplifies fruit tannins, whereas extended barrel aging, especially in newer barrels, accentuates the wood tannins.

Serve bitter foods with tannic wines.

Foods that have been grilled, charred, or blackened are excellent vehicles for showing off bitter-edged wines. Ingredients that are implicitly bitter, like arugula, endive, and sautéed broccoli rabe, are great, too. There's nothing like a charcoal-grilled steak with a full-bodied, tannic Cabernet Sauvignon.

Counterbalance tannins with fat and protein.

This is the fancy way of saying drink red wine with red meat! Those hard and astringent tannins are tamed when paired with rare to medium-rare red meat (ample in fat and protein) or many cheeses (also chock-full of both). If the wine is too tannic, however, the tannins can still dominate. Also, certain hard, sharp, or pungent cheeses—such as aged Parmesan or Romano, French goat cheeses, aged Spanish Manchego, or aged dry Cheddar or Gouda—can give the tannic red wines a metallic character. If you serve a very tannic wine alongside a dish containing little or no protein (a vegetarian entrée, for example), the tannins can react chemically with the available protein (on your tongue and the inside of your mouth) and come across as even more tannic.

Tannin and fish oil usually aren't happy together.

This lesson requires no subtle training of the palate. Generally, all it takes is one bite of fish alongside a rich, tannic wine to provoke the unpleasant "sucking on a penny" reaction between fish oil and tannin. Red wines with less tannin (Pinot Noir is a prime example) fare far better in this challenging pairing of wine and food.

KEY 5. OAK

Although plenty of wines are not aged in wood barrels, many winemakers claim it's impossible to create a fine wine without oak. The vanilla and coconut that you may detect in Chardonnay and the smoke and chocolate identifiable in Cabernet Sauvignon are not from the grapes: the flavors we associate with our favorite wines are often due to the extended time spent in oak. With respect to oak and food:

Oaky flavors are exaggerated by food.

Sooner or later every wine lover runs into a wine that seems too oaky or heavy-handed. Food amplifies the oak in wine, making it stand out as a distinct flavor component. Try any extremely oaky wine with virtually any entrée, and lo and behold, you'll have wine, food, and a lumberyard!

Oaky wines need very specific foods to show them at their best.

This is not to say you can't enjoy oak-aged wines with food; you simply need to choose carefully. Oak imparts tannins (bitterness) that can easily dominate food and need to be balanced out. If you want to show off an oaky wine (a spanking new Cabernet Sauvignon or a modern-style Italian Barolo, for example), simply tailor the food to handle it: serve grilled meat and similar dishes.

With oak, match the flavors in the wine (toast, char or smoke, caramel, and so on) by using cooking techniques, or ingredients cooked with those techniques, that also impart those flavors: grilling, smoking, caramelizing, and so on.

Lightly oaked or even unoaked wines are the easiest to pair.

Most of the time, I prefer to serve wines that are low in oak, extremely well-balanced, or un-oaked (that is, made and aged in stainless-steel tanks or in very old wooden barrels that impart no flavor). Minimizing oak creates a level playing field, allowing you more flexibility in matching your wine with different foods and methods of preparation. An unoaked Chardonnay can work with foods ranging from simply poached fillet of sole to tandoori chicken to veal piccata, served with lemon, capers, and garlic, whereas an oakier version of the Chardonnay would pair well only with the sole.

Oak adds smoothness and roundness of texture to wines.

Wines that spend no time in oak, or very limited time, are much more austere. Wines aged in oak are more mouth-filling and voluptuous. You can play off this added texture by complementing, for example, a silky, oak-aged Chardonnay with a dish accompanied by a cream sauce or compound butter. A velvety Merlot can be sublime when served with a slow-cooked osso buco or other slow-braised dishes of similar personality.

KEY 6. ALCOHOL

Alcohol is what distinguishes wine from grape juice, and a wine's alcohol content is the primary determinant of body and weight. As a rough guide, the higher the wine's alcohol content, the fuller-bodied the wine seems. As with fat content in dairy products, an increase in alcohol content increases the perception of density and texture. A milder wine (7 to 10 percent alcohol) is significantly less weighty and textured on the palate than one of 13 to 14 percent.

Match wines and foods of equal "weight."

This principle is somewhat intuitive. You shouldn't crush a gentle Pinot Noir with a stick-to-the-ribs beef stew. Nor should you match light, simple fillet of sole with an amply textured Chardonnay, which might obliterate the fish. Try to keep the mouth-weight profiles of the wine and food on a par. For example, medium-bodied red wine such as a Merlot or Chianti is successful served with a medium-weight dish such as roast chicken. So is a full-flavored risotto with scallops and cream served with an equally rich barrel-fermented white Burgundy like a Meursault. As the wine's alcohol content increases, the food-pairing options decrease.

We know now that our perception of a wine's alcohol is amplified by food, specifically by salt and by spicy heat. If a very powerful wine is paired with spicy dishes, you may feel as though someone poured gasoline on the fire! Lots of salt creates a similar effect. In general terms, medium-bodied wines (those of medium alcohol content, 11 to 13 percent), and even lighter wines are easier to work with at the table.

THE KEYS TO UNDERSTANDING FOOD

Which comes first, the food or the wine? This question, like the chicken-and-egg dilemma, can lead people in circles, because the synergy between food and wine makes it impossible to make decisions about either one in isolation. But to know how a food might affect the way we perceive a good wine, we need to understand how various flavors and preparation techniques contribute to the taste of a finished dish. Now that we know how to define a wine's ability to go with food, we need to get a handle on how to understand a dish.

Recipes are as different as snowflakes; it's impossible to pair up every recipe with a single perfect wine. As with wines, in thinking about any recipe the rationale remains the same: identify certain basic characteristics. Rather than get caught up in thinking about a dish in all its complexity, it's far easier to look at the three food keys and then determine how to proceed.

KEY 1. INGREDIENTS

We have been "trained" to think about a dish primarily in terms of its ingredients. From a wine and food perspective, this approach allows you to think about pairings in a formulaic way: if you know the ingredients, you know the correct wine selection, right? Red meat with red wine, and white meat and fish with white wine. Well, sort of.

Certainly, when you're pairing wine and food, what's cooking is important, and it's often the main consideration. Of course, the wine you choose to accompany rock cod will be the polar opposite of what you'd choose to go with leg of lamb. However, within the broad "red" and "white" categories of meat, fish, and poultry, there are many shades of pink. For example, some fish are strongly fishy (sturgeon, mackerel, anchovies, and bluefish), while others are mild (rock cod, halibut, sole, and trout).

Red meat can be strong, like lamb, or mild, like a filet of beef. White meat (pork and veal) is very different from red meat in personality, often acting more like chicken, semineutral in character and much influenced by the supporting cast of ingredients. Poultry also may vary from mild (chicken) to pungent (squab). Then there are other categories, such as offal (sweetbreads, liver, and so on), vegetables, grains, and legumes. So it really is more complicated than choosing a red wine for dinner because you're having meat.

A handful of very useful ingredients can inform—and hedge—your wine and food pairings. Often referred to as "bridge ingredients" or "wine links," these allow you to play Merlin in the kitchen. See the table on page 22 for a list of "magic" ingredients and their effects.

KEY 2. COOKING METHODS

Although the selection of ingredients is important, it's only one element of the overall plan. And while it's true that the primary ingredient in the food may determine the wine selection, just as

GARLIC AND ONIONS (SLOW-COOKED) . . .

- Add creaminess and roundness to a dish. When braised, roasted, or sweated, they add sweetness. When caramelized, they add sweetness and smoky flavors.
- "Pop" red or white wines with riper fruit and/or slight sweetness.
- Meld nicely with oak-aged and oak-influenced wines.
- Help form a bridge between foods and wines with more weight and texture.
- Provide a link to earthier wines, such as classically styled European wines (true of raw and quickly sautéed garlic and onions as well).

OLIVES . . .

- Can swing dishes toward pairing with either red or white wines. Green olives create a white wine affinity (especially with Sauvignon Blanc, Pinot Gris, and unoaked Chardonnay), and black olives create a red wine affinity (especially with Merlot, Cabernet Sauvignon, and Syrah).
- With flavored cures (such as those incorporating peppers and herbs) can lend another dimension of compatibility to a dish. Strong cures (especially those very high in acid or vinegar) are best rinsed off.

CURED MEATS (PROSCIUTTO, BACON, PANCETTA, AND OTHER CHARCUTERIE) . . .

- Can tilt "white wine" dishes (fish, poultry, veal, pork) toward pairing with red wines. Prosciutto-wrapped fish or shellfish with bacon, for example, can pair beautifully with soft, bright reds and rosés.

CHEESE AND OTHER DAIRY INGREDIENTS . . .

- Add texture and richness to a dish when used in cooking.
- Can be a bridge between salads or vegetables and higher-acid white wines. Try using a small amount of goat cheese, feta, or gorgonzola.

HERBS (FRESH OR DRIED) . . .

- That are fragrant (chervil, dill, tarragon) pair best with whites like Riesling and Chardonnay.
- That are more pungent (basil, thyme, rosemary) go best with Sauvignon Blanc and many reds (especially Merlot and Cabernet Sauvignon).

LENTILS, BEANS, AND OTHER LEGUMES . . .

- Can pair beautifully with white wines.
- If prepared with herbs, can swing a dish toward white wine; if prepared with meat (bacon, ham, pancetta, sausage), can swing a dish toward red wine.
- Can provide a clean backdrop for fuller-bodied white wines. Waxy white beans are a good example.
- Can enable fish to pair with red as well as white wines. Try serving fish over a bed of green lentils.

MUSHROOMS . . .

- Add earthiness and a natural affinity for earthy wines.
- That are darker (especially reconstituted dried mushrooms) make almost all foods red wine friendly.
- That are light-colored, creamy, and textured (shiitake, chanterelles, oyster, button) help dishes go well with white wines, especially those with texture (Chardonnay, oak-aged Sauvignon Blanc, and Pinot Gris).

NUTS . . .

- When toasted and added to a dish (as a crust on a piece of fish, for example) pick up on the nutty nuances imparted by oak-barrel-aged wines and show off oak-aged wines.
- With the skin on (especially walnuts and almonds) have an inherent bitterness that softens the perception of bitter tannins in red wines and some strongly oak-aged whites.
- That are powdered and used in cooking (as in moles and other Latino and world foods) make dishes wine-friendly and can favor lightly oak-aged wines.

often it's not the only or the main basis for the choice. Preparation of the ingredients can just as frequently play a part. Savory marinades can transform the taste of the primary ingredient(s), drawing out new or different flavors. But the cooking method may overshadow everything.

Some cooking techniques, such as steaming, poaching, and boiling, impart minimal flavor and are what I refer to as "low-impact." Others, like smoking, grilling, and blackening, are dominant, "high-impact" techniques that can transform the flavors in foods. Smoking can add sweet as well as smoky elements. Grilling will impart a bitter, slightly acrid, taste and an outer crust. Sautéing is fairly neutral: it can add mild sweetness, but the flavors in the resulting dish have more to do with the ingredient profile. Deep-frying adds a hint of sweetness and intriguing texture, and braising, roasting, and baking fall somewhere in the middle.

To taste the differences, take three chicken breasts, salt and pepper them all in the same way, and prepare one with a low-impact cooking method, one with a medium-impact method, and one with a high-impact method. Then try each with a series of different wines and note how your preference in wine varies with the cooking method.

KEY 3. SAUCES AND CONDIMENTS

A sauce is a trump card: it invariably dictates the wine match. Varied in personality, sauces may be cold, room temperature, or hot. They may be vinaigrettes, salsas, chutneys, or reductions. They may contain herbs, spices, fruit, or any combination thereof. Some contain cream or butter; others may be based on stock, flavored infusions, or wine. Some are smooth in texture; others are chunky and coarse. In any form, sauces want to run the show. Every sauce can be analyzed and broken down into its basic taste components. From that analysis, you can reach an informed choice about wine.

For example, vinaigrette-based and citrus-based sauces share the common element of acid: there is sharpness at the core. Rather than try to find a wine that works with all the ingredients, it would be wiser to find one that pairs well with sourness, for that will be the basic personality of the dish. In chutneys, sweetness may dominate, whereas in a salsa, harissa, or any other sauce based on hot peppers, the dominant characteristic, and the one that will govern wine choice, will be heat.

Matching a wine with the basic tastes in a sauce is a fairly straightforward principle that can also apply to textures. A butter- or cream-based sauce, with its silky and rich texture, may, like emulsified sauces (such as mayonnaise and aioli), pair best with similarly rich-textured wines such as Chardonnay, Pinot Gris, and Viognier.

To demonstrate these principles, return to the chicken-breast experiment. This time sauté three chicken breasts identically and serve them alongside three very different sauces: salty (soy-based), sweet (such as a fruit chutney), and spicy (harissa, salsa picante, or another hot sauce). Next, line up an array of wines. As you work through the permutations, you'll note the dramatic impact of saucing.

AND THOSE DEVILISH SIDE DISHES

Global travel, food experimentation, and increasingly daring palates, supported by the year-round availability of fresh ingredients from around the world, mean that we live in an intriguing food time. I am often astounded by restaurant menus. Not only can these dining establishments lay on the lavish "menu-speak" descriptions, but the dishes themselves may have four to six accompanying items that have personalities as compelling as that of the central item. I have been surprised and at times disappointed to discover that the entrée I ordered had to take a back seat to a more intensely flavored side dish. Surprises like this can wreak havoc on wine choices, so when you're dining out, it's important to read the menu carefully; when you're planning an elaborate meal at home, remember that side dishes and condiments can, like a sauce, influence the wine selection even more than the main ingredient or its preparation.

WINE IN THE COOKING

Having explored how cooking influences wine pairing, we need to look at the use of wine *in* the cooking. There are three fundamental applications of wine in cooking: cooking with or in wine, marinating foods with wine, and macerating foods in wine.

COOKING WITH WINE

Like your good olive oil and vinegar, your cooking wine should not be stored next to the stove. Heat detracts from the wine's flavors and accelerates spoilage; the convenience of having the wine right at hand does little to justify the sacrifice of integrity. Also important is what's in the bottle. Hands off any "cooking wine" from the shelf of the local market! Such wines are almost always chock-full of added salt and bring nothing to the party. Never cook with wines that you wouldn't be willing to drink.

The two most common applications of wine in cooking are as a flavoring component of a sauce (as in a beurre blanc or beurre rouge) and as a cooking or stewing liquid (as in the classic coq au vin or boeuf bourguignon). In both cases, once the wine is cooked (and the alcohol and most of the water evaporated off), what's left bears little resemblance to what was in the bottle. Compulsive chefs who want to tie a dish and a wine together by cooking with the wine that they intend to serve are, in my opinion, fooling themselves. Here's the making of a lively dinner party conversation: cook down a cup each of Sauvignon Blanc and Chardonnay to a saucelike consistency. Add a touch of butter to emulsify each, and serve the two sauces to all. Ask your guests to identify which is which, and watch the sparks fly.

This transformation is even more pronounced when a dish is stewed for hours. A simple but tasty table wine will be fine to pour into that boeuf en daube. There's no need to use a sixty-dollar Napa Valley Cabernet. Hooray for life's little bargains!

But surely, people ask, there must be a way to sense the pedigree of the wine when cooking?

In one single case the answer is definitely yes: when the wine is incorporated into the dish at the last moment, and therefore not cooked. Many recipes either require or suggest this use for wine, and in this case alone I would recommend using a very fine wine or the wine being served with the meal, as there will be a strong reference.

A couple of principles are important when cooking with wine.

- *If you cook with an off-dry wine or a sweet wine, the residual sugar will have an effect on the dish*. This sweetness may or may not be desirable.
- *High oak and high tannins will add a perceptible note of bitterness*. I generally avoid monster reds and Chateau Two-by-Four super-oaky whites for cooking, as I don't enjoy the added acrid notes.

MARINATING AND MACERATING

Marinating and macerating both use uncooked wine. With marinades, the ingredients spend time in the wine and are then removed from the wine and cooked. With macerating, the ingredients spend time in the wine and are generally served in the maceration liquid in the final presentation. As when cooking with wine, most people grab whatever's open and pour in the required quantity, regardless of quality. And although it is true that added ingredients such as chiles, dried spices, herbs, garlic, and onions may overshadow the flavors of the wine, the wine's quality will nonetheless influence the final dish.

Marinating is a wonderful technique. It creates great complexity of flavor and gives the impression that you slaved over a dish for hours when in fact you might have put the marinade together in twenty minutes yesterday or the day before. In wine marinades, it pays to use a better wine: it will add a more complex flavor to the dish.

Usually used for meat but often also for fish or fowl, marinades provide layers of flavor while tenderizing and adding texture. The acids in wine act to break down the toughness of the meat, so the higher the acidity of the wine, the more dramatic and effective the marinade will be.

With macerating, too, the quality of the wine has a dramatic effect on the final dish. The two most popular examples of macerating with wine are that lovely concoction sangría, and fresh or dried fruits macerated in wine.

While using a bottle of Château Lafite Rothschild is not necessary, a tasty, juicy, and appropriately fruity red will make a difference: a local Spanish Rioja *joven,* a zesty Beaujolais, or a plump Italian Dolcetto makes a welcoming base for those cut-up oranges, lemons, and other flavorings for sangría. Similarly, when you're serving a dessert of fresh summer peaches floating in Moscato d'Asti, a cheap, soapy-tasting bottling will take away from the dish; using a better wine will pay off in spades.

. . . . .

This chapter covers a lot of material. To make the information easier to refer back to, I've created the following cheat sheet, which summarizes the key points of this chapter and adds a few other tips.

WHEN THE WINE IS . . .

TART

- Select dishes that are rich, creamy, high in fat, or salty to counterbalance the wine.
- Match the wine with tart food (sharp ingredients, vinaigrettes and other sharp sauces).
- Use the wine to cut the heat in mildly spicy dishes.
- Try skipping the lemon wedge that you might otherwise serve with the dish (with fish, chicken, veal, pork, vegetables, and grains).

SWEET

- If you're serving the wine with dessert, choose a dessert that's less sweet than the wine, or else the wine will taste sour.
- If the wine is not too sweet (closer to off-dry), try serving it with foods that are slightly sweet to complement it, or dishes that are mildly hot or spicy as a foil.
- Try playing the wine against dishes that are a little salty; you may find some fun combinations, especially with cheeses and many Asian and Nuevo Latino, North African, Floridian/Caribbean, or Hawaiian-influenced "tropical" preparations.

HOT/ALCOHOLIC

- Ensure that the dish being served is ample in personality and weight, or it will be overwhelmed.
- Don't serve very spicy-hot food, or you'll be sorry!
- Remember that food will make the wine appear even hotter.
- Avoid excessive salt, which will exaggerate your perception of the wine's heat (alcohol).

TANNIC

- Counterbalance the tannins by serving foods that are high in protein, fat, or both.
- Remember that an entrée relatively low in protein or fat may make the wine come off as even more tannic.
- Remember that tannin and spicy heat can clash brutally.
- Use pepper (cracked black or white) to counterbalance tannins, as it's somewhat bitter by nature.
- Serve foods that are bitter (eggplant, zucchini, chard, endive, broccoli rabe, and so on) or prepare ingredients in a way that accentuates bitterness (blackening, cooking over a wood fire, or grilling) to achieve taste symmetry.

OAKY

- Because really oaky wines will always seem "bigger" with food, accompany them with bold recipes.
- Play up the oak through the choice of ingredients (include nuts or sweet spices) or cooking methods (lightly grilling or smoking).
- Remember that oak aging adds rich texture that can be nice with rich and textured sauces and dishes.

AGED AND RED

- Serve rare preparations of meats to fill in the flavor gaps left by the drying out of the youthful fruit that occurs as the wine develops in the bottle.
- Remember that because tannins soften over time, an aged red gives you a broader range of food options than a tannic young wine does.
- Bear in mind that wines become more delicate as they age; choose simpler preparations to show them off rather than make them compete for attention with complex recipes.

AGED AND WHITE

- Serve the wines with dishes that feature similar flavors (nuts, sherry, and dried fruits) to mirror the flavor profile.
- Compensate for the lost acidity in the mature wine with acidity in the dish: a squeeze of lemon, a spoonful of verjus, or a splash of vinegar.

WHEN THE FOOD IS . . .

TART

- Serve a wine which is equally sharp or even more so, or the wine will taste off and shattered.
- Avoid red wines, except those of a sharper nature (Sangiovese, Pinot Noir, Gamay).
- Don't overlook dry rosés and sparkling wines as options.

SLIGHTLY SWEET

- Make certain that the wine accompanying the food shares its personality traits: choose a wine that is slightly sweet, such as a Chenin Blanc, Riesling, or even sake.
- If you really want a dry wine, serve one that's young and very, very ripe.
- Remember that sometimes a wine with oak can work if the wood's *sweetness* mirrors that of the dish; however, success is not guaranteed.

SALTY

- Pick wines with low to moderate alcohol content, as the wine's heat will be exaggerated by the salt.
- Play with wines that have some sweetness; salt and sweet can enjoy each other's company!
- Avoid wines with high levels of oak or tannin.

SPICY OR HOT

- The spicier the dish, the more difficult it is to pair with wine. Select young wines with low to moderate alcohol content, minimal (or no) oak, and, if possible, some residual sugar (for whites and rosés).
- Among still wines, stick to off-dry whites and rosés; sparkling wines can also be nice foils for heat.
- You may have to forgo wine with Texas five-alarm chili or those Thai, Indian, and Korean dishes that make your hair stand on end. Opt instead for beer and yogurt-based drinks, along with large, large bowls of rice!

BITTER

- Select wines with bitter components (oak aging, tannins) to complement the personality of the recipe.
- Try wines with high acidity. This doesn't always work, but it's better than the opposite extreme. After all, tannin is an acid.

DOMINATED BY A STRONG SAUCE OR CONDIMENT

- Forget the main dish and match the wine to the sauce or condiments and side dishes.

SERVED VERY HOT

- Allow the dish to cool off, or it will ruin your enjoyment of the wine and make the alcohol (by heating it) seem overwhelming.
- Serve chilled wines if it's essential that the dish be served very hot.

OVERVIEW OF THE WINE JOURNEYS

The heart of this book is a sequence of journeys through twelve varietals (grape types), along with sparkling wines and dessert wines. Hundreds of grape varieties are used to make wine around the globe. In these sections I focus on the grapes used to make the wines people most often consume on a regular basis, in still, sparkling, and sweet or dessert styles. Within the categories of white and red, the varietals are arranged in order of popularity and prestige in the wine world. Each journey presents a practical approach to understanding wines made from the grape type, interpreting varied styles, and applying those insights to pairing the wines with food. But first, here's an explanation of the itinerary for each journey and how to follow the road map!

WINE-GROWING AREAS First I look at the countries, regions, states, appellations, and subappellations where the grape is grown and wines are produced. Tables showing the wine-growing areas for each varietal can be found in the chapter titled "Principal Wine-Growing Regions." These tables list U.S. regions first, followed by other areas in order of importance. These lists aren't exhaustive; they emphasize what is commercially produced and widely available.

VINTNER CHOICES This section lists the fundamental options and decisions facing a winemaker and his or her team that determine the style, taste, and flavor of the wine. Many of these choices are addressed as comparative scenarios, such as the use of oak or no oak, blended or 100 percent pure varietal, or barrel rather than stainless-steel fermentation. For sparkling wines and dessert wines, I also explain how these types of wines may be vinified. Definitions of the more technical and specialized terms used in these descriptions are provided in the glossary at the back of the book.

As this is not a encyclopedic wine book but one about matching food with wine, I don't go into detail about most aspects of wine production. For example, long before the grapes are harvested, vineyard decisions must be made about trellising, irrigation, root-stock selection, leaf picking, and other basic viticultural practices. For more detail on these matters, you may want to consult comprehensive wine books such as Tom Stevenson's *Sotheby's Wine Encyclopedia* or Jancis Robinson's *Oxford Companion to Wine*. These books offer excellent discussions of the wine-making process and preproduction vineyard practices.

FLAVOR LEXICON Although the flavors elicited from a wine are quite subjective, there is an accepted working vocabulary for describing grapes and their resultant wines. In this section I try to provide some of the most common flavor descriptors associated with a particular varietal or style. These listings are by no means exhaustive, and you may find yourself developing and inventing your own words to describe the wines. That's not only OK; it's encouraged and applauded.

WINE AND FOOD PAIRING The final component of the journeys addresses real-life scenarios at home or in a restaurant. While I do offer my own point of view and attempt to "get into your mouth," the truism still holds: nobody experiences aroma and taste in the same way as anybody else. As each person's threshold for saltiness, bitterness, heat or spice, sweetness, and tartness is different, so too are the perceptions of how these factors react with wine and food on individual palates.

Each of the varietal chapters concludes with four tasty, easy-to-make recipes that have been designed specifically to go with different stylistic versions of the grape. For sparkling wine, I provide four recipes to accompany different styles of sparkling wine and Champagne, and the dessert wine chapter includes six recipes. Each recipe is followed by Joyce's discussion of the dish and my rationale for the pairing.

RECOMMENDED PRODUCERS Following each recipe, where the information is germane, is a short list of reliable producers whose wines are consistently made in the relevant style. I have purposely avoided specifying a particular vintage, vineyard, or bottling, because the availability of many wines varies radically in different areas of the country—and from year to year. Instead of listing specific prices, which are also highly variable, I give three price ranges, as shown below.

Everyday	$5–15
Premium	$16–39
Splurge	$40 and up

In a few cases, no producers make wines in a certain price category, and so no recommendations are made for that category. For example, there are no "splurge" white Zinfandels.

I have tried to select producers with reasonably comprehensive distribution who produce sufficient quantities of wine. Nothing is more frustrating than falling in love with a wine and then finding out that only ten cases were produced, and those were sold exclusively to those who live in the right places and know the secret handshake.

part one

A SPARKLING WINE JOURNEY

SPARKLING WINES

Champagne and other types of sparkling wine, which make up the bubbly category, are different from varietals: in addition to being effervescent, these wines are almost always blends rather than single-grape (varietal) bottlings. And they are fantastic with food! But unfortunately, most of us reserve our enjoyment of these bubblies for celebrations or drink them like cocktails, without food. We should consider these sparklers more frequently, because they have an amazing affinity for many dishes.

Where do the bubbles come from? When grape juice is fermented into wine, the yeast organisms convert sugar into alcohol. In the process, carbon dioxide gas is released. In the making of still wines, this gas is allowed to dissipate into the air. In sparkling wines, it is retained. To make Champagne and Champagne-style wines, still wine is placed into a bottle with a small amount of sugar and live yeast. The carbon dioxide produced from this second fermentation is trapped in the bottle as effervescence. In other styles of sparkling wine, the carbon dioxide is trapped at other stages, using different processes.

WINE-GROWING AREAS

Most people believe that all sparkling wines are Champagne. This belief is true only to the extent that the region of Champagne, in northeastern France, is universally revered as the spiritual home of bubblies. It is the birthplace of the "Champagne method" (the *méthode champenoise*, pronounced "me-*tud* cham-pen-*woz*")—the production process by which a secondary fermentation is induced in the same bottle in which the still wine is bottled after blending. The result is a sparkling wine of complexity and great elegance.

You can say that all Champagne is sparkling wine (virtually all of it is), but you *cannot* say that all sparkling wine is Champagne. In order to be labeled as such, it must come from this prestigious appellation.* In other parts of France, sparkling wines are produced using the same method (identified on the label as the *méthode traditionnelle*). However, these producers often use different grapes, and the wines don't have Champagne's uniquely layered character of toasted brioche, hazelnuts, tart citrus, and chalky earth, rooted in the holy trinity of Champenois grapes from which the wines are produced: Chardonnay, Pinot Noir, and the indigenous Pinot Meunier. Many of the other French sparkling wines, labeled as Crémant (for example, Crémant de la Loire, Crémant d'Alsace), are nevertheless excellent. The Cava appellation in the Catalonia region of Spain produces more *méthode traditionnelle* wine than any other country in the world; it bears the eponymous name of Cava. More rustic, uniquely savory, and with flavors of mineral, spice, and earth, Cava makes use of the indigenous Spanish grapes of Xarel-lo, Viura, and Parellada and is always a great value. Italy's sparkling wine industry is based in the northwestern region of Piedmont surrounding the town of Asti; its Muscat-based wine is known as Asti Spumante (*spumante* simply means "sparkling" in Italian). Asti Spumante is almost always sweeter than other sparkling wines and redolent of the flavors of white Muscat grapes: lychee, apricot, and ripe tangerine. It is also based on a different method of production, by which the wine achieves its effervescence within a pressurized, closed tank: this is the *cuve close,* Charmat, or bulk process, which preserves all the fresh, primary fruit flavors. A slightly less bubbly relative, Moscato d'Asti, has a similar flavor profile but less prickle on the tongue and makes for enjoyable summer al fresco dining. Italy's other celebrated sparkling wine is Prosecco. Made from the eponymous grape and produced primarily in Veneto but also in the Friuli–Venezia Giulia and Trentino–Alto Adige regions, Prosecco utilizes the same bulk method as Asti Spumante, but produces a wine slightly drier to the tongue, with earthy nuances and more apple and pear notes.

Other countries and regions around the world make sparkling wines using the *méthode traditionnelle* with excellent results: the United States (with California leading the charge), Australia, New Zealand, South Africa, South America, the rest of Italy (primarily Lombardy's Franciacorta region), and less obvious places like Portugal (which also utilizes the *continuous method,* described below) and even India. Although the flavor profiles (and in some cases, the grapes) vary from country to country, all these wines share a level of complexity that results from the traditional production method, which adds a creaminess and sophistication to the wine.

There are two other important methods for getting bubbles into the bottle. A process called the *transfer,* or Kriter, method, named for the German winemaker who invented it, is similar to

---

* Until recently, all U.S. producers of sparkling wines could legally use the term *Champagne,* but, counterintuitively, it usually denoted a cheap product. Under the terms of a 2005 U.S.–E.U. trade agreement, U.S. producers who have historically called their product *Champagne* may continue to use the term, but new producers may not. Almost all of the best U.S. producers who use the *méthode traditionnelle* label their wines as "sparkling wine."

the *méthode traditionnelle,* except that the wine is moved from the secondary fermentation bottle into a larger tank to filter out the yeast sediment before being returned to the bottle. Commonly used for speed and efficiency in the past, it is less frequently used today. More common in modern sparkling wine production is the *continuous method,* by which the secondary fermentation occurs in a series of pressurized tanks, to which additional live yeast is continually added to keep the fermentation going. It is fast, efficient, and economical. This technique is employed increasingly in Germany and Portugal.

In Germany many grapes are used, notably Riesling for the best-quality wines. Alas, most German bubbly is simply labeled as *Sekt* (which can be produced from grapes from any country), produced inexpensively from a mélange of grapes utilizing the bulk method, and is inexpensive and of fair quality. The best German sparkling wines are labeled as *Deutscher Sekt,* which must be made from grapes grown in Germany.

Some inexpensive wines are not made according to any of the traditional methods but are simply carbonated (just like soda pop). These have little to offer. Fortunately, by U.S. law, they must be labeled as "carbonated wine," so if you see those words on a bottle, avoid it.

A table of principal wine-growing regions for sparkling wines appears on pages 263–64.

VINTNER CHOICES

*Early or late picking; method of production; vintage or nonvintage; style of wine—
brut, blanc de blancs, rosé (blanc de noirs), or prestige cuvée; length of time
"on the yeast"* (tirage); *oak or no oak; dosage level (dry, off-dry, or sweet)*

Several winemaking decisions determine the style of the final effervescent product. Although practices vary by region and country, in general the grapes for sparkling wines are picked earlier and slightly less ripe than those intended for still wine, for two reasons. First, sparkling wines are in part defined by sharper acidity levels, which make them tart but also carry and help sustain their delicate flavors and lingering aftertaste, or *finish,* as well as define their character. Second, because the secondary fermentation increases the alcohol level by a percentage point or so, starting out with grapes that are less ripe, and therefore lower in sugar, helps control the alcohol content.

Many different sparkling wines result from using various permutations of grape types and production methods (see the table on page 35). The most complex wines are those employing the *méthode champenoise* or *traditionnelle.* Around the world, the countries that emulate the model of the Champagne region and employ the classic blend of grapes produce multifaceted sparkling wines. In this classic blend, Pinot Noir adds the spice, red fruit flavors (strawberry, raspberry, cherry), and complexity, while Chardonnay contributes backbone (acidity) and sharp

PRODUCTION OF CHAMPAGNE AND OTHER SPARKLING WINES

METHOD OF PRODUCTION	COUNTRY	REGION (APPELLATION)	PRINCIPAL GRAPE(S)
Méthode champenoise (méthode traditionnelle)	France	Champagne	Chardonnay, Pinot Meunier, Pinot Noir
		Loire	Cabernet Franc, Chardonnay, Chenin Blanc
		Alsace	Pinot Blanc, Pinot Gris, Pinot Noir
		Languedoc (Limoux)	Blanquette, Chardonnay, Chenin Blanc, Mauzac
		Rhône (Die)	Clairette, Muscat
		Bordeaux	Muscadelle de Bordelais, Sauvignon, Semillon
		Burgundy	Chardonnay, Gamay, Pinot Noir
	United States	California	Chardonnay, Pinot Noir
		Oregon, Washington, New Mexico	Chardonnay, Pinot Gris, Pinot Noir, Riesling
	Italy	Lombardy (Franciacorta)	Chardonnay, Pinot Nero (i.e., Pinot Noir)
	Spain	Catalonia (Cava)	Chardonnay, Parellada, Viura, Xarel-lo
Transfer method	Germany	Various	Müller-Thurgau, Riesling
	United States	Various	Various
Continuous method	Germany	Various	Various
	Portugal	Bairrada	Bical
Cuve close (bulk or Charmat)	Italy	Asti	Muscat
		Veneto, Friuli–Venezia Giulia, Trentino–Alto Adige	Prosecco
	United States	California	Chenin Blanc, Colombard, Muscat, Thompson Seedless
		New York	Catawba, Delaware

fruit nuances (green apple and citrus). Pinot Meunier adds texture and ripe fruit and fills in any flavor gaps; it's almost like a winemaker's spackle. Wines using local fruit (French Crémant wines and Spanish Cava, for example) have different flavor profiles and *terroir* nuances. Wines made using the bulk, or Charmat, method, most notably Prosecco and Asti Spumante, do so not to save money or time (though the method does both) but because this is the best method for showing off those grapes. Finally, the continuous process, utilized in Germany and Portugal, is unique, quick, and cost-effective, too.

Most sparkling wine is nonvintage, that is, produced from grapes from more than one year's harvest. The reason for this goes back, like so many traditions in bubbly, to Champagne, where the unpredictable weather forced vintners to save still wines from prior years in case Mother Nature decided to be uncooperative in a given harvest. Still wines from that year's vintage were then blended with some of the older still wines to produce a *cuvée* (French for wine blend) that conformed to a consistent flavor profile or signature house style. Because these wines contain less than the 95 percent of a single year's grapes that is required for a wine to qualify as a vintage, the resulting wine is labeled a blended nonvintage (or multivintage, as it's now fashionable to say). What matters is that the wine be consistent in taste from year to year. In exceptional years a vintner may choose to capture the vintage's personality in a bottle by declaring a vintage, that is, making a sparkling wine exclusively out of grapes from that year's harvest. These wines are the only sparkling wines that bear a year on the label, and that is the year in which the grapes were picked.

Besides the country and region of origin, the choice of production method and grapes employed, and the decision to make a nonvintage or vintage wine, sparkling wines also vary in style. Almost all are of the nonvintage brut type. *Brut* suggests wines that are dry to the palate and blended according to regional grape varieties and specifications; they are frequently a blend of red and white grapes. Some wines, however, have additional information on the label. Blanc de blancs (literally "white of whites") are made exclusively from white grapes (most often Chardonnay). They are delicate and citrus-flavored with racy acidity and a zesty vibrancy, and they are very light in appearance. Rosé wines are primarily made from red grapes and are either a blush or rosé color. These wines, although most often spicy, rich, and dry, can also be slightly riper or sweeter, in which case they are often labeled "blanc de noirs" ("white of darks"). Blanc de noirs wines are produced almost exclusively in the United States.

The Rolls-Royce of any given winery is called its *prestige cuvée,* or *tête de cuvée.* Included in this category are Möet et Chandon's Dom Perignon and Roederer's Cristal from France; Schramsberg's J. Schram from California; Bellavista's Gran Cuvée Pas Opere from Italy; and Rimarts' Cava Uvae from Spain. These are always vintage wines and represent the best and most distinctive of what a house can make. While there are also *prestige cuvée* wines that are rosés and a few blanc de blancs, most are very high-end, classic brut interpretations.

STYLE (LABELING)	PERCEPTION	APPROXIMATE *DOSAGE* (SUGAR AS % OF 750 ML BOTTLE)
Brut zero or *sauvage*	Bone-dry	0.0–0.5
Brut	No sweetness	0.5–1.5
Extra dry	Off-dry	1.2–2.0
Demi-sec	Slightly sweet	1.7–3.5
Sec	Sweet	3.3–5.0
Doux	Very sweet	More than 5.0

In the *méthode champenoise,* once the wines are produced, but before they are corked and sold, they spend time resting on their spent yeast deposits (a by-product of the secondary fermentation in the bottle). During this time the wine is said to be *en tirage* (on its yeast). The amount of *tirage* time will add personality to the wine as the dead yeasts break down and their amino acids are absorbed into the wine, a process called *autolysis*. The remaining yeast deposit is removed by a process called disgorging (in French, *dégorgement*) before the wine is considered finished. In general, the longer the *tirage* time, the more complex and creamy the wine is, and the smaller and more refined the bubbles are. Some wines are known for their extended *tirage* times, and the label may make reference to this with terms such as *RD* or *late disgorged*.

Although almost all sparkling wines and Champagnes are made without any aging in wood barrels or casks, some noteworthy exceptions are made with oak-aged still wines. The great Champagne houses of Krug and Bollinger are respected advocates of the judicious use of wood, and their wines are known for the resulting roundness and richness.

The style of a sparkling wine is ultimately determined by the amount of sweetening (sugar) added after disgorging and just before the wine is cork-finished (see the table above). This step determines how dry or sweet the wine actually is. In wine lingo this addition is referred to as the *dosage* (doh-*sahj*), and it is important in determining personal tastes as well as wine and food pairing. (For more on the sweet styles of sparkling wine, see the dessert wine journey.)

FLAVORS

Fruit: Cherry, lemon, lime, citrus (grapefruit, citron), apple (green, yellow), pear, pineapple, passion fruit, lychee, raspberry, strawberry, cucumber

Floral: Honeysuckle, rose, gardenia, freesia, apple blossom, lime blossom, mint

Earth: Mineral, chalk, dust, mushroom

Extended age (tirage): Toast, brioche, French bread (baguette), biscuit, hazelnut, almond, walnut, vanilla wafer, nougat, gingerbread, dried fruit (fig, raisin), coffee

Other: Yeast, dough/raw bread, soy, cream, Vegemite, plain yogurt, vanilla, honey, blond tobacco, melted butter

WINE AND FOOD PAIRING

Sparkling wine is like Rodney Dangerfield: it gets no respect, at least when it comes to pairing wine and food. I strongly believe that sparkling wine has a bigger role to play at the table than simply being sipped for a toast. Its brilliant combination of effervescence, ample acidity (tartness), and lighter weight (low alcohol) make for beautiful pairings. Add the dimension of the *dosage,* and bubbly can offer a range of pairing options.

At bottom, sparkling wines are all about the fizz. The bubbles can contrast beautifully with the textures of deep-fried foods, puff pastry, or phyllo dough. The tactile play of the food's crackle and the wine's effervescence is satisfying in the mouth. And many pastry items incorporate plenty of butter, an ingredient that works well with sparkling wines. Additionally, the bubbles can counterbalance spicy heat (peppers).

Next, the sharpness (acidity) is the perfect foil for preparations that are salty, thick or rich (such as cream sauces and many soft cheeses), or a little oily (fish, caviar, and fried foods). The nutty and toasty aromas that predominate in French styles and more developed or aged American and antipodean examples are excellent with sautéed dishes and those with "toasty" elements, such as grains, nuts, and especially corn.

Sparkling wines that are more fruit-driven (especially those that come from the United States, Australia, and New Zealand) are very compatible with exotic and Asian cuisines such as Indian, Thai, Vietnamese, and Singaporean. Finally, if you're serving a dish that is relatively spicy, off-dry bubblies can be very enjoyable and help tame the heat.

The fact that virtually all sparkling wines are produced without any oak makes for tremendous all-around flexibility, and the lighter weight and lower alcohol content also allow for a wide range of matching options.

PAIRING POINTERS

Bubbly works well:
- To counterbalance salt, moderate heat, richness and cream, and grease, butter, and deep-fried foods.
- To replace any other highlighting acid (citrus) with fish or shellfish.
- To accompany raw fish—sushi, sashimi, oysters, ceviche, and some caviars.
- To match tart foods: citrus and other tart fruits, vinegars, pomegranate, dill, capers, tomatoes, leeks, and zucchini.

- To match many Latin dishes (such as empanadas, ceviche, and mole), and the cuisines of Florida, the Caribbean, and Hawaii. Especially successful are the fruit-forward styles from the United States, New Zealand, and Australia.
- To match many Asian cuisines (Japanese sushi, tempura, and gyoza; Chinese deep-fried dishes, seafood dishes, and some poultry; Thai crepes, fish cakes, and some coconut-milk-based curries; Indian samosas and papadams). Again, the fruit-driven New World styles work best here.
- To accompany many cheeses, especially hard cheeses like Parmesan, really rich cheeses (like triple-cream St. André) and salty cheeses (such as Greek or Bulgarian feta).
- To match dishes with crunchy texture (phyllo pastry and deep-fried foods such as Southern fried chicken, tempura, and Italian fritto misto).
- To harmonize with dishes that have an inherent toasty character, like the bubbly itself (toasted canapés or puff pastry dishes).
- To accompany dishes that imply sweetness or have lightly sweet condiments or treatments. Again, New World styles work best.
- To accompany foods difficult to match with other wines, such as egg dishes and soups.
- To pair with rustic or coarsely textured foods: polenta, pesto, hummus, and baba ghanoush. Sparkling wine goes well with Middle Eastern foods in general.

Bubbly isn't good with:
- Extremes. Dishes that are too rich or flavorful squash its subtlety. Dishes that are too spicy eviscerate the wine.
- Dishes that are too sweet (unless they are paired with the sweeter styles of wine).
- Some strong-tasting fish, other strong flavors, and certain vegetables, especially bitter vegetables, which can make the wines taste metallic (broccoli, escarole, and radicchio).
- With rich red meats. Many chefs pair rosé styles with these foods, but they are not always complementary.

FOR FRUIT-FORWARD, DRY BUBBLIES (BRUT-STYLE)

CRAB SALAD IN ENDIVE LEAVES

SERVES 4 TO 6

⅓ cup mayonnaise, or as needed to bind
1 tablespoon Dijon mustard
½ pound crabmeat, picked over and cartilage removed
⅓ cup finely diced celery
Grated zest of 1 lemon plus 1 to 2 tablespoons lemon juice
2 tablespoons chopped fresh chives
1 tablespoon chopped fresh flat-leaf parsley
Salt and freshly ground black pepper to taste
Cayenne pepper to taste
12 to 18 Belgian endive leaves

In a large bowl, combine the mayonnaise and mustard, and then add the crabmeat, celery, lemon zest, lemon juice, chives, and parsley. Add the salt, black pepper, and cayenne pepper to taste. Cover with plastic wrap and refrigerate until ready to serve. (The crab salad can be prepared up to 1 day ahead of time, though it's better when served within 6 hours.)

Just before serving, spoon the crab salad onto the endive leaves and arrange on a platter.

VARIATION For an alternative presentation, spread the crab mixture on slices of toasted bread.

· · · · ·

This salad is an easy hors d'oeuvre that requires no cooking. Bitter endive provides a fine contrast for the sweet crab and tart lemon. Textures are diverse, contrasting the creaminess of the mayonnaise and the crunch of celery and endive. —Joyce

This dish is one that I love serving to make the flavors of New World sparkling wines "pop." The crab should be fresh (rather than canned) to maximize the wine's fruit flavors. If your wine's a bit tart, increase the lemon juice (or zest if you prefer the mixture a little drier). If your endive is very bitter, you can substitute toasted or grilled bread. Sparkling wines with ample Chardonnay in their blend meld particularly seamlessly with this dish, but I've had many others that sing equally well. The mustard is an "earthy" bridge that can allow you to serve this dish with Champagne-style wines as well, but I do prefer it with the New World styles. Finally, the bubbles offer a nice contrast to the crispness of the endive and celery. —Evan

RECOMMENDED PRODUCERS

Fruit-Forward, Dry Bubblies

EVERYDAY	PREMIUM	SPLURGE
Domaine Chandon (Napa Valley, California)	Roederer Estate (Mendocino County, California)	Schramsberg (Napa Valley, California)
Lindauer (multiple appellations, New Zealand)	Mumm Napa (Napa Valley, California)	J Wine Company (Sonoma County, California)
Domaine Ste. Michelle (Greater Columbia Valley, Washington)	Gloria Ferrer (Sonoma County, California)	Iron Horse (Sonoma County, California)

CAVIAR AND CREAM CHEESE ROLL

YIELDS 12 TO 14 SLICES

**4 tablespoons unsalted butter,
plus 1 to 2 tablespoons for buttering the pan
2 cups milk
½ cup all-purpose flour
½ teaspoon salt
Freshly ground black pepper to taste
5 eggs, separated
8 ounces cream cheese, room temperature
2 tablespoons sour cream
8 ounces salmon roe (caviar)
2 tablespoons minced chives (optional)
Sprigs of watercress for garnish**

Preheat the oven to 375 degrees.

Using about 1 tablespoon of the butter, butter a 10 × 15–inch jelly roll pan and line with baker's parchment. Using another 1 tablespoon or so of butter, butter the parchment.

In a small saucepan over low heat, warm the milk.

In a medium saucepan over low heat, melt the remaining 4 tablespoons butter. Whisk in the flour, salt, and pepper and gradually add the milk. Simmer to cook the flour and thicken the sauce, 2 to 3 minutes. Remove from heat.

In a small bowl, whisk the egg yolks to blend. Gradually add the yolks to the milk mixture, whisking well.

In the bowl of an electric mixer, beat the egg whites until stiff. Stir one-third of the whites into the milk and egg mixture, and then carefully fold in the rest.

Spread the batter evenly in the prepared pan and bake until puffed and golden, 30 to 40 minutes.

Remove the cake from the oven and cover it with a damp dish towel. Chill in the refrigerator for about 10 minutes or cool at room temperature.

To make the filling, use a fork to mash the cream cheese and sour cream together in a small bowl to blend. Add 2 tablespoons of the caviar and mash it to break it down slightly, then fold in the remaining caviar. Fold in the chives, if desired.

Turn the cooled cake out onto the towel. Remove the parchment. Spread the cream cheese filling over the cake and roll up lengthwise, using the towel as a guide. Roll it onto a long cutting board or platter. Cover with plastic wrap and refrigerate until ready to serve. (Can be prepared up to 8 hours ahead of time.)

To serve, slice the roll crosswise into 1-inch slices and transfer the slices to appetizer plates. Garnish with sprigs of watercress.

· · · · ·

This roll is a spectacular starter for a festive meal. You don't have to splurge on the most expensive caviar for this dish to be delicious. The saltiness of the salmon roe is tempered by the cream cheese and the sour cream. One caveat: do not substitute inexpensive black lumpfish caviar, as it will stain the filling a weird shade of purple. —Joyce

Many people think of caviar and Champagne pairings and cheer. Others cringe and claim the caviar makes the wine taste metallic. This dish should make everyone happy. The cream cheese softens the ultrasalty blow that caviar can deliver by itself and adds a creamy texture that frames the wine nicely. Finally, the toasty nature of the cake roll itself is sublime with the wine. —Evan

RECOMMENDED PRODUCERS
Biscuity, Toasty, Nutty Bubblies

EVERYDAY	PREMIUM	SPLURGE
Charles de Fère (Languedoc, France)	Taittinger (Champagne, France)	Krug (Champagne, France)
Gratien & Mayer (Loire Valley, France)	Perrier-Jouët (Champagne, France)	Salon (Champagne, France)
Monmousseau (Languedoc, France)	Pol Roger (Champagne, France)	Bollinger (Champagne, France)

CRUNCHY FRIED MOZZARELLA
AND ANCHOVY SANDWICHES

SERVES 6 AS AN APPETIZER

12 slices baguette or rustic bread, cut about ¾ inch thick
6 oil-packed anchovy fillets, chopped
6 slices fresh mozzarella cheese, cut ½ inch thick
1 cup all-purpose flour
1 cup milk
3 eggs, lightly beaten
Oil for frying

Arrange 6 bread slices on a work surface. Spread the bread with chopped anchovies, and then top each with 1 slice of cheese and 1 of the remaining bread slices. Skewer closed with toothpicks.

Put the flour in a shallow bowl. Put the milk in another shallow bowl and the eggs in a third shallow bowl.

In a large saucepan, pour the oil to a depth of 3 inches. Heat the oil to 365 degrees.

Dip each sandwich into the flour, then into the milk, and then into the eggs. Let the sandwiches absorb the eggs for 1 to 2 minutes. Deep-fry the sandwiches in batches in the hot oil until golden, turning once, about 4 to 5 minutes total. Drain on a plate lined with paper towels. Carefully remove the toothpicks. If the sandwiches are large, cut them in halves or quarters. Serve while hot.

VARIATION Instead of using bread as the outer part of the sandwich, use slices of cooked polenta.

. . . . .

These crispy sandwiches are a specialty of Rome. The anchovies provide salt, the cheese a creamy component, and the bread a wonderful crunch. —Joyce

You can have these delicious sandwiches with Champagne, too, though when we were doing the tasting and testing for this book, earthier and more rustic wines like Spanish Cava and Italian Prosecco were the favorites. The anchovies coupled with the crackly texture of the deep-fried bread are natural crowd pleasers for bubblies. Let the sandwiches absorb the milk and egg washes thoroughly to add an extra richness and a stronger match with the wine. I have always thought anchovies cry out for a less refined bubbly, and, while many Cavas and similar wines are less tart, you don't really need the higher acidity with this match. Although fresh mozzarella is recommended, other kinds of cheese (such as smoked mozzarella or Fontina) can mix it up and are fun to try with a variety of wines. —Evan

RECOMMENDED PRODUCERS
Earthy, Somewhat Rustic Bubblies

EVERYDAY	PREMIUM	SPLURGE
Segura Viudas (Cava, Spain)	Mionetto (Veneto, Italy)	Ca' del Bosco (Veneto, Italy)
Codorníu (Cava, Spain)	Ferrari (Trentino–Alto Adige, Italy)	Bellavista (Veneto, Italy)
Cristalino (Cava, Spain)	Domaine Laurent (Languedoc, France)	

ASIAN-INSPIRED SHRIMP SALAD

SERVES 4

3 cups dry white wine or water or a combination
1 pound (about 16 to 20) large shrimp, peeled and deveined

VINAIGRETTE
⅔ cup peanut or olive oil
6 tablespoons fresh lime juice
Grated zest of 2 limes
2 tablespoons brown sugar
½ teaspoon red pepper flakes or diced jalapeño chile, or more to taste
Salt to taste

2 ripe papayas or mangos, or 1 cantaloupe
6 cups assorted lettuces
6 tablespoons torn fresh mint leaves
6 tablespoons torn fresh basil leaves

In a saucepan, bring the wine to a simmer over medium heat. Add the shrimp and poach until they turn pink, about 3 minutes. Using a slotted spoon, transfer the shrimp to a bowl. Refrigerate until cold, at least 1 hour and up to 1 day. Discard the poaching liquid.

For the vinaigrette: In a large bowl, whisk the peanut oil, lime juice, lime zest, brown sugar, and red pepper flakes to blend. Season to taste with additional red pepper flakes, if desired, and salt.

Peel, pit, and dice or slice the selected fruit. If using papayas, cut them in half and scoop out and discard the seeds. Dice or slice the flesh. If using a mango, cut off the flesh on either side of the central pit. With a sharp paring knife remove the peel and dice or slice the fruit. If tropical fruit is unavailable, you can substitute slices of cantaloupe.

In a large mixing bowl, combine the lettuces, mint, and basil.

Toss the shrimp with ¼ cup of the vinaigrette and marinate for 5 minutes.

Add half of the remaining vinaigrette to the bowl with the lettuces and herbs. Toss to coat, and divide among individual salad plates. Top with the shrimp and fruit. Drizzle the remaining vinaigrette on top and serve.

VARIATION If you don't want to use fruit, you may substitute thinly sliced cucumbers, marinated for about 10 minutes in the vinaigrette before you assemble the salad.

· · · · ·

A salad of tangy fruit and chewy shrimp dressed with a spicy, sweet, and tart vinaigrette makes for a nice, light beginning to a special meal. The shrimp can be poached the night before or earlier in the day. The fruit can be diced or sliced and the vinaigrette prepared hours ahead of serving time. Assemble the salad at the last minute. —Joyce

This is always a crowd-pleasing combination. I opt for slightly sweet wines here because of the mild heat and the sweetness of the fruit. The riper the fruit, the sweeter the wine should be, so ripe mangos require a slightly sweeter wine than most papayas and melons. But if you choose to substitute cucumbers for the fruit, you can go with quite a dry wine, though I would go with a New World bubbly rather than one from Europe. And, just as the sweetness of the fruit is important to your wine selection, so is the heat of the peppers. Sugar takes the edge off the heat, so the hotter the kick in your dressing, the more sweetness you may need to counterbalance it. Try preparing the dish a few times to find the balance that works best for you. —Evan

RECOMMENDED PRODUCERS
Off-Dry (Slightly Sweet) Bubblies

EVERYDAY	PREMIUM
Fontanafredda (Piedmont, Italy)	Ceretto (Piedmont, Italy)
Zonin (Piedmont, Italy)	Möet et Chandon (Champagne, France)
Michele Chiarlo (Piedmont, Italy)	Mumm Napa (Napa Valley, California)

part two

THE WHITE JOURNEYS

CHARDONNAY

Chardonnay (shar-doh-*nay*) is the darling of white wines to American palates. This grape and its wines are fashionable for many reasons: the name is easy to pronounce, and the wine is readily accessible stylistically, gussied up with lots of delicious and enticing oak. Whatever the reason, Chardonnay is the most popular white wine in the United States, and it is enjoyed and admired globally.

WINE-GROWING AREAS

Although Chardonnay is thought by some wine experts to have its roots in Persia, most of us associate it (correctly) with France, and specifically with the globally respected Côte de Beaune, the southern portion of Burgundy's celebrated Côte d'Or. Chardonnay is, in winespeak, an older grape with an ancestry that is in part noble (the Burgundian Pinot family of grapes) and in part plebeian (its Pinot ancestry having been conjoined long ago with the unremarkable Gouais Blanc grape originating in central Europe). Once established in the Côte d'Or, however, the wines from such heralded appellations as Montrachet, Meursault, and Corton Charlemagne became benchmarks. Long-lived and infinitely complex when well made, great white Burgundies (almost all of them Chardonnays) are mosaics of mineral-scented earth, ripe citrus and tree fruit (apples and pears), and an intricacy of spice, toast, and varying levels of butter or butterscotch from the small oak barrels *(barriques)* in which they are aged. Additionally, the less oaky (or unoaked), more earth-driven styles of Chablis to the north and the Chardonnays of the Côte Chalonnaise and Mâconnais to the south present other interpretations, which are often excellent values. Wines coming from the Loire Valley and other parts of France, such as the Ardèche, don't have the depth or complexity of their Burgundian cousins, but have the same unique *terroir*-driven palate and a similar quality of ripe but tart fruit. Finally, in the Champagne region, Chardonnay (especially from the Côte des Blancs) provides the sharp fruit and lemony backbone of many *cuvées* and is also used in making sparkling wine. Chardonnay is also used in the Burgundy region's interpretation of sparkling wine: the local Crémant de Bourgogne is both affordable and delicious. For the rest of the world, it's indeed the two French regions—Burgundy for still wines and Champagne for sparkling wines—that have supplied the road map.

Chardonnay is grown in the northeast of Italy (in Friuli–Venezia Giulia, among other regions), where clean and refreshing wines are styled much like the local Pinot Grigio: light, pure, and crisp. In Italy, as everywhere, there are examples of wines that are Burgundy-style, and these are most often found in Tuscany. Many other European countries have their own versions of Chardonnay. Those from Germany's Pfalz, Austria's Styria, and Spain's Navarra are among the most successful, displaying ample weight and aromatics and employing varying levels of oak. Cava, the appellation of the workhorse sparkling wine from Spain's Catalonia, has since the mid-1990s permitted the use of Chardonnay in its *méthode traditionnelle* wines, which were historically blended only from local grapes such as Xarel-lo and Viura, and the results have been very good.

Australia is producing some of the finest Chardonnay anywhere, ranging from the rich, oak-laden styles of the Hunter Valley to the crisper, tree-fruit-nuanced examples of the Clare Valley. Australia was once known for the same overdone, overoaked interpretations that plagued California early on, but Australian winemakers have, over the past two decades, blown that provincial approach out of the water. Instead of the old Chateau Two-by-Fours, world-class efforts are being vinified in microclimates as widespread as Western Australia's Margaret River, the Adelaide Hills of South Australia, and the island of Tasmania, where Chardonnay is used for both still and sparkling wines. Complex stone fruit, tree fruit, and citrus flavors, rich, waxy textures, and a deft use of oak identify Australia's best bottlings today. Look for the tropical-scented wines of New Zealand's Gisborne region and the Auckland area (Kumeu-Huapai), as well as South Africa's Stellenbosch and Paarl—countries and regions considered young and emerging stars in Chardonnay whose wines are getting better with each vintage.

The Americas, both north and south, are avid players in the Chardonnay arena. A sound majority of the fifty U.S. states bottle Chardonnay. While, in my opinion, the best of the breed still come from California (the Carneros vineyards of Napa and Sonoma, Sonoma's Russian River, Santa Ynez's Santa Rita Hills, and Mendocino's Anderson Valley, among other areas), formidable wines are being made in unexpected states, including New York, Virginia, Maryland, and even Texas. American wines have, like their Australian counterparts, benefited from the discovery of cooler microclimates within the regions where Chardonnay has traditionally flourished. The range of styles is immense: Carneros Chardonnays exhibit a green-apple and lemon personality with bright acidity, while those that come from Santa Barbara exhibit tropical pineapple and guava flavors with secondary notes of peach and pear, and the Russian River Valley wines are waxy and lush with a note of dense melon and apple fruit. Continuing up the Pacific coast, Oregon and Washington's best Chardonnays are distinct, with slightly less body but great structure, as you might expect at more northerly latitudes, and some of the recent examples of British Columbia's best Okanagan Valley Chardonnays show promise.

Chardonnays from Chile and Argentina as a general rule display personality traits somewhere between those of California and those of northern Italy, with the best examples rivaling the Burgundy-style interpretations from the latter area. For now, the most notable efforts come from Chile's Casablanca region and Argentina's Mendoza, especially the higher-altitude vineyards of Argentina such as the Uco Valley.

A table of principal wine-growing regions for Chardonnay appears on pages 265–67.

VINTNER CHOICES

*Still or sparkling; clones or selections; skin contact or none; wood or no wood;
new or older wood; type and size of wood; use and percentage of barrel fermentation;
use and percentage of malolactic fermentation (ML); lees stirring*

The most significant choice for the vintner is whether to make still or sparkling wine. For sparkling wines, the decisions on production techniques and ripeness of the grapes at harvest will be made long before the crushing and pressing begin, because the grapes for bubbly require many viticultural choices. Chardonnay for sparkling wine is always picked at lower sugar levels and pressed quickly but gently, while the grapes for still wine are left out on the vine longer to ripen and develop more mature flavors. Prior to fermentation, the wine may also be left in contact with the skins for longer to extract more flavor. Deciding on the selection or clone of Chardonnay is important, as Chardonnay is generally not blended with other varietals (grape types): complexity is achieved through blending grapes from different vineyards, choosing smaller lots within vineyards, and using differing selections of Chardonnay. Selections of Chardonnay are like relatives within a family. Although they come from the same ancestors and are genetically similar, environment and experience also affect their character: siblings may differ from one another emotionally and physically as much as oil does from vinegar.

Vintners sometimes leave the fermenting wine *must* (the combination of grape pulp and solids) in contact with its skins. In white wine production, this process "pops" the fruit character of the wine by extracting components from the skins that make the wine very opulent and flashy. The downside is that, over time, the wines often brown and oxidize (that is, age) more quickly and can ultimately seem more like sherry than Chardonnay.

Oak, the wood employed for most wine barrels, contributes key elements to many wines. The butter or butterscotch flavors that many people identify with Chardonnay come not from the grape but from the oak, from the aging or actual fermenting of the wine in the barrel. Oak bestows a waxy, velvety texture and can add a sweet buttercream flavor to the wine. The flavors of charring or toasting picked up when the staves of the barrels are bent over an open flame, a common technique for making wine barrels, also influence the wine. As a rule, the heavier the toasting or charring of the staves, the greater the effect on the wine. Heavily toasted barrels impart more intense roasted and toasted flavors (think caramel, molasses, toffee, coffee, and burnt sugar) to the wine. The age of the barrels employed is also significant, as new oak contributes much more flavor than older, previously used oak—which, depending on the wine and the grapes, may be a better choice. The size of the oak vessel is critical: the smaller the barrel, the larger the surface area of wine exposed to the wood, and the stronger the oak influence. Then again, some producers want minimal or no oak used, as they feel it distracts from the purity of the fruit. Many winemakers in Chablis (France) and other producers around the world now making wine labeled as "unoaked" vinify their Chardonnay in this manner.

The implementation of malolactic fermentation (or ML) can soften the wine's acidic edge and adds a strong buttered-popcorn flavor. It can be entirely prevented in the winemaking process or allowed to happen in some portion of the wine, which is then blended with the rest; again, this is a vintner's choice. ML, by converting wine's malic acid (the same sharp acid found in tart green apples) into milder lactic acid (that in sour cream, yogurt, etc.), reduces the tartness of the wine and contributes a velvety smooth texture that for many wine lovers is a source of great enjoyment. This smooth texture of the wine is commonly referred to as its *mouthfeel*. It's considered particularly important in Chardonnay and Pinot Noir.

During alcoholic fermentation, as the yeast metabolizes the sugar and produces alcohol, the dead yeast cells *(lees)* tumble slowly to the bottom of the fermentation vessel. When the wine is stirred or agitated, they can add additional toasty flavors, along with more texture and yet another dimension of complexity. Lees stirring, as this process is called, is an increasingly common practice that originated in Burgundy.

FLAVORS

Fruit: Lemon, lime, grapefruit, tangerine, Mandarin orange, peach, nectarine, pear, apple, pineapple, fig, guava, melon, banana, marmalade, pie fruit, mango, passion fruit, kiwi, quince, cucumber

Floral: Mint, lemongrass, verbena, lemon thyme, aromatic white flowers, lemon, lime, or citrus blossoms, blond tobacco

Earth: Minerals, stones, gunflint, steel, mushrooms, chalk, forest floor (humus)

Wood (oak): Smoke, cream, vanilla, custard, caramel, bread crust, burnt sugar, molasses, maple syrup, honey, toast, coconut, hazelnut, almond, walnut, cashew, nutmeg, ginger

Other: Popcorn, butter, butterscotch, yeast, plain yogurt, cornmeal, oatmeal, flan, lemon curd

INGREDIENTS AND STYLES

First off, it is easy to "lose" Chardonnay behind food. Chardonnay's personality and flavors can be easily dominated by dishes that are too rich, strong, or bold for its forward yet subtle personality. Chardonnay is best matched with foods that are enhanced by its round, full, and often silky character. Various shellfish (lobster, scallops, prawns, and shrimp) are classic and time-honored table partners, especially when accompanied by a rich sauce: drawn butter or a modification of a cream or butter sauce. The same is true for milder poultry (chicken, quail, and turkey), white meat (veal and pork), fish (halibut, trout, and swordfish), and other meats (sweetbreads and rabbit). Pastas, risotto, and other starches (winter squash and polenta) provide a great textural backdrop for many Chardonnays when paired with compatible food ingredients.

The cuisines of Hawaii and South Florida, with their reliance on tropical tastes, are particularly well suited to young fruit-forward Chardonnays, such as those coming from the United States, Australia, New Zealand, and South Africa. Nuevo Latino cooking, with its myriad sources of sweet and implied sweet ingredients, is another great partner for many similar Chardonnays and for the Chardonnays from Chile and Argentina.

METHODS OF COOKING

As so many Chardonnays spend some time in the barrel, knowing how to play off the wood or oak aging is useful. Try oak-aged Chardonnays with lightly smoked or grilled dishes and those with traits similar to those imparted by the oak: sweet spices, toast, caramel, and vanilla. It is said that the acclaimed French chef Alain Senderens developed his globally renowned lobster in vanilla sauce specifically to match the countless white Burgundies served in his former restaurant, L'Archestrate. If the Chardonnay you have selected is influenced by malolactic fermentation (that is, it has a buttery or buttered-popcorn aroma and flavor), attempt to match that core personality by sautéing or poaching with butter or incorporating butter into the dish. The use of nut oils can pick up nicely on the toasted and nutty oak characters of many a Chardonnay, and you can also add raw nuts to a dish as a last-minute ingredient rather than cooking with them. I prefer to toast the nuts first, both to preserve the texture and to echo those elements in the wine itself. Other methods of cooking that set the stage well for oak-aged Chardonnay are plank roasting, slow braising, and gentle stewing.

Please remember that not all Chardonnays are created the same. Many European versions are more austere, stressing mineral and earth components: these wines are less overtly oaky and show best with simple and clean flavors in food. Good choices here would be a roast chicken with garlic or a sautéed snapper served simply or with a tart sauce or a wedge of lemon. These styles of Chardonnay are also exceptional at diminishing the richness of thick-textured dishes and counterbalancing sauces based on cream, butter, emulsification, or reduction.

Finally, if the wine is aged and shows more developed Chardonnay flavors (almond, hazelnut, sherry, and dried fruit), it's best to keep the food as neutral as possible or, again, attempt to mirror the flavor profile of the wine. Using nuts (as a coating, as an ingredient, or in powdered form as a thickening agent) or drizzling on a nut oil is almost always a slam dunk. Because the acidity of the Chardonnay will be mitigated by age, its effectiveness in cutting the richness of a heavy dish is lessened. Dishes such as Chinese prawns with cashews, macadamia-crusted fried chicken, and fillet of sole amandine are good options for pairing with a developed Chardonnay.

PAIRING POINTERS

Chardonnay works well:

- With dishes that have rich textures and flavors, especially if the Chardonnay has texture (as from oak aging or lees stirring).
- To counterbalance rich dishes by "cutting" richness with higher acidity (especially unoaked, cooler-climate examples).
- With most mild and sweet shellfish, including lobster, prawns, shrimp, and steamer clams; but choose unoaked types when matching with mussels and most oysters.
- With butter, cream, melted cheeses, and anything adding coarse texture (such as white beans, macaroni, polenta, or grits).
- With many sweet spices, which mirror the flavors derived from oak barrels, including nutmeg, cinnamon, five-spice powder, and dried ginger.
- With nuts, and recipes incorporating nuts. As an inherent flavor characteristic of Chardonnay, nuts of various kinds, and especially toasted nuts, are sublime, especially with aged and older, developed wines.
- With milder white mushrooms (standard button mushrooms, chanterelles, shiitakes, oyster mushrooms, etc.), especially when they are sautéed with butter. Other textured and mild ingredients are also great platforms for Chardonnay, including avocado and squash.
- With onions and garlic; served with earthy Old World examples (such as those from Burgundy or northern Italy), these pick up on the wine's *terroir*.

Chardonnay doesn't work:

- If it is too oaky to match with food. If you are serving a rich and oaky Chardonnay, play to it with ingredients that mirror the flavors of the wine or, better still, with cooking methods that match well with the oak (such as grilling and smoking).
- In showing off hot or spicy dishes. The explosion of capsaicins, the heat-invoking elements in chiles, blows out the subtlety while accentuating the oak and the alcohol in the wine.

- With very sharp ingredients. Most oak-aged Chardonnay is diminished when paired with items such as leeks, olives, asparagus, capers, zucchini, tomatoes, and broccoli rabe. Unoaked and sharper examples, however, can be brilliant.
- When paired with overtly sweet foods. Oak, Chardonnay, and sugar in the mouth aren't a happy combination. Opt for something other than oaky Chardonnay when sitting down to Easter or Thanksgiving dinner or digging into a sweet Thai coconut curry.
- With many cheeses in a cheese course. Really. To show off oaky Chardonnay, serve a smooth unaged Brie, a nutty Swiss Emmenthaler, a French Comté, or a mild and creamy Italian Teleme. Avoid pungent cheeses and those high in acid, such as goat cheese.

FOR EARTHY, MINERALLY CHARDONNAYS (BURGUNDY-STYLE)

GRILLED, HERB-MARINATED FISH
ON A BED OF WHITE BEANS

SERVES 4

MARINADE

½ cup extra virgin olive oil

4 sprigs thyme

4 sage leaves

2 small bay leaves, broken up

1 to 2 tablespoons coarsely chopped rosemary

1 tablespoon finely chopped garlic

Grated zest of 1 orange

Salt and freshly ground black pepper

4 6-ounce fillets of albacore tuna, swordfish, or sea bass

Cooked White Beans (see recipe below)

4 lemon wedges

In a small saucepan, bring the olive oil, thyme, sage, bay leaves, and rosemary to a simmer over medium heat. Reduce heat to low and simmer 2 to 3 minutes to infuse the oil with the herbs. Remove from the heat and cool to lukewarm. Add the garlic, orange zest, and salt and pepper to taste. Let the marinade cool completely. Reserve 2 tablespoons of the marinade to drizzle on the fish later.

Place the fish fillets in a shallow dish or bowl. Pour the herbed oil over the fillets. Marinate in the refrigerator for 2 to 3 hours.

Preheat the broiler or prepare a charcoal or gas grill. Remove the fish from the marinade. Sprinkle with salt and pepper. Cook the fish until it is opaque in the center when pierced with a knife, about 3 to 4 minutes per side.

Place a serving spoonful of white beans on each dinner plate. Top with the cooked fish. Drizzle with the reserved marinade and add a few grinds of black pepper. Serve lemon wedges on the side.

COOKED WHITE BEANS

½ pound (1 cup) dried cannellini, great northern, or other white beans

2 to 3 quarts water

3 whole sage leaves or 1 bay leaf

½ onion (optional)

2 whole cloves garlic, peeled (optional)

1 teaspoon salt, plus more to taste

5 tablespoons extra virgin olive oil

Freshly ground black pepper

3 cloves garlic, minced

3 fresh sage leaves, chopped

Additional olive oil

Overnight method: In a large pot, soak the beans in 1 quart water overnight in the refrigerator.

Quick-soak method: If you need beans in a hurry, and you don't want to use canned, use this method. In a large pot, combine the beans with 2 quarts of water and bring to a boil. Boil for 2 minutes, then remove from the heat, cover the pot, and let the beans stand for 1 hour.

After completing either method of soaking, drain the beans, transfer them to a saucepan, and cover with 1 quart cold water. Bring to a gentle boil. Add the whole sage leaves, and the onion and whole garlic cloves, if desired, and reduce the heat to low. Skim off the foam, cover the pot, and simmer gently until the beans are tender, 40 to 60 minutes. Add 1 teaspoon of salt after 15 minutes of cooking.

When the beans are tender, discard the garlic, onion, and sage leaves. Drain the excess liquid from the beans, keeping them in about 1 cup of bean cooking liquid. Transfer the beans to a bowl. While the beans are still warm, add 3 tablespoons of the olive oil and toss to coat. Season to taste with additional salt and pepper. (Can be prepared up to 2 days ahead of time. Cover and refrigerate.)

In a small sauté pan, heat the remaining 2 tablespoons olive oil over low heat. Add the minced garlic and sauté until fragrant, about 3 minutes. Add the cooked beans with their liquid and the chopped sage leaves. Simmer 15 minutes. Taste and reseason. Drizzle with extra oil and serve.

. . . . .

All over the Mediterranean—in Italy, France, Greece, Turkey, Spain, and North Africa—fish is rubbed with oil and fresh herbs and grilled over a wood fire. Citrus juice may also be added to the marinade. A broiler will work fine if you don't have the time or inclination to set up the grill. To provide a textural contrast, serve the fish atop a bed of creamy white beans. In a pinch, canned beans can be dressed with oil, garlic, and herbs and substituted for the Cooked White Beans recipe. This dish is set off nicely with an accompaniment of mild sautéed greens, such as spinach or Swiss chard, or simply grilled Japanese eggplant. —Joyce

Garlic and fresh herbs are two key ingredients that will always set off and frame a more classic, Old World Chardonnay. I love this particular dish with this style of wine, as the firm acidity in the wine highlights the herbal components of the dish and echoes an earthy character in the wine, while heightening the inherent sweetness of the fish itself. If the wine is acidic, you need not add any citrus to the marinade. If it is a little lacking in sharpness, adding lemon or lime juice to the marinade can compensate. The white beans give you a great excuse to opt for a richer and more textured Chardonnay (one that has spent some time in oak), as it can handle and balance the richness of the beans' texture. If the Chardonnay is mild in flavor, play down the herbs a bit and avoid the pungency of charcoal grilling. —Evan

RECOMMENDED PRODUCERS

Earthy, Minerally Chardonnays

EVERYDAY	PREMIUM	SPLURGE
Labouré-Roi (Burgundy, France)	Domaine Olivier Leflaive (Burgundy, France)	Jean-Marc Boillot (Burgundy, France)
Cave de Lugny (Burgundy, France)	Château Fuissé (Burgundy, France)	Louis Jadot (Burgundy, France)
Antonin Rodet (Burgundy, France)	Ramey (Sonoma County, California)	Patz & Hall (Napa Valley, California)

ROAST LOBSTER WITH TARRAGON-LEMON BUTTER

SERVES 4

4 lobsters, about 1½ pounds each
½ cup tarragon vinegar
2 tablespoons finely minced shallot
2 tablespoons finely chopped fresh tarragon
¼ cup fresh lemon juice
1 tablespoon grated lemon zest
½ pound (2 sticks) unsalted butter, room temperature
Salt and freshly ground black pepper

Bring a very large pot of heavily salted water to a boil. Drop in the lobsters and parboil for 7 to 8 minutes. Meanwhile, fill the sink with ice water. When the lobsters are done, use tongs to transfer them to the sink of ice water to cool. Transfer 1 lobster to a work surface. Cut it in half lengthwise and remove the gravelly sac at the base of the head. Remove the claws. Crack and remove the meat, transferring it to a bowl. Discard the claw shells. Remove the meat from the body cavity, cut it into bite-sized pieces, and transfer to the bowl. Stir the meat to combine and put it back into the body shells. Repeat with the remaining lobsters. Wrap tightly and refrigerate.

Combine the vinegar, shallot, and tarragon in a small saucepan and bring to a boil over high heat. Boil until the liquid is syrupy and almost totally absorbed, about 5 minutes. Stir in the lemon juice and zest and cool to room temperature. Using a food processor, beat the butter until creamy. Add the tarragon-lemon mixture and beat until incorporated. Season the butter to taste with salt and pepper.

Preheat the oven to 350 degrees. Spread the butter over the lobster meat in the shells. Cover loosely with foil and roast in the oven for 8 minutes. Serve immediately.

. . . . .

You can't go wrong with a classic seafood and Chardonnay pairing, especially one as irresistible as this. When you want to serve your finest bottle, lobster is the way to go. For the compound butter, Meyer lemons are ideal, as they are less tart than regular Eureka lemons. If you can't get Meyer lemons, you may use half lemon and half orange juice, or just use regular lemons. The richness of the butter will counteract excessive tartness. Anise-scented tarragon heightens the sweetness of the lobster. Though it's fine to serve nothing with this lobster except a few slices of crusty baguette, an uncomplicated side of pan-fried or roasted potatoes adds richness and texture. —Joyce

Ahh . . . lobster and Chardonnay. This is one of those quintessential matches that almost everyone knows and loves. Although most Chardonnays pair well with this dish, I find that the sweet, rich meat of the lobster, the ample butter, the subtle sweetness added by the oven finishing, and the bright sweet "pop" of the lemons make this dish sing with the fruit-forward examples we find in the New World (the Americas, Australia, New Zealand, and South Africa). As Joyce says, Meyer lemons, if available, really make this dish shine and let you serve riper and tropical-fruit-scented wines. If you're using traditional lemons, more classically citrus-scented examples of Chardonnay (such as New Zealand's Hawkes Bay or California's Carneros) may be preferable. —Evan

RECOMMENDED PRODUCERS
Opulent, Fruit-Forward Chardonnays

EVERYDAY	PREMIUM	SPLURGE
Gallo of Sonoma (Sonoma County, California)	Kumeu River (Auckland, New Zealand)	Lewis (Napa Valley, California)
Chateau Ste. Michelle (Greater Columbia Valley, Washington)	Catena Zapata (Mendoza, Argentina)	Leeuwin (Margaret River, Western Australia)
Lindemans (multiple appellations, South Australia)	Sanford (Southern Central Coast, California)	Paul Hobbs (Sonoma County, California)

POLENTA WITH SMOKED FISH
AND CRÈME FRAÎCHE

SERVES 4

1½ cups fresh corn kernels (from about 2 ears of corn),
or 1½ cups frozen corn kernels (optional)
Oil for baking sheet
1 cup cornmeal (not instant or superfine)
4 cups cold water
Salt and freshly ground black pepper
4 tablespoons butter
2 medium red onions, cut in ¼-inch slices
12 ounces smoked trout fillets, broken into 2-inch pieces (from about 2 trout),
or 12 ounces smoked salmon, cut into 2 × ½–inch strips
¾ cup crème fraîche
¼ cup minced fresh chives

If using the corn kernels, cook them in a pot of boiling salted water until tender and cooked through, about 1 to 2 minutes. Drain well, transfer to a clean dish towel, and pat dry. (If the corn is too wet it will weaken the final polenta.)

Lightly oil a small baking sheet. In a heavy saucepan, combine the cornmeal and 4 cups cold water. Bring to a boil over medium heat, reduce the heat to low, and cook the polenta, stirring often, until thickened and no longer gritty, about 30 minutes. When the polenta is done, stir in the corn kernels, if using. Season to taste with salt and pepper. Pour onto the prepared sheet and refrigerate until firm, about 2 hours. (Can be prepared up to 1 day ahead of time. After the polenta has set, cover with plastic wrap and refrigerate.)

Meanwhile, in a large skillet over medium heat, melt the butter. Add the red onions and sauté for 10 minutes, then lower the heat to low and sauté another 10 minutes, until lightly golden and caramelized.

To serve: Preheat the grill or broiler. Cut the polenta into 8 triangles or strips. Grill or broil until golden brown around the edges, turning once, about 5 minutes total. Or heat the oven to 350 degrees, place the polenta on an oiled baking sheet, and heat until warm, about 10 minutes. Transfer the polenta to individual salad plates. Top with strips of smoked fish and caramelized onions, dividing evenly. Drizzle with crème fraîche and sprinkle with minced chives.

. . . . .

This polenta is an ideal first course to launch a special-occasion dinner. Choose either smoked salmon or smoked trout. Fresh corn kernels and caramelized onions add sweetness, which plays nicely off the smokiness of the fish. Drizzle with tart crème fraîche, add a sprinkle of chopped chives, and you have a wonderfully complex-tasting dish. —Joyce

Because I often recommend Chardonnay as the ideal first-course wine (carried over perhaps from hors d'oeuvres or a reception), this is a dish I serve frequently. It contains many elements that highlight rich, oaky Chardonnays: smokiness (smoked fish), toastiness (polenta and, if you use it, fresh corn), creaminess and tartness (crème fraîche), and the roasted, sweet, or torrefied flavors of caramelized onions. Select a smoked fish that's not ultrapungent (a milder trout or salmon as opposed to one that's fishy or heavily smoked), as the fish can otherwise dominate the wine. The fresh corn adds a pleasant sweetness that echoes the Chardonnay's fruit while adding another grain dimension to the polenta. The thread that pulls this match together is the crème fraîche, which I always use generously. If your Chardonnay is very buttery, stir a few tablespoons of butter into the polenta while it's cooking. This will enrich the flavor and add a smooth, rich texture to the polenta itself. —Evan

RECOMMENDED PRODUCERS
Rich, Oaky, Buttery Chardonnays

EVERYDAY	PREMIUM	SPLURGE
Concha y Toro (Central Valley, Chile)	Au Bon Climat (Southern Central Coast, California)	Miner Family (Napa Valley, California)
Clos du Bois (Sonoma County, California)	Casa Lapostolle (Central Valley, Chile)	Gary Farrell (Sonoma County, California)
Rosemount (multiple appellations, South Australia)	Wolf Blass (multiple appellations, South Australia)	Talbott (Northern Central Coast, California)

BAKED RICOTTA WITH TOAST

SERVES 4

1 tablespoon extra virgin olive oil, or as needed
1 pound fresh soft ricotta cheese
Salt and freshly ground black pepper
1 tablespoon chopped fresh herbs (optional)
12 slices grilled or toasted bread

Preheat the oven to 300 degrees. Lightly oil a 4-cup ceramic crock or soufflé dish.

Stir the ricotta cheese with a fork and add salt and pepper to taste. Stir in the herbs, if desired. Pack the cheese into the crock and drizzle with olive oil. Bake until warm and a little quivery, about 15 minutes.

Serve with grilled or toasted bread.

• • • • •

This baked ricotta and toast is a classic Italian appetizer and is simplicity itself. All that's required is fresh ricotta cheese, sweet and soft in texture. Once it is baked, spread it on toast or bruschetta—grilled bread rubbed with extra virgin olive oil and garlic. I also love the ricotta on rosemary or walnut bread, but any rustic loaf will do. If you are in the mood, add some chopped fresh herbs such as basil, mint, parsley, or chives. Often, though, the simplest can be best, especially if you want the wine to shine. —Joyce

Why not an elaborate main course dish? Well, I have worked for years to find the perfect pairing for the delicate and evolved nuances of an aged Chardonnay. As with many things in life, less is more with older Chardonnay, and this simplest of dishes is a real crowd pleaser. Ricotta is a wonderful platform for Chardonnay, and with its implicit savory sweetness it seems to infuse a little life into older wines, with fruit that is more developed and dried. The toasted bread, of course, can pick up on any oaky, toasty, nutty, or other oxidative characteristics in the wine, and the warm temperature of the dish is a lovely and sexy backdrop. But do give it a few minutes out of the oven to cool off, or you'll find yourself with singed taste buds and no appreciation of either the wine or the dish! If you have Burgundy-style wine (earthy, Old World), adding the herbs can enhance its rustic charm. Walnut bread, with its slight bitterness, will also show off these rustic wines. And a fruitier, less sharp olive oil is almost always better with the New World interpretations.

Although this dish is my personal choice to accompany wines of this style, you may want a more substantial dish to serve as an entrée. In that case simplicity is still key—a minimally adorned roast chicken, lightly sautéed or poached trout or sole, or a clean-tasting seafood risotto would be appropriate and interesting without upstaging the wine.

When you're selecting Chardonnays to cellar—although this advice goes against just about everything I believe—price is often a reliable guide. The best and most age-worthy Chardonnays by definition come from specific areas and are made with artisanal techniques, employing the best grapes and the most expensive barrels. I list a few reputable producers below, but it's worth doing a little research of your own on wineries whose Chardonnays age well: consult a trusted friend, a good retailer, or a knowledgeable sommelier. —Evan

RECOMMENDED PRODUCERS
Developed, Mature Chardonnays

EVERYDAY	PREMIUM	SPLURGE
Acacia (Napa Valley, California)	Mayacamas (Napa Valley, California)	Michaud (Northern Central Coast, California)
Columbia Crest (Greater Columbia Valley, Washington)	Hanzell (Sonoma County, California)	Domaine Leflaive (Burgundy, France)
Evans & Tate (Margaret River, Western Australia)	William Fèvre (Burgundy, France)	Comtes Lafon (Burgundy, France)

SAUVIGNON BLANC

I am so happy that more and more wine drinkers are developing a fondness for this prominent white grape. This affection owes a lot to Sauvignon Blanc's versatility in matching with food as well as to its relative affordability.

Once considered the next big thing in white wines, Sauvignon Blanc (soh-veen-*yown blahn*), or Fumé Blanc, as it's often called (yes, they are the same wine), has found a happy place in the world of white wines and at the table. Sauvignon Blanc is my desert-island wine—if I could pick only one white wine, this would be it. I never tire of its forthright and bold personality, and it rarely disappoints. Indeed, to this day, two of my all-time fondest wine-touring memories are in Sauvignon Blanc areas: the eastern Loire Valley in France and Marlborough in New Zealand.

WINE-GROWING AREAS

Like Chardonnay, Sauvignon Blanc has its ancestral home in France; also like Chardonnay, it is at home in two regions of France: the Loire Valley and Bordeaux. These two regions are associated with two different styles of Sauvignon Blanc. The Sauvignons of the Loire Valley are 100 percent Sauvignon (no blending is permitted); they are rarely made with any oak aging; and they tend to be very characteristic of the varietal, with grass, gooseberry, olive, and lemon or grapefruit flavors. The bold green flavor found in these wines, and in similarly styled Sauvignon Blancs from other parts of the world, is attributable to high concentrations of methoxypyrozines, a chemical component inherent to the grape that is found in greater concentrations in cooler climates. Managing these methoxypyrozines is the key in Loire Valley styles of wine, as they can be offensive if overly dominant.

Sauvignon Blanc wines from Bordeaux's Graves and Entre-Deux-Mers regions are generally blended with Semillon (and some Muscadelle) and may well see some oak aging. The flavors here lean more toward earthy, sweet citrus, green and yellow apple, and some green melon, and, if the wine is oaked, may be accompanied by a richer, rounder texture. Outside France, this style of Sauvignon Blanc is often referred to as the Graves style.

Sauvignon Blanc performs extremely well in New Zealand (Marlborough's examples have quickly become well established and globally popular). In New Zealand, Sauvignon Blanc has two decidedly different styles. In Marlborough, it comes off pungent with gooseberry, green olive, and other methoxy nuances but is also framed with flavors of guava, passion fruit and, in ripe vintages, nectarine and peach. In Hawkes Bay, the wine is decidedly more citric. Both versions are most often 100 percent varietal or blended with just a few percentage points of related grapes (such as Semillon).

Sauvignon Blanc is not a significant grape in Australia. In South Africa, however, it is a rising star, and the examples coming from Stellenbosch and Elgin are worth a look—and a taste. Stylistically, they resemble those from New Zealand.

In Europe (outside France), the grape has done well in northeastern Italy, making wines that resemble Pinot Grigio in personality, with a decidedly bright Sauvignon flavor. Many bottlings from Austria are downright stunning and readily available. And the most memorable whites I had while in Moldova and Bulgaria some years back were Sauvignon-based.

From Chile come great everyday sipping wines: lighter-bodied and sharper, with a defined fruit character, an angular and austere structure, and a lightness that make them food-friendly. In Chile most Sauvignon Blanc is blended with a French selection called Sauvignon Vert (or Sauvignonasse), which is musky and pungent. Some wines are more Vert than Blanc!

In California, the same Loire or Graves choice separates regions and styles: the bold herbal varietal nature of Sonoma's Dry Creek contrasts with the sharp citric qualities of Amador County in the Sierra foothills, the stylized, oak-aged examples of Napa Valley, and the in-between interpretations of the Southern Central Coast. One of my favorite areas for Sauvignon Blanc is Mendocino County's Potter Valley, where the grapes are in harmonious balance, ranging across the whole flavor rainbow; the underrated Lake County also excels. Up-and-coming examples from the Pacific Northwest are also definitely worth exploring, as are the lovely wines coming from Israel, where the Sauvignon Blanc wines are world-class and not just a Passover treat.

A table of principal wine-growing regions for Sauvignon Blanc appears on pages 268–69.

VINTNER CHOICES

Graves- or Loire-style; wood or no wood; new or older wood; type of wood; blended or 100 percent varietal; sweet or dry; Chardonnay wannabe or not; skin contact

The decision to emulate a Loire or a Graves model will drive most of the vintner's other decisions. The principal choices are whether to age in oak and whether to blend with Semillon (or, increasingly in California, Chardonnay and Viognier). If winemakers do use oak, the principles used in making Chardonnay also come into play here. Larger oak barrels impart less oak flavor than smaller ones. Newer oak is much more dramatic than older oak; winemakers can hedge their bets by using a combination of younger and older barrels to temper the effect of the new oak on the wines. If the oak influence is played up a lot, those of us in the biz say that the wine becomes a "Chardonnay wannabe." In this style of Sauvignon Blanc, many of the vintner choices listed for Chardonnay apply here, too.

Leaving the wine in contact with the skins of the grapes (often referred to as *skin contact* or by the French technical term *macération pelliculaire*) will make the wine more fruit-forward and approachable in its youth. However, like Chardonnays treated in this way, the wine may not age well. That said, for Sauvignon Blanc, age is often moot, as few people cellar and store these wines for the long haul.

If a winemaker is intent on making a sweet dessert wine, patterned after Bordeaux's celebrated Sauternes or its surrounding (great value!) appellations, then many different decisions need to be made to accommodate that style of wine. Grapes will be harvested late to allow them to become sweet and possibly botrytized. Then clusters of grapes (and even individual grapes) are selected, vinified, and aged in oak to produce wines intended for consumption at the end of the meal (though people occasionally enjoy a sweet wine as a counterpoint to a savory first course such as foie gras). And although Sauvignon can make a lovely late-harvest wine on its own, more often than not it plays a supporting role to Semillon, which is the grape that generally drives dessert blends.

FLAVORS

Fruit and vegetable: Grapefruit, lemon, lime, citron, melon, guava, passion fruit, quince, gooseberry, kumquat, green banana, papaya, fig, green bean, green pea, green olive, artichoke, flower stem, asparagus, bell pepper, fennel, caper, celery, celeriac (celery root), grass, hay, straw, alfalfa

Floral: Mint, menthol, dill, coriander, basil, green-tea leaf, lemongrass, lemon verbena, lemon thyme

Earth: Wet wool, wet dog, cat box,* gunflint, mineral

Wood (oak): Smoke, vanilla, toast, sweet spice (pie)

In dessert styles: Apricot, peach, ripe pear, honey, caramel, flan/crème brûlée, sultana (golden raisin), marmalade, vanilla, sweet spice, citrus peel, nut, dry fig

* Yes, occasionally Sauvignon can have the sweet, putrid smell of a cat's litter box!

INGREDIENTS AND STYLES

Sauvignon Blanc is one of the best wines to drink with food. Indeed, many of my friends who aren't fond of it as a sipping or cocktail wine are miraculously converted when they have it with a meal.

"Classic" Sauvignon Blanc (young, minimally oaked or unoaked, redolent of bright "green" flavors, with tangy acidity) is sublime with most salads, vegetarian dishes (especially those including peppers, eggplant, zucchini, asparagus, or leeks), and the freshest and simplest seafood and fowl. It performs well with most shellfish and light poultry and shows beautifully with white meats (pork and veal) if they are prepared in a manner that spikes its flavors (with citrus, capers, garlic, olives, and ginger). A green salad with goat cheese, a pasta with green beans, tomatoes, and pesto, and flash-fried rock cod fillets are all prime candidates. When you want to bring out the best in a dish, a Sauvignon Blanc can highlight a recipe without masking its character. Additionally, many sharp, soft-rind, or lightly-washed-rind cheeses are lovely tablemates. Sauvignon pairs well with feta, ricotta salata, Fontana, Jarlsberg, and any shape, age, and size of goat cheese.

With the recent arrival of the "small plates" phenomenon, I find Sauvignon Blanc to be a great equalizer. It's as happy alongside a variety of Middle Eastern *mezze* as it is with Spanish tapas or Italian antipasto. And if you don't have a bottle of chilled fino sherry for shooting the breeze over nuts and olives, you need look no farther than a Sauvignon.

Sauvignon styles that are rich from blending with other grapes (Semillon, Chardonnay, and Viognier) can marry well with richer preparations such as risotto, lightly smoked or grilled white meat, fish and poultry, and many pan or oven roasts. With their fuller body and zippier tartness and acidity, these wines mirror the texture, personality, and main flavors of such dishes.

The richer oak-aged styles, fuller in flavor and texture and verging in personality on a Chardonnay, should be treated like Chardonnays in pairing. Strong Chardonnay wannabes are almost identical to Chardonnay in their food affinities.

Aged Sauvignon Blanc is an acquired taste. Long gone are the tangy green and citrus flavors of youth. They are replaced by the more developed nut, yellow and green vegetable, and fino sherry tastes. With these I prefer slightly more pungent fish, dishes with stronger sauces, or flavorful vegetarian dishes with texture (think eggplant parmigiana or vegetarian lasagna).

METHODS OF COOKING

Unlike Chardonnay, Sauvignon Blanc can handle it all. Low-impact methods of cooking generally highlight ingredients, and Sauvignon's ample acidity makes it a natural partner for these preparations. Almost any steamed dish will be lovely, as the wine will bring out the delicate flavors of the ingredients. Sautéing is fine, and Sauvignon Blanc wines are bold enough to stand up to stronger cooking treatments such as grilling, smoking, and charring.

Ahhh . . . *dessert!* I explore this area more deeply in the dessert wine section. Having said that, being a huge fan of dessert, I enjoy a sweet Sauvignon Blanc both as an accompaniment to select savories (such as cheeses and foie gras) and with desserts highlighting stone or tree fruits, such as a peach tart, poached pears, or a compote of yellow and red plums. Many cookies and some nut-based desserts can be lovely with aged Sauternes and Sauternes-style oak-aged wines. And with pure, creamy vanilla ice cream, few wine selections marry better.

PAIRING POINTERS

Sauvignon Blanc goes well:

- With most vegetarian soups (especially minestrones and simple purées). Soup can be tricky, and Sauvignon is one of the best wines to pair it with. Avoid serving Sauvignon with broth-based soups unless you plan to add substance to them (pieces of vegetable, pasta, etc.).
- With anything emphasizing or enhanced with fresh herbs, such as a salad, a dish grilled with or over herbs, or a dish served with a sauce, even a bold one such as salsa verde, an herbal pesto, or guacamole!
- With a dish served with a vinaigrette dressing, be it a dressed salad or grilled fish, meat, or poultry with a vinaigrette spooned on top (especially grilled dishes served at room temperature). The acidity of a vinaigrette dressing can be reduced through the use of citrus or verjus (made from unfermented grapes) in lieu of vinegar, or simply by using the wine you'll serve with the meal as the basis of your dressing.
- With dishes that are spicy and hot. Sauvignon Blanc's brighter acidity levels and generally lower alcohol cleanse and refresh your palate.
- With sharper or more acidic ingredients: citrus, dairy (yogurt, crème fraîche, and sour cream), dill, sorrel, capers, olives, tomatoes, zucchini, summer squash.
- To cut through richer dishes. To counter cream- and butter-based sauces, often a clean and bright Sauvignon Blanc is the way to go.
- To show off pure and clean ingredients. Try a Sauvignon with a plate of oysters, a bowl of steamers, simply grilled swordfish, or the first ripe tomatoes of summer (which will be better still with a little fresh basil and mozzarella!).
- At the start of a meal. This wine not only pairs well with an array of starter courses but also allows you to progress from lighter to heavier (and from white to red) wines as the meal continues.
- With sooo many cheeses. I often switch back to a dry Sauvignon Blanc when serving the cheese course, or I opt for a sweet interpretation that can pair with both dessert and cheese.

Sauvignon Blanc isn't good:

- With classic red meat dishes. Although it's possible to fool your palate (by squeezing lemon on a steak or serving lamb with a citrus treatment and marinade), it's simply not the slam dunk that red wine would be.
- With savory dishes that border on the sweet. Like Chardonnay, Sauvignon Blanc isn't the number-one choice for holiday foods and sweetish ethnic dishes (Asian, North African, Latin American). It also doesn't taste best against caramelized onions, roasted garlic, or slow-cooked and sweet squash and root vegetables.
- With dishes that are extremely rich. This grape pairs best with leaner foods, and sweet or creamy dishes can sometimes make the wine taste tart.
- When you pick the wrong style for a dish. The oakier, blended styles and the bright, pure, 100 percent varietals can't simply be interchanged. Oakier versions follow the Chardonnay rules more closely.
- On its own (sometimes). Many people find it too intense and won't enjoy it as a cocktail sipper. Always have some food to accompany it!

PASTA WITH GREENS, CHICKPEAS, TOASTED BREADCRUMBS, AND PECORINO

SERVES 4 TO 6

8 cups escarole, chard, or arugula, cut into 1-inch strips and washed,
or 1 large bunch broccoli rabe, washed and cut into 1½-inch pieces
1 pound orecchiette or penne pasta
⅔ cup extra virgin olive oil
3 tablespoons finely minced garlic
3 tablespoons finely chopped anchovy
Pinch red pepper flakes
1 cup cooked chickpeas or white beans (see recipe on page 58),
or drained canned chickpeas or white beans
1 cup Toasted Breadcrumbs (see recipe below)
1½ tablespoons grated lemon zest
1 teaspoon freshly ground black pepper
½ cup grated Pecorino cheese

Bring a large pot of salted water to a boil. Add the greens or broccoli rabe and cook until tender, 8 to 10 minutes. Using a slotted spoon, transfer the greens to a colander. Run under cold water to stop the cooking. Drain.

Bring the cooking water back to a boil and add the pasta. Stir once and cook over high heat until al dente, about 10 minutes.

Meanwhile, make the vegetable sauce. In a large sauté pan, heat the olive oil over low heat. Add the garlic, anchovy, and red pepper flakes and sauté 2 minutes. Add the greens and sauté 3 to 5 minutes. Add the chickpeas, half of the breadcrumbs, the lemon zest, the pepper, and some of the cheese and stir for 1 minute.

When the pasta is al dente, reserve 1 cup of pasta cooking water and drain the pasta. Add the pasta to the greens mixture and toss well. Add some of the reserved pasta cooking water if the pasta seems dry, and toss. Add the remaining breadcrumbs, if desired, and toss to incorporate. Transfer to warmed pasta bowls. Pass the remaining cheese at the table.

TOASTED BREADCRUMBS

2 cups cubed crustless day-old Italian or French bread
¼ cup olive oil
1 teaspoon salt
1 teaspoon freshly ground black pepper

Preheat the oven to 350 degrees.

In a food processor, pulse to process the bread to coarse crumbs. In a large bowl, toss the crumbs with the oil, salt, and pepper. Spread the crumbs on a baking sheet. Bake until golden, stirring occasionally for even browning, about 20 minutes. Can be made up to 4 days ahead of time. Store in an airtight container at room temperature.

. . . . .

Not every Italian pasta sauce includes meat, cream, or tomato. Many pastas are simply tossed with vegetables and extra virgin olive oil. Especially refreshing is this traditional southern Italian pasta dish made with bitter greens and accented with a hit of hot pepper, saltiness from anchovy and cheese, and a hint of tartness from fresh lemon zest. Toasted breadcrumbs add crunchy texture and the beans provide a creamy contrast to the crunch. —Joyce

This is a yummy dish and one that is great for "classic" Sauvignon Blanc. I prefer it with the bitterest of greens (broccoli rabe and escarole being among my favorites), though you can also get excellent results with chard and mustard greens, and I even like to toss in a little arugula for the peppery taste. The lemon zest picks up on the wine's tart-fruit character, while the saltiness of the anchovy is more food-friendly than table or sea salt. If you are generous with the toasted breadcrumbs, a little oak on the wine can add a nuance of complexity. The wine's inherent zestiness will cut through the buttery richness of the breadcrumbs while taking the edge off the heat, which will work great with the wine as long as it's not over the top (personal preference is the key here). If your wine choice is clean and pure, you can leave out the breadcrumbs. —Evan

RECOMMENDED PRODUCERS
Grassy, Herbal Sauvignon Blancs

EVERYDAY	PREMIUM	SPLURGE
Château du Sancerre (Loire Valley, France)	Henri Bourgeois (Loire Valley, France)	Dagueneau (Loire Valley, France)
Sauvion et Fils (Loire Valley, France)	Mason (Napa Valley, California)	Pascal Jolivet (Loire Valley, France)
Neil Ellis (multiple appellations, South Africa)	Mulderbosch (Coastal Region, South Africa)	Source-Napa (Napa Valley, California)

CALAMARI WITH GARLIC AND PEAS

SERVES 4

3 pounds peas in the pod (about 3 cups shelled)
½ cup extra virgin olive oil
6 to 12 cloves garlic, peeled
2 slices bread, crusts removed
¼ cup blanched almonds
1 small onion, finely chopped
3 ripe tomatoes, peeled, seeded, and chopped,
or 1½ cups chopped canned tomatoes (see note below)
⅓ cup dry white wine, or more as needed
¼ cup chopped fresh flat-leaf parsley
¼ cup chopped fresh mint
1½ pounds squid, cleaned and cut into ¾-inch rings

Shell the peas and cook in a pot of boiling salted water until tender, 3 to 5 minutes, depending on their size. Drain and rinse with cold water.

In a large sauté pan over medium heat, heat the oil. Add the garlic and fry until pale gold, 3 to 4 minutes. Using a slotted spoon, transfer the garlic to a bowl and set aside. Add the bread and almonds to the same oil and fry until golden, about 5 minutes. Using a slotted spoon, transfer the bread and almonds to a plate lined with paper towels.

Add the onion to the oil and sauté until soft, about 8 minutes. Add the chopped tomatoes and ⅓ cup wine and bring to a simmer.

Pound the fried garlic, almonds, and bread in a mortar with a pestle or puree in a food processor. Add this paste (called a *picada*) to the tomatoes. Stir in half the parsley and half the mint. Simmer over low heat until slightly thickened, about 10 minutes. The sauce needs to be liquid in consistency. If it is too thick, add a little water or additional wine. Increase the heat to medium-high, add the squid and the peas, and stir well. Cook until the squid is opaque, 1 to 2 minutes. (Do not overcook or the squid will be tough.) Serve immediately, topped with the remaining chopped fresh mint and parsley.

VARIATION To serve this with clams: In a large pot, combine 4 pounds manila clams and 1 cup white wine. Cover, bring to a boil, and steam until the clams open, about 5 minutes. Using a slotted spoon, remove the clams from the pan as they open and add them to the tomato sauce. Strain the clam juices through a cheesecloth-lined strainer and add to the warm tomato sauce along with the peas.

NOTE Taste the liquid in which the tomatoes are packed. If it is too salty, too tart, or metallic-tasting, discard. Tomatoes packed in puree may be sweeter, but taste to make sure. Muir Glen is a good brand.

. . . . .

Spanish cooks love to play with variations on the theme of shellfish, peas, and mint. Clams and cuttlefish are popular, but calamari (squid) are especially appealing. The tomato sauce is thickened with a traditional mixture called a picada, *made up of fried garlic, almonds, and bread. In Rome, calamari and peas are a springtime favorite, but much less garlic is used, and there are no tomatoes or mint. This dish is good served with rice or potatoes. —Joyce*

In all candor, I selected this dish by accident. I was having it for dinner with a Spanish Rueda (a wine made from a grape called Verdejo that has a remarkable Sauvignon-like character). Although the match was almost right, the dish needed a wine with a little more texture and richness. When I tried it with a fuller-bodied Graves, I thought I had died and gone to heaven! While the squid is a Sauvignon Blanc natural, the mélange of the peas (which add texture in addition to a sweet flavor) and the picada *calls for a wine that's richer and more rustic than a classically styled Sauvignon Blanc. The mint reinforces the varietal character, and the fruitier the olive oil, the greater the possibilities for serving with New World interpretations. If you like a lot of garlic, or if the garlic that you are using is a little hot, opt for an Old World wine. Cut back on the garlic a little to broaden your wine choices. —Evan*

RECOMMENDED PRODUCERS
Earthy, Pungent, Waxy-Textured Sauvignon Blancs

EVERYDAY	PREMIUM	SPLURGE
Michel Lynch (Bordeaux, France)	Château Carbonnieux (Bordeaux, France)	Château Smith-Haut-Lafitte (Bordeaux, France)
Château Bonnet (Bordeaux, France)	Château La Louvière (Bordeaux, France)	Château de Fieuzal (Bordeaux, France)
Covey Run (Greater Columbia Valley, Washington)	Cakebread Cellars (Napa Valley, California)	Domaine de Chevalier (Bordeaux, France)

SEAFOOD SALAD

SERVES 4

½ pound squid, cleaned and cut into ½-inch pieces,
tentacles separated
½ pound medium shrimp, peeled and deveined
2 pounds clams, well scrubbed
2 pounds mussels, debearded
½ cup dry white wine or water
½ cup extra virgin olive oil
3 to 4 tablespoons fresh lemon juice
Salt and freshly ground black pepper
¼ teaspoon red pepper flakes (optional)
4 to 5 celery stalks, thinly sliced, cut on the diagonal
2 tablespoons chopped fresh flat-leaf parsley

Bring a pot of salted water to a boil. Add the squid and cook until opaque, 1 to 2 minutes. Using a slotted spoon, transfer the squid to a strainer and rinse with cold water. Transfer the squid to a large bowl. Return the pot of water to a boil. Add the shrimp and cook until pink, 2 to 4 minutes depending on size. Drain the shrimp, rinse with cold water, and add to the squid in the bowl.

Discard any open clams and any mussels that do not close when tapped with a spoon. In a large pot, combine the white wine, clams, and mussels. Place over medium-high heat, cover, and steam until the shellfish open, 3 to 5 minutes. (They won't all open at once, so keep checking.) As they open, use a slotted spoon to transfer them to a second large bowl. Continue steaming until all have opened. (Clams can be stubborn; after 5 minutes, turn off the heat and cover the pan. Discard any clams that haven't opened within 10 minutes.)

When they are cool enough to handle, remove the clams and mussels from their shells and add to the bowl with the cooked squid and shrimp. Discard the shells.

In a small bowl, whisk together the oil and lemon juice and season lightly with salt and pepper. (Clams are a bit salty, so don't add too much salt.) Add the red pepper flakes, if desired.

Combine the celery with the shellfish. Pour the oil and lemon dressing over the shellfish and celery and toss to coat. Sprinkle with chopped parsley. Serve at room temperature.

VARIATION Use fennel instead of celery. Use mint or basil instead of, or in addition to, parsley.

. . . . .

A seafood salad is a light and refreshing way to start a meal. It could be part of an antipasto assortment or served solo on a bed of lettuce. The ancient Romans loved celery and believed it was an aphrodisiac. Though I can't vouch for that particular property, here it adds crisp, cool green notes and a textural contrast to the rich shellfish and olive oil, the tart lemon, and the very mild heat of the pepper flakes. —Joyce

Anybody who has been to New Zealand can attest to the implicit affinity of their zippy Sauvignon Blanc wines and the bountiful seafood. Here we play that up by providing a perfect platform for Sauvignon Blanc. The parsley and celery reinforce the varietal nature of the wine, while the lemon juice "pops" the fruit character. Instead of the lemon juice, try lime or a lime- and lemon-juice combination to bring out different nuances of the wine. If the wine is relatively high in alcohol, I wouldn't recommend the hot pepper, but, if it's not, you may want to play around with the degree of heat. Finally, substituting fennel for the celery is very successful for Sauvignons that share its licorice and light pepper character. —Evan

RECOMMENDED PRODUCERS

Herbal, Tropical Sauvignon Blancs

EVERYDAY	PREMIUM	SPLURGE
Geyser Peak (Sonoma County, California)	Hanna (Sonoma County, California)	Araujo (Napa Valley, California)
Frog's Leap (Napa Valley, California)	Brancott (Marlborough, New Zealand)	Spottswoode (Napa Valley, California)
Babich (Marlborough, New Zealand)	Isabel (Marlborough, New Zealand)	E & M Tement (Styria, Austria)

BAKED GOAT CHEESE IN A WALNUT CRUST WITH GREENS AND APPLE

SERVES 4

CHEESE

4 2-ounce rounds of fresh mild goat cheese, each about 1 inch thick,
or 1 8-ounce log, cut into 1-inch rounds
1 to 2 tablespoons extra virgin olive oil, or as needed
½ cup walnuts, toasted and finely chopped
¼ cup Toasted Breadcrumbs (see recipe page 73)
1 teaspoon chopped fresh thyme

VINAIGRETTE

6 tablespoons walnut oil
2 tablespoons extra virgin olive oil
2 tablespoons balsamic vinegar
1 tablespoon sherry vinegar
Salt and freshly ground black pepper

½ cup walnut halves
4 to 6 cups mixed salad greens
1 tart green apple (such as Pippin or Granny Smith)

To prepare the cheese: Coat the cheese rounds with olive oil and let stand on a plate at room temperature for 30 minutes.

Combine the chopped walnuts, breadcrumbs, and thyme on a plate. Dip the cheese rounds into the nut mixture, making sure all sides are evenly coated. Gently press the coating into the cheese. Place the cheese on a baking sheet lined with baker's parchment.

For the vinaigrette: In a small bowl, whisk together the walnut oil, 2 tablespoons olive oil, and both vinegars. Season the vinaigrette to taste with salt and pepper.

Just before serving, preheat the oven to 400 degrees.

Spread the walnut halves out on a small baking pan and toast until fragrant, about 8 minutes. When cool enough to handle, chop them coarsely. Put them in a small bowl and toss with enough vinaigrette to coat.

Bake the nut-crusted cheese until the cheese is softened and the nut mixture is aromatic, about 10 minutes.

Place the salad greens in a bowl. Reserve 3 tablespoons of the vinaigrette. Toss the greens with the remaining vinaigrette and distribute evenly among individual salad plates.

Cut the apple in half, remove the core and slice the apple, with the peel on, into thin half rounds. Place about 6 slices atop the greens on each plate and drizzle the reserved vinaigrette on the apples. Top with the pre-dressed walnuts. Place 1 or 2 warm goat cheese rounds adjacent to each salad or on top of it. Serve immediately.

· · · · ·

Creamy and tart goat cheese, bitter and crunchy walnuts, bitter greens, and sweet-tart apple combine for a delightful first course or after-dinner salad. Store walnut oil in the refrigerator, as it goes rancid fairly quickly. For the same reason, store nuts in the freezer if you do not use them quickly or often. —Joyce

Nuts and nut oils are great link ingredients for oak, whether the wine is a Sauvignon Blanc, Chardonnay, or Pinot Gris. The goat cheese calls for a wine with high acidity, and Sauvignon, with its zingy acidity, is a perfect partner. Although you could substitute almonds or cashews, I like the walnuts because of their bitter character, which is always enhanced by oak. A milder and less acidic cheese, such as a young Brie or Camembert (with the crusts cut away so that the nuts will stick), would be lovely if you chose to tweak this recipe to serve with a Chardonnay or Pinot Gris. Regarding the fruit, green apples are the best bet, though if you find your Sauvignon Blanc to be a bit deficient in tartness, opt for a sweeter yellow apple such as a Golden Delicious. Finally, the toasted breadcrumbs work well when served with an oak-aged and higher-acid wine. —Evan

RECOMMENDED PRODUCERS
Rich, Oaky Sauvignon Blancs

EVERYDAY	PREMIUM	SPLURGE
Chateau St. Jean (Sonoma County, California)	Merryvale (Napa Valley, California)	François or Pascal Cotat (Loire Valley, France)
Ferrari-Carano (Sonoma County, California)	White Oak (Napa Valley, California)	Peter Michael (Napa Valley, California)
Markham (Napa Valley, California)	Greenwood Ridge (Mendocino County, California)	Alphonse Mellot (Loire Valley, France)

RIESLING

The white grape responsible for making some of the greatest wines in the world has a devoted but limited audience. Always a favorite in restaurants, Riesling (*rees*-ling) is arguably the most versatile white wine for pairing with food. It comes in many interpretations, from the driest of dry wines to unctuously sweet versions. Its intrinsic acidity showcases food, and, in spite of widespread reluctance to try it ("Oh yeah, Riesling . . . I don't like sweet wines"), all it takes to convert most people is getting a delicious and representative glass into their hand. Watch their opinions change forever after the first sip.

WINE-GROWING AREAS

Whether it belongs to Germany or France depends on the period of history in question, but Riesling is indigenous, and prevalent, in the central plateau around the Rhine and Mosel rivers. As with Chardonnay and Sauvignon Blanc, there are two main styles.

The wines of Germany's Rhine and Mosel-Saar-Ruwer river areas, universally considered the best Rieslings in Germany, are lighter (7 to 11 percent alcohol in general) and can run the gamut from bone-dry (*Trocken,* literally "dry") to the off-dry (*Kabinett* and *Spätlese*) to sticky sweet (*Eiswein, Auslese,* and *Trockenbeerenauslese*). They have extraordinarily balanced acidity to keep them from being cloying, and they explode on the palate with a bevy of flavors that scream fruit (peach, apricot, nectarine, and green apple) while being firmly underscored by slatey and petrol-like earth notes.

France's Alsace is the other model, and its examples are thicker (closer to 12 or 13 percent alcohol) and almost always bone-dry. While their fruit profiles are similar to those of Germany's Rieslings, Alsace Rieslings are riper and, although dry, may come off as having sweeter fruit than their easterly neighbors. The two off-dry examples of Alsace Riesling are *vendange tardive* (translating to "late harvest") and *sélection des grains nobles* (SGN), which translates to "selected noble (that is, botrytized) grapes." The former is off-dry and the latter of serious, dessert-wine-level sweetness. Both styles are rare, made only in years when the harvest yields exceptionally ripe fruit (known as ripe years).

These European models extend into other global areas, with the Alsace model being more prevalent in warmer Australia and New Zealand and the German model predominant in cooler Lower Austria and Central Europe (including Hungary and Romania).

Down under, Australia's examples have surprised many skeptics. Considered by many to be too warm, Australia is today the source of many great bottles of world-class Riesling, primarily from the cooler Clare and Eden Valleys, the Adelaide Hills, and Tasmania (which is farther south and so has a chillier climate). With abundant ripe fruit and ample to very high acidity, Australian Rieslings manage to be weighty without being over the top. In New Zealand, wines from the Central Otago region of the South Island are floral, apple-scented and razor-sharp, while those from Marlborough at the north end of the same island are packed with peach and pear fruit and have the classic, racy acidity of all Kiwi whites.

Led by those from the Wachau, Austria's Rieslings, which are a bit weightier than their German counterparts, are world-class and finally acquiring the recognition they deserve. As in Germany, Austrian Rieslings encompass a range of sweet styles as well as dry wines. The Rieslings of Central Europe tend to be lighter, fragrant, floral, and clearly identifiable as Riesling, though some of the selections or clones are different from those of Germany and France.

In North America, styles are all over the board, so you need to experiment. From the West, I prefer the wines of Washington State, British Columbia's Okanagan Valley, and California's Mendocino and Central Coast areas (especially the drier styles). Many of America's consistently best Rieslings are being made in upstate New York, around the Finger Lakes area, and in Michigan, throughout the Old Mission and Leelanau Peninsulas. Although these comments mainly apply to the dry and off-dry bottlings, there are also excellent sweet wines being made in the United States and in Canada, where Riesling *Eisweins* are a specialty of Ontario's Niagara region.

A table of principal wine-growing regions for Riesling appears on pages 270–71.

VINTNER CHOICES

Sparkling or still; dry, off-dry, or sweet; wood aging (minimal)

Riesling simply doesn't provide as many winemaking options as either Chardonnay or Sauvignon Blanc. For the volume of average-quality Riesling that is made into bubbly (called *Sekt* in Germany, where it's big business), harvest and production decisions must be made early on. Decisions about whether to produce a late-harvest style of dessert wine are made as the season progresses, and grapes are picked and the harvest vinified accordingly.

For Riesling table wine, a vintner will either ferment the wine dry (in the Alsace style) or, for off-dry styles, leave a certain amount of residual sugar in the wine that will determine the final sweetness. With Riesling, oak aging is not an issue. The only wood casks found in wineries that produce Riesling are so old and so large that they have no impact on the flavor of the wines. Of course, there are exceptions to the rule, and some winemakers do employ small-barrel aging, but they are unusual and have limited success. Riesling is a very delicate grape, and too much oak makes the wine taste like . . . too much oak.

FLAVORS

Fruit: Apricot, peach, nectarine, green and yellow apple, pear, yellow plum, loquat, kiwi, golden raisin, lemon, tangerine, lime, passion fruit, lychee, guava

Floral: Mint, honeysuckle, geranium, rose, pine, juniper, anise, clove, jasmine, lavender, green tea

Earth: Kerosene or fusel oil, asphalt, smoke, earth, flint, stone, slate, musk

Wood: Not applicable (as a rule)

Other: Cream

In dessert styles: Dried apricot, dried peach, raisin, caramel, quince, candied citrus, marmalade

WINE AND FOOD PAIRING

INGREDIENTS AND STYLES

Whereas Chardonnay and Sauvignon Blanc are made in a bevy of styles, and many options in production affect their final flavor profile, Riesling's diversity comes predominantly from its range of sweetness. Consequently, there's an amazing array of ingredients the wine can accompany, from the obvious, including fish (sole, trout, snapper, and rock cod), shellfish (scallops, shrimp, and prawns), and mild poultry (turkey, chicken, game hens, and quail), to the less obvious, including white meat (pork, ham, and veal), rich fowl (duck and goose), and charcuterie (sausages and cured meats). Vegetables that are sweet or imply sweetness are lovely with Riesling, including corn and root vegetables such as sweet potatoes, yams, and slow-roasted turnips or rutabagas.

Bone-dry Rieslings are lean, bright, and refreshing and will easily stand in wherever a squeeze of lemon or lime would enhance the dish—a plate of oysters, scaloppine of pork or veal, or a simply poached salmon. The significant issue here is whether you are serving a more generous style from a warmer climate (Australia or California) or a lighter and less ample wine from Germany, Austria, or New Zealand. Remember the basic rule of matching the level of alcohol with the richness of the food.

The off-dry Rieslings (*Kabinett* or *Spätlese* or those simply labeled off-dry) are magnificent at foiling spicy heat (as in an Indian tandoori or Szechuan shrimp) or mimicking sweetness (think tamarind- or pomegranate-glazed pork roast, white fish with fruit salsa, or a sweet Korean barbecued chicken). Additionally, off-dry Riesling is sublime with smoked items (especially salmon, trout, and pork) or recipes made with them, like pasta dishes. Moderate levels of salt can also be balanced with these off-dry styles of wine.

The very sweet dessert style wines are wonderful for pairing with desserts based on tropical fruit, white stone fruit (peach, nectarine, and plum), and tree fruit (especially in tarts, poached fruit, and compotes) or custards such as crème brûlée or a not too caramelly crème caramel. Sweeter citrus dishes (such as candied oranges) are also extraordinary with Riesling, as is almost any fruit prepared in honey. Avoid chocolate, coffee, and mochas, as they bury the subtlety of the Riesling. And, as always, ensure that the dessert is less sweet than the wine.

PAIRING POINTERS

Riesling goes well:
- With almost all fatty poultry, but especially with goose, duck, and other rich, gamy birds.
- As a counterbalance to rich, salty meats and meat treatments—ham, sausage, charcuterie, and the like. It also works with mildly salty cheeses: mildly pungent blue-veined cheeses such as Gorgonzola dolcelatte are sublime.
- With aromatic and distinctive marinades or sauces, especially plays of sweet and sour, sweet and salt, and sweet and spicy aromatics (chiles). And it's great with almost all sushi served on sweet vinegared sushi rice!
- With most picnic dishes, from pâté to sliced ham, from cold chicken to tuna-salad sandwiches.
- With many exotic and flavorful spices. Try Rieslings with foods seasoned with curry, cardamom, cinnamon, clove, mace, star anise, cumin, and turmeric.
- With many initial courses, which tend to stress salt, fat, and flavors that fall between savory and sweet (such as pâtés, savory mousses, sauces with sweet notes, and preparations with scallops and shrimp).
- With foods which are slightly sweet, from American holiday fare to Thai, and from Malaysian to Nuevo Latino.
- With crab, lobster, prawns, and other sweet shellfish. The wine's real or implied sweetness pops the ingredients.
- With quiche. Riesling is one of the few wines that can hold its own with egg dishes.

Riesling isn't good:
- With dishes that are overpowering. It can be lost behind a dish that's too rich and dominant. Most Rieslings are subtle.

- When you pick the wrong one. A sharp, dry, and puckery Riesling is great with a plate of oysters, whereas an off-dry and semiluscious interpretation will be much less successful.
- With dishes that are very peppery. Too much cracked black pepper overpowers most Rieslings, though off-dry examples may fare better.
- With most green vegetable preparations, unless they are slightly sweet (like snap peas with a slightly sweet Asian sauce).
- With traditional red-meat dishes. While a sauce or a long braise could steer the dish the right way, Riesling is not at its best with simply sautéed or roasted lamb, beef, or venison.

ROAST PORK LOIN WITH CREAMY ONION SAUCE AND SAUTÉED APPLES

SERVES 6

1 4-pound bone-in pork loin
3 large cloves garlic, slivered
Salt and freshly ground black pepper
8 tablespoons (1 stick) unsalted butter
2 cups diced yellow onions
2 cups diced red onions
2 cups sliced leeks (white part only)
1 cup (about) chicken stock
¼ teaspoon freshly grated nutmeg, or more to taste
2 to 3 tablespoons cream (optional)
2 apples, peeled, cored, and sliced
¼ cup chopped fresh chives

Preheat the oven to 400 degrees.

With the tip of a sharp knife, cut slits all over the pork loin. Insert the garlic slivers into the slits. Sprinkle the meat with salt and pepper and place in a roasting pan. Roast until an instant-read meat thermometer registers 140 degrees, about 1 hour.

While the pork roasts, make the sauce and sauté the apples.

For the sauce: Melt 4 tablespoons of the butter over low heat. Add the yellow and red onions and cook very slowly until the onions are meltingly tender and very sweet, 30 to 40 minutes. In another sauté pan, melt 2 tablespoons butter and cook the leeks over low heat, covered, until tender, about 20 minutes. Puree the onions and leeks in a food processor. Thin to desired consistency with chicken stock. Stir in ¼ teaspoon nutmeg. Season the sauce to taste with additional nutmeg, salt, and pepper. If you like, add cream to round it out.

For the apples: In a large sauté pan, melt the remaining 2 tablespoons butter over medium heat. Add the apple slices and sauté until lightly browned, about 10 minutes. Keep warm.

To serve: Transfer the roast pork to a cutting board. Slice the pork between the bones and transfer to plates. (Or remove the pork from the bones, slice, and serve the bones separately to those who want them.) Spoon on the sauce. Sprinkle with chives. Place apple slices alongside the pork, dividing evenly, and serve.

. . . . .

This pork loin is served with a delicious onion sauce. After long cooking, onions develop a wonderful sweetness. Please do not rush them. Taste before you stop the cooking process, and if the onions are not sweet enough, keep them on the stove a little longer. Serve the pork with sautéed apples and potato pancakes. If time is tight, pan-fried or roasted potatoes will do nicely. —Joyce

This dish exemplifies the Alsatian style of preparing pork. The slow cooking of the onions creates a rich texture and brings out a natural, caramelized sweetness that pairs well with the Riesling's fruit character. While using a mixture of different onions is essential to the complexity of the puree, you can play up the leeks if the wine is less ripe and downplay them if the wine is very ripe. The apples bridge the meat and the wine with their balance of tart and ripe flavors. Yellow and green apples hold their flavor and shape and are lovely when paired with dry Riesling. —Evan

RECOMMENDED PRODUCERS
Earthy, Minerally, Dry Rieslings

EVERYDAY	PREMIUM	SPLURGE
Schlumberger (Alsace, France)	Alsace Willm (Alsace, France)	Zind Humbrecht (Alsace, France)
Pierre Sparr (Alsace, France)	Claiborne & Churchill (Southern Central Coast, California)	Trimbach (Alsace, France)
Jean-Baptiste Adam (Alsace, France)	Hugel (Alsace, France)	Marcel Deiss (Alsace, France)

CHINESE CHICKEN SALAD

SERVES 4

4 boneless, skinless chicken breast halves
Salt and freshly ground black pepper
Vegetable oil for frying (such as canola or olive oil)

GINGER-SOY DRESSING
1 teaspoon finely minced garlic
3 tablespoons finely minced peeled fresh ginger
2 tablespoons hot mustard
1 tablespoon sugar
2 tablespoons soy sauce
2 tablespoons white or rice vinegar
2 tablespoons sesame oil
1½ cups vegetable oil (such as canola, peanut, or grapeseed oil)
Salt to taste

1 large cucumber, peeled, seeded, and cut on the diagonal into ¼-inch slices
2 small heads romaine, coarsely shredded
1 cup bean sprouts
¼ cup minced green onions (mostly green parts)
¼ cup fresh coriander (cilantro) leaves
2 tablespoons toasted sesame seeds

For the chicken: Lightly pound the chicken breasts between sheets of plastic wrap to a uniform thickness. Sprinkle the chicken with salt and pepper. In a large sauté pan, pour the oil to a depth of ¼ inch and warm over medium-high heat. Add the chicken breasts and fry until golden and cooked through, turning once, 4 to 5 minutes per side. Drain the chicken on a plate lined with paper towels. When cool, shred into a large bowl.

For the dressing: Puree the garlic and ginger in a small food processor. Add the mustard, sugar, soy sauce, vinegar, and sesame oil and pulse to combine. Gradually beat in the vegetable oil, a drop at a time, until the mixture emulsifies. Season the dressing to taste with salt.

To serve: Add the cucumber slices to the chicken in the bowl and toss with ½ cup or more of the dressing to moisten the mixture well. Combine the romaine, bean sprouts, green onions, and fresh coriander in another bowl and toss with ½ cup of the dressing. Distribute the greens mixture evenly among salad plates. Place the chicken and cucumber mixture atop the greens.

Drizzle with some of the remaining dressing if desired. (This recipe makes more dressing than you will need. Refrigerate any remaining dressing for another salad. Bring it to room temperature before using.) Garnish with toasted sesame seeds and serve.

VARIATION You can broil or grill the chicken breasts instead of frying them. You can also poach them, though they are best with a bit of texture on the outside. Try some sweet sliced jicama in place of the cucumber, and use toasted pine nuts as a sweeter substitute for toasted sesame seeds.

· · · · ·

This chicken salad is an ideal hot-weather main-course dish, and it deserves a good glass of wine. Mild chicken, cool, crisp romaine, slightly bitter cucumber, cilantro, and green onions are tossed with a creamy sesame-ginger dressing for a perfect balance of flavors. —Joyce

This is a wonderfully harmonious match. The crispness of the Riesling is splendid against the crunchy romaine and cucumber (or my personal preference, jicama). The off-dry sweetness of the wine balances perfectly with the slight earthy sweetness of the sesame-ginger dressing, while the wine's fruit flavors are set off gently by the toasted sesame seeds. The greens are nice for making this dish into a salad but are not the focal point. I've mixed a bit of the extra dressing into some mayonnaise, spread it on bread, added a lettuce leaf for crispness, and used this salad for a marvelous twist on the chicken-salad sandwich. It makes a perfect picnic combination when you add sun, a beautiful location, and a few good friends. —Evan

RECOMMENDED PRODUCERS
Apple- and Apricot-Flavored, Dry (or Slightly Off-Dry) Rieslings

EVERYDAY	PREMIUM	SPLURGE
Dr. Bürklin-Wolf (Pfalz, Germany)	J. J. Prum (Mosel-Saar-Ruwer, Germany)	Robert Weil (Rheingau, Germany)
St. Urbans-Hof (Mosel-Saar-Ruwer, Germany)	Zilliken (Mosel-Saar-Ruwer, Germany)	Franz Künstler (Rheingau, Germany)
Navarro (Mendocino County, California)	Grosset Wines (multiple appellations, Australia)	Gunderloch (Rheinhessen, Germany)

TANDOORI-STYLE SHRIMP

SERVES 4

MARINADE
1 cup nonfat plain yogurt
2 jalapeño chiles (leave seeds in for extra heat), chopped
3 tablespoons fresh lemon juice
2 large cloves garlic, chopped
2-inch piece of peeled fresh ginger, sliced thinly across the grain
1 tablespoon ground cumin
½ teaspoon salt
¼ teaspoon turmeric

1½ pounds large shrimp, shelled and deveined
1 tablespoon sweet paprika
Lime or lemon wedges

Place the yogurt, jalapeños, lemon juice, garlic, ginger, cumin, salt, and turmeric in the container of a food processor and pulse to combine. Place the shrimp in a large nonaluminum container. Add the marinade and toss to coat. Marinate in the refrigerator for 1 hour.

Soak bamboo skewers in water for 30 minutes.

Preheat the broiler or prepare a charcoal or gas grill. Thread the shrimp on two parallel bamboo skewers for easy turning. Broil or grill until pink and firm, turning once, about 2 minutes per side. Sprinkle with paprika and serve with lime wedges.

VARIATION If your budget is tight, fish cubes can be substituted. The fragrant but spicy yogurt marinade is also excellent for boneless chicken breasts, cut into cubes and skewered. While chicken can marinate for 4 to 5 hours, fish and shrimp need only a 1- to 2-hour marinade, as the yogurt and citrus have a tenderizing effect.

This tandoori-style shrimp is an ideal dish for a family barbecue. Everyone loves shrimp. The bitter spices are balanced by the tartness of lemon and yogurt and the sweetness of the shrimp. Serve this dish with saffron rice and sautéed spinach for a main course or alone as an appetizer, with a few wedges of lemon or lime. —Joyce

We served this dish at a family gathering, and everyone cheered. But be careful in choosing your wine: if you pick one that's too dry, it will taste very tart. So a bottle with ample sweetness—like a Spätlese—is necessary. Given the right degree of sweetness, the Riesling's flavors accentuate the bevy of exotic spices while bringing out the natural sweetness of the shrimp. This dish also works well, though with slightly less impact, with chicken or fish instead of shrimp. The accompanying lime wedge is a big deal. If the wine's a bit on the sweet side, squeeze the lime immediately on the shrimp. Otherwise, try the shrimp alone and then with the lime to find your personal preference. —Evan

RECOMMENDED PRODUCERS

Floral, Peach-Flavored, Distinctly Off-Dry (Slightly Sweet) Rieslings

EVERYDAY	PREMIUM	SPLURGE
Columbia Crest (Greater Columbia Valley, Washington)	Domaine Weinbach (Alsace, France)	Schlossgut Diel (Mosel-Saar-Ruwer, Germany)
Hogue (Greater Columbia Valley, Washington)	Dr. H. Thanisch (Mosel-Saar-Ruwer, Germany)	Selbach-Oster (Mosel-Saar-Ruwer, Germany)
Dr. Pauly-Bergweiler (Mosel-Saar-Ruwer, Germany)	Dr. Loosen (Mosel-Saar-Ruwer, Germany)	Johanishof (Rheingau, Germany)

BAKED ROCKFISH WITH SPICY PEANUT SAUCE

SERVES 4

SAUCE
½ cup smooth, unsalted peanut butter
¼ cup finely chopped dry-roasted peanuts
2 tablespoons (packed) brown sugar
⅔ cup chicken stock or water
½ cup coconut milk, or more as needed
⅓ cup soy sauce
3 tablespoons fresh lemon juice
½ teaspoon finely minced garlic
1 teaspoon red pepper flakes, or more to taste
1 teaspoon ground cumin
1 teaspoon ground coriander

FISH
2 teaspoons minced garlic
1½ teaspoons salt
½ teaspoon freshly ground black pepper
1½ pounds rockfish fillets
Oil for baking dish

For the sauce: In a small saucepan, place the peanut butter, peanuts, and brown sugar. Gradually stir in the stock, ½ cup coconut milk, soy sauce, lemon juice, garlic, 1 teaspoon red pepper flakes, cumin, and coriander. Bring to a boil, reduce heat to low, and simmer 2 minutes to combine well. Season to taste with additional red pepper flakes if desired. If the sauce is too thick, thin with additional coconut milk or water. It should be the consistency of heavy cream. (The sauce may be made ahead of time and will keep in the refrigerator for up to 1 week. Thin and rewarm before using.)

Preheat the oven to 450 degrees.

For the fish: In a small bowl, stir the garlic, salt, and pepper to combine. Rub the paste into the fish fillets. Place them in an oiled baking dish large enough to hold the fish in one layer. Spoon half the sauce over the fish. Bake until the fish feels firm and looks opaque when the point of a knife is inserted in the thickest part, 10 to 15 minutes. To serve, spoon a little of the warmed sauce over the fish.

VARIATION This recipe is also delicious when made with Alaskan halibut, sea bass, or ling cod. Instead of baking the fish, you can grill or broil it, brushing with some of the sauce. Spoon a little more sauce on after cooking.

· · · · ·

This baked rockfish recipe is influenced by Southeast Asian cooking, which has seduced the dining public. We are now in love with its traditional flavor combinations of sweet, tart, salty, and hot. They enliven a mild fish and transform it into a stellar creation. Serve with sweet and crunchy corn fritters, or corn on the cob rubbed with lemon, red pepper flakes, and butter. —Joyce

This delicious and exotic fish dish shows well against most aromatic white wines: Viognier, Gewürztraminer, and even Austrian Grüner Veltliner. All have their floral and tree fruit flavors lifted by the food, but no pairing surpasses in affinity that of this dish with a richer New World Riesling. The magic combination of tastes is sublime against the bright, ripe flavors of an Australian or similar bottling. The brown sugar together with the coconut milk adds texture and mouth richness, which call for a fuller-bodied wine. You may want to play down the heat a touch if your wine is very high in alcohol (over 13 percent). —Evan

RECOMMENDED PRODUCERS
Rich, Fruit-Forward, Dry to Off-Dry Rieslings

EVERYDAY	PREMIUM
Stoneleigh (Marlborough, New Zealand)	Eroica (Greater Columbia Valley, Washington)
Snoqualmie (Greater Columbia Valley, Washington)	Trefethen (Napa Valley, California)
Annie's Lane (Clare Valley, South Australia)	Dr. Konstantin Frank (Finger Lakes, New York)

PINOT GRIS

Pinot Gris (*pee*-noh *gree*), or Pinot Grigio, depending on geography and interpretation, has just recently caught America's fancy. Formerly found exclusively in Italian restaurants and among the partisan locals of Alsace in France and the state of Oregon, Pinot Gris/Grigio is becoming increasingly and widely available in stores and restaurants. It is easy to like: clean, refreshing, and vibrant, or rich, spicy, and tangy, depending on its origin. Almost any version will give you a rewarding glass of wine.

WINE-GROWING AREAS

Originally a mutation of Pinot Noir, Pinot Gris is a grape that has proved itself to be one of the great cosmopolitan varietals of Europe. In Italy, where it is called Pinot Grigio, it predominates in the north, although it is now being grown in different regions of the country. Once unique to the Trentino–Alto Adige and Friuli regions, Pinot Grigio is now being planted in Tuscany and locales in the south of Italy to satisfy the public's passionate love affair with this crisp, lemony, and refreshing wine style.

In France, Alsace makes exemplary Pinot Gris. Here the wines are full-bodied, fleshy, and broadly flavored, with a tangy, spicy character evocative of the grape's red Pinot Noir ancestry. If Pinot Gris is indeed mutated Pinot Noir, it is natural that it should be at home in France.

Germany's examples, locally called Ruländer, tend to be in between the Italian and French styles, though closer to the Italian model. Experiments with reduced yields and some oak aging are resulting in wines more akin to Alsace's Pinot Gris and an opulent Chardonnay. Austria's interpretations are lean, dry, and moderately rich, while those of Central and Eastern Europe are decidedly more in the Italian vein.

Oregon's Willamette Valley is the dominant Pinot Gris region of the United States. Oregon's winemakers label the wine only as Pinot Gris, although the state produces three distinctive styles: the Italian, the Alsatian, and the in-between one that can, I suppose, be called the Oregonian style. You will require a little trial and error (or a retailer's guidance) to know which wines are which, as style is not typically identified or discussed on the label. California is making progressively better wines, labeled as either Pinot Grigio or Pinot Gris, depending on the style the winery attempts to emulate. Farther north, in British Columbia, there are increasingly refined interpretations made in the Okanagan Valley. Recent efforts in New Zealand fall somewhere between the Alsace and Italian styles, though many are particularly zippy and piquant—not surprising, given the tart acidity common in New Zealand wines.

A table of principal wine-growing regions for Pinot Gris appears on page 272.

VINTNER CHOICES

Wood or no wood; skin contact; fermentation temperature;
dry, off-dry, or sweet; style (interpretation); malolactic fermentation

There are few clear-cut winemaking choices beyond the interpretive ones listed above. Although this varietal is occasionally aged in wood, many vintners argue that its personality is easily lost behind staves of oak and that it's best left in a more natural state, fermented and aged either in stainless-steel vats or in older, relatively inert oak casks.

Increasingly, vintners are using skin contact as a technique to add more fruit aroma and flavor. And, more and more, winemakers are fermenting the grapes more slowly and at cooler temperatures, an approach that enhances the fruit and floral components in the wines. While some vintners are experimenting with malolactic fermentation, it is by no means prevalent, and the topic is likely to cause a food fight at a convention of Pinot Gris producers. Although I have tasted examples with some residual sugar to brighten the perception of fruit, I've yet to try an intentionally off-dry or sweet style that knocked my socks off, apart from late-harvest Alsatian wines. And those wines are rare and expensive.

FLAVORS

Fruit: Lemon, lime, green melon, green apple, pear, pineapple, peach, yellow plum, kumquat, loquat, star fruit, tangerine

Floral: Honeysuckle, citrus blossom, rose petal, violet, ginger, lemongrass, lemon thyme

Earth: Mineral, stone, asphalt, flint, slate, musk

Oak (if used): Smoke, toast, vanilla, sweet spice

Other: Honey, plain yogurt, sour cream, raw nut, white pepper

WINE AND FOOD PAIRING

INGREDIENTS AND STYLES

With respect to wine and food pairings, the most significant factor is the wine style. The Italian versions and others patterned on them tend to resemble Sauvignon Blanc, without the grassy or herbal notes. Because of their acidity, they are good at cutting through the fullness of richer recipes and butter and cream sauces and highlighting the simplest of quality ingredients. In the summer, I enjoy Pinot Grigio with plates of sweet heirloom tomatoes and fresh mozzarella and for refreshing my palate alongside a rich, sautéed chicken breast sauced with a reduction of white wine, butter, and a dash of stock. Of course, in keeping with the lemon-wedge rule, a plate of oysters or tuna carpaccio is very content with a Pinot Gris, as is a simply sautéed rainbow trout or the classic Oregon match of Pinot Gris with plank-smoked northwestern salmon.

The more viscous, tangy, and spicy examples from Alsace, California, and Oregon demand slightly richer dishes but not necessarily pungent and highly seasoned ones. As with fine Chardonnay, the flavor of Pinot Gris is easy to lose in the mix. Simple pastas, fowl, shellfish, and white meats are sure bets, especially when accompanied by mildly rich sauces, reductions of pan juices, or light additions of fresh herbs. I enjoy Pinot Gris as a foil for a lemon mayonnaise or a light aioli. If the wine is indeed treated like a Chardonnay, with oak treatment and possibly some malolactic fermentation, then treat it as you would a Chardonnay of similar personality.

Although I am always willing to be convinced, I have yet to taste many bottles of aged Pinot Gris or Pinot Grigio that I felt merited the time in the cellar! So avoid hanging on too long; instead, serve these wines fresh and bright, when they show at their finest. What's too long? Of course, maturity is a subjective matter, but I think these wines don't last well more than two years after release to consumers—except in Alsace, where, counterintuitively, they may show well for up to a decade.

PAIRING POINTERS

Pinot Gris goes well:

- With almost any food that works with a Loire-style Sauvignon Blanc (100 percent varietal, unoaked), as long as the Pinot Gris likewise is crisp, zesty, and unoaked.
- With Chardonnay-friendly dishes, if the Pinot Gris is more unctuous, rich, and textured, like those from Alsace and some from Oregon and California.
- With many Asian preparations. The more austere versions cut richness and highlight great ingredients (like stir-fried crab with garlic or black bean sauce), while the richer interpretations do well against flavorful, textured dishes (clay-pot treatments, dishes thickened with arrowroot or cornstarch, and coconut-milk-based curries).

- With most simple shellfish dishes, including those based on oysters, clams, and mussels.
- With raw fish dishes such as tuna tartar, salmon carpaccio, and ceviche. The wine's acidity pops the naturally flavorful fish.
- Against sweet-tart sauces such as applesauce, or sweet-salty sauces such as Japanese *ponzu* and other sweet, soy-based dipping sauces.
- With semihard cheeses like Gruyère, Comté, and Emmenthaler.
- With picnic fare, especially on a warm summer day!

Pinot Gris is not good:
- With thick and bold preparations. While its texture may hold up (especially in the Alsace or Oregon styles), the flavors are intrinsically subtle and may well get lost.
- When the wrong wine is selected. Pick bright and refreshing examples for simpler, sharper, or leaner preparations and the richer versions for more textured, sauced, and thicker dishes.
- When the dish is overly sweet. If you have a recipe that is blatantly sugary, opt for a wine with some residual sweetness, such as a Riesling, rather than a dry Pinot Gris, or select an Alsatian *vendange tardive* interpretation.
- When served at the wrong temperature. The Italian and Italian-style wines are best served cool; they fall apart if served too warm. Those that are oilier in body are muted if too cold and their flavors will be lost behind the meal.
- With big red meats. As with many other white wines, avoid Pinot Gris/Grigio with classic roasts of lamb, beef, or venison.

BUTTERNUT SQUASH RISOTTO
WITH GORGONZOLA CHEESE

SERVES 6

7 cups vegetable broth

4 tablespoons (½ stick) unsalted butter

2 tablespoons olive oil

1 small onion, chopped

2 cloves garlic, minced

2 tablespoons chopped fresh sage

3 cups peeled butternut squash cut in ¾-inch cubes

Salt

2 cups Arborio rice

½ cup dry white wine (optional)

½ cup cream

3 ounces crumbled Gorgonzola dolcelatte or other mild, creamy blue cheese

6 tablespoons grated Parmesan cheese

¼ cup chopped toasted walnuts (optional)

Freshly ground black pepper

Pour the broth into a large saucepan and bring to a simmer; adjust the heat to maintain a gentle simmer.

In a deep sauté pan, melt the butter and olive oil over medium heat. Add the onion, garlic, and sage and sauté until the onion is almost tender, 5 to 6 minutes. Add the squash, sprinkle with salt, and stir for 1 minute. Add the rice and stir until the rice is opaque, about 3 minutes. Add the white wine, if desired, and cook until it evaporates, about 3 minutes. Add a ladleful of the simmering broth (about 1 cup), and stir until the broth is absorbed. Reduce the heat to low. Continue to add broth 1 ladleful at a time, until the rice is al dente in the center and creamy on the outside, about 20 minutes total. (Do not attempt to rush the cooking of the rice. It takes at least 20 minutes to achieve the proper chewy yet creamy consistency.) Stir in the cream, Gorgonzola, 4 tablespoons of the Parmesan cheese, and the walnuts, if desired. Simmer until the cheeses are melted, about 2 minutes. Season to taste with salt and pepper. Sprinkle with the remaining 2 tablespoons grated Parmesan cheese and serve immediately.

. . . . .

Risotto is Italian comfort food at its best. The rice provides a neutral foil for the other flavors, in this case the sweet squash and salty Gorgonzola. For a contrast in texture, and a hint of bitterness, add some chopped toasted walnuts.

If you want the squash to become soft and melting, add it at the start of cooking. If you want to keep some texture, parboil it separately in the vegetable broth and add it to the rice along with the last addition of broth. —Joyce

There are so many directions to go when pairing this flexible white with food. Here the wine's balanced acidity is put into play in several ways. First, it will indeed cut through the richness of this dish and refresh the palate between bites. Second, the bright acidity frames the sweet, rich squash and cheese, and, third, any excessive saltiness from the Gorgonzola dolcelatte will be effectively neutralized. A culinary trifecta! With a fuller-bodied Pinot Gris interpretation, the wine should match perfectly with the richness and intensity of the dish. The walnuts add texture and are delightful if the wine demonstrates any bitterness imparted through skin contact during production. —Evan

RECOMMENDED PRODUCERS

Textured, Spicy, Tangy Pinot Gris

EVERYDAY	PREMIUM	SPLURGE
Foris (Rogue River Valley, Oregon)	Domaine Weinbach (Alsace, France)	Zind Humbrecht (Alsace, France)
Pierre Sparr (Alsace, France)	Keuntz-Bas (Alsace, France)	Marcel Deiss (Alsace, France)
Jean-Baptiste Adam (Alsace, France)	Dopff & Irion (Alsace, France)	Josmeyer (Alsace, France)

SCALLOP CEVICHE WITH GRAPEFRUIT AND AVOCADO

SERVES 4

1 pound bay scallops

½ cup fresh lime juice

½ cup fresh grapefruit juice

1 small red onion, finely diced

2 jalapeño chiles, seeded and minced (leave seeds in for extra heat)

¼ cup olive oil

3 tablespoons minced fresh mint or coriander (cilantro)

1 teaspoon grated peeled fresh ginger (optional)

1 teaspoon salt, or more to taste

2 small grapefruits, peeled and sectioned

2 avocados, pitted, peeled, and diced

With a sharp paring knife, trim the foot muscles from the scallops and place the scallops in a nonreactive container. Cover with the lime and grapefruit juices and marinate in the refrigerator for 3 to 4 hours.

Add the onion, jalapeños, oil, mint or coriander, ginger (if desired), and 1 teaspoon salt and marinate for another hour. Then toss in the grapefruit sections and avocado. Season to taste with additional salt, if desired, and serve immediately.

VARIATION While bay scallops are best for this ceviche, sea scallops will work, too. Just cut them crosswise if they are very thick, and cut in half if they are very wide as well. This dish can also be made with ½-inch chunks or slices of a firm white fish such as snapper, rock cod, or halibut.

• • • • •

This ceviche is a refreshing appetizer salad that plays with the elements of sweetness (the scallops), tartness (the citrus), and hints of bitterness (the onion and jalapeños). Avocado adds a creamy contrast to the shellfish and grapefruit. For the herb garnish to echo the sweetness, use mint; for a bitter accent, choose fresh coriander. —Joyce

This match is a slam dunk. Here the goal is to not conflict with the subtleties and layers of complex flavor in this simple but very tasty preparation. The cleaner, racier versions of Pinot Gris do exactly that, bringing out the sweetness of the scallops, resonating with the sharp nuances of the citrus, and accentuating the ginger and the mint or fresh coriander. The waxiness of the fresh avocado and the tart sweetness found in the grapefruit segments frame both the dish and the wine. —Evan

RECOMMENDED PRODUCERS

Clean, Racy, Citrusy Pinot Gris

EVERYDAY	PREMIUM	SPLURGE
Zenato (Veneto, Italy)	Bottega Vinaia (Trentino–Alto Adige, Italy)	Jermann (Friuli–Venezia Giulia, Italy)
Chateau Ste. Michelle (Greater Columbia Valley, Washington)	Alois Lageder (Trentino–Alto Adige, Italy)	
Collavini (Friuli–Venezia Giulia, Italy)	Vie di Romans (Friuli–Venezia Giulia, Italy)	

MOROCCAN-INSPIRED FISH WITH OLIVES AND LEMON

SERVES 4

1½ pounds fillets of white fish such as halibut, snapper,
cod, sole, flounder, or sea bass

Oil for baking dish

¼ cup water

½ teaspoon saffron threads, crushed

4 cloves garlic, finely minced

1 teaspoon ground cumin

1 teaspoon kosher salt

½ teaspoon freshly ground black pepper

1 tablespoon extra virgin olive oil, or as needed

2 juicy lemons, peeled and seeded, sliced into paper-thin rounds

⅔ cup cured green olives, pitted and halved

¼ cup chopped fresh coriander (cilantro)

Fish stock or water

Preheat the oven to 475 degrees. Place the fish in an oiled baking dish large enough to hold the fish in one layer.

Pour the ¼ cup water into a small saucepan and bring it to a simmer. Remove the saucepan from the heat, add the saffron, and let steep 10 minutes.

Meanwhile, in a small bowl, stir together the garlic, cumin, salt, and pepper and add enough olive oil to make a paste. Rub the paste on the fish. Top the fish with the lemon slices, pressing them to release a bit of juice. Sprinkle with the olives and fresh coriander, and spoon on the saffron infusion. Drizzle liberally with olive oil and add enough fish stock to the dish to reach a depth of ¼ inch. Bake until the fish looks opaque when the point of a knife is inserted into the thickest part, 10 to 15 minutes.

· · · · ·

This fish is flavored by bitter saffron and fresh coriander, tart lemon, fragrant cumin, and mild briny olives—all traditional ingredients in Moroccan fish cookery. To balance these assertive flavors, serve the fish with couscous or steamed new potatoes. Another wonderful accompaniment to this tasty fish is a side of sautéed Swiss chard and roasted red peppers. —Joyce

Several of the key elements in the recipe (lemon, coriander, and olive) are intrinsic to the wine, while others (saffron, cumin, and garlic) are complementary when used in the correct amounts, as they are here. If the olives are especially briny, rinse them first, or you may find that the excessive salt distorts the match. Halibut is an excellent choice for this recipe, adding a bit of meaty resilience and being flavorful but not too fishy. However, you can easily substitute snapper, rock cod, or other flaky fishes, or even try monkfish or swordfish if you'd prefer something meatier for a more generous wine. —Evan

RECOMMENDED PRODUCERS
Pinot Gris Somewhere In Between

EVERYDAY	PREMIUM
Firesteed (Willamette Valley, Oregon)	King Estate (Willamette Valley, Oregon)
Oak Knoll (Willamette Valley, Oregon)	Ponzi (Willamette Valley, Oregon)
Boeger (Sierra Foothills, California)	MacMurray Ranch (Sonoma County, California)

BOUILLABAISSE-STYLE SEAFOOD STEW

SERVES 6

¼ cup white wine
¼ teaspoon saffron threads, crushed

SOUP BASE

3 tablespoons olive oil
2 leeks, cut in half lengthwise,
sliced crosswise into ¼-inch pieces, well washed
2 onions, diced
2 stalks celery, diced
4 cloves garlic, finely minced
2 to 3 strips orange zest, ½ × 3 inches each
8 to 9 cups Fish Stock (see recipe below)
2 cups diced canned plum tomatoes
8 sprigs fresh thyme
1 bay leaf
2 teaspoons ground fennel seed
½ teaspoon red pepper flakes
Salt and freshly ground black pepper

1½ pounds firm white fish such as monkfish, flounder,
bass, or snapper, cut into 2-inch pieces
3 lobsters, about 1½ pounds each, boiled for 8 minutes,
or 2 large crabs, boiled for 12 to 15 minutes, cleaned, cut into chunks
with the shells on, and cracked where needed (optional)
24 shrimp, shelled and deveined
24 sea scallops, foot muscles removed
2 to 3 pounds mussels, scrubbed and debearded
Dry white wine
2 fennel bulbs, quartered, cored, and parboiled until tender (optional)
½ cup chopped fresh flat-leaf parsley for garnish
¼ cup chopped fennel fronds for garnish
24 slices toasted French bread, rubbed with garlic
2 cups Aïoli or 1 cup Rouille (see recipes below)

For the saffron infusion: Pour the wine into a small saucepan and bring it to a simmer. Remove the saucepan from the heat, add the saffron, and let steep 10 minutes.

For the soup base: In a large, heavy pot, heat the olive oil over medium heat. Add the leeks, onions, celery, garlic, and orange zest and sauté until tender, about 10 minutes. Add the saffron infusion, fish stock, plum tomatoes, thyme, bay leaf, ground fennel seed, and red pepper flakes. Stir well and bring gently to a boil. Reduce the heat to low and simmer 15 to 20 minutes. Season to taste with salt and pepper. (The soup base can be prepared up to 2 days ahead of time. Cool, then cover and refrigerate.)

To serve: Bring the soup base to a simmer and add the fish and the lobster or crab, if using, and cook for 2 to 3 minutes. Add the shrimp and scallops and cook an additional 3 to 4 minutes, until the seafood is firm and the fish is opaque.

Discard any mussels that do not close when tapped with a spoon. In a saucepan, pour the white wine to a depth of $1/2$ inch and add the mussels. Cover and bring to a boil over high heat. Steam until the mussels open, 3 to 5 minutes. Discard any that haven't opened within 10 minutes. Using a slotted spoon, transfer the opened mussels to the stew. Strain the cooking liquids through cheesecloth and add to the stew as well. Add the cooked fennel bulbs, if using, and top with chopped parsley and fennel fronds. Garnish with toasted bread croutons and generous dollops of aïoli or rouille.

VARIATION You can replace half of the French bread croutons with 12 to 18 boiled new potatoes.

AÏOLI

1 tablespoon finely chopped garlic
Pinch of salt, or more to taste
2 large egg yolks
3 to 4 tablespoons lemon juice
2 cups mild olive oil, or part canola oil and part olive oil

Place the garlic in a mortar and grind to a fine paste with a pinch of salt.

Put the egg yolks in the container of a blender or food processor. Add 3 tablespoons lemon juice and blend. With the machine running, gradually add the olive oil, a few drops at a time, until the mayonnaise is emulsified. Add the garlic mixture and remaining lemon juice to taste. Season to taste with additional salt. Thin if needed with a bit of water.

SIMPLE ROUILLE

2 tablespoons tomato paste
1 teaspoon cayenne pepper
1 cup aïoli

Combine tomato paste, pepper, and aïoli in a bowl.

ALTERNATE ROUILLE

3 slices bread, crusts removed
4 cloves garlic, finely minced
1 teaspoon cayenne pepper
8 tablespoons olive oil
2 tablespoons tomato paste
Fish Stock (see recipe below)

In a food processor, combine the bread, garlic, cayenne pepper, olive oil, and tomato paste. Gradually add enough fish stock to make a spoonable sauce.

FISH STOCK

6 to 8 pounds fish frames with heads and tails (from mild-flavored fish
such as snapper, rockfish, or halibut), gills removed
2 tablespoons mild olive oil
2 quarts water, or more as needed
4 cups dry white wine
3 medium onions, chopped
4 ribs celery, chopped
5 sprigs fresh flat-leaf parsley
3 strips lemon zest
2 sprigs fresh thyme
10 peppercorns
4 coriander seeds
3 allspice berries
1 bay leaf
1 teaspoon fennel seeds (optional)

Rinse the fish frames well. In a large heavy pot, heat the olive oil over medium heat and cook the fish frames, stirring often, until the frames give off some liquid, about 10 minutes. Add the

2 quarts water, white wine, onions, celery, parsley, lemon zest, thyme, peppercorns, coriander seeds, allspice berries, bay leaf, and fennel seeds, if desired. Add additional water to cover if needed. Bring to a boil. Reduce the heat and simmer uncovered for 30 minutes, skimming the surface occasionally. Strain the stock through a cheesecloth-lined strainer. Refrigerate and cover when cold. Refrigerate for up to 2 days or freeze for up to 3 months. *Makes about 10 cups*

· · · · ·

While shellfish traditionally are not used in Provençal bouillabaisse, they certainly make a fish stew more festive. Allow about ½ pound of assorted fish per person if using only fish, and use ¼ to ⅓ pound of fish per person if combined with shellfish. If you are in the mood to splurge, add a lobster or crab to the seafood assortment. Steamed new potatoes and fennel are good choices for accompaniments. Grilled or toasted bread, and, of course, rich, garlicky aioli or spicy rouille are the final garnishes for this sumptuous stew.
—Joyce

I admit it: sometimes it can be more work than you want to do to try and figure out what style of wine your bottle best fits. And with some grapes, Pinot Gris being one, subtleties can be difficult to discern. So if you simply want a dish that will work for just about any style, here it is. The bounty of the sea is always successful with Pinot Gris, and with bouillabaisse, you have it all. Again, saffron is an attractive accent spice with this grape, while the mild heat in the rouille is just enough to set off the bevy of flavors in the recipe, and the wine's sharpness prevents the rouille from being too assertive. The rouille and croutons add more layers of texture and should be served in copious amounts. —Evan

RECOMMENDED PRODUCERS
Excellent All-Around Pinot Gris

EVERYDAY	PREMIUM
Beringer (Napa Valley, California)	Chehalem (Willamette Valley, Oregon)
Clos du Bois (Sonoma County, California)	Willakenzie (Willamette Valley, Oregon)
Plozner (Friuli–Venezia Giulia, Italy)	Jermann (Friuli–Venezia Giulia, Italy)

GEWÜRZTRAMINER

I have often thought that if more people attempted to pronounce Gewürztraminer (gah-*vertz-trah-mee*-ner), more of the wine would be consumed. Those who dare, despite sweaty palms and foreheads, are generally happy that they tried. The wine that sounds like a sobriety test is remarkable in its accessible, delicious, and straightforward character. It's unmistakable and refreshingly forthright. And in spite of its intimidating Germanic name, Gewürztraminer is not an intimidating wine. While perhaps less flexible in pairing with food than other white wines, its flavors and personality are forceful, and I like that in a wine.

WINE-GROWING AREAS

The origins of Gewürztraminer are peculiar. Most people believe it to be German by birth. However, long ago the Italians exported the local grape of Tramin (or Termeno, as it's sometimes referred to), a town in the northeastern Trentino–Alto Adige region, to Germany, and lo and behold, it became more noteworthy outside Italy than within it! The prefix *gewürz*, which means spicy, was added in Germany, as the wine has a very spicy bouquet. The spices of Germany, however, aren't of the hot coriander and cumin variety but rather are of the sweeter cinnamon, clove, and nutmeg variety.

France's Alsace is the home of the quintessential Gewürz. It's a wine of more generous weight than the German style, with an exotic and pungent aroma of ripe tree fruit (apples and pears), exotic and fragrant flowers, and sweet spice. It has an oiliness of texture and a flavor that is distinctive and powerful. Although Gewürztraminers are almost invariably dry, off-dry (*vendange tardive*) and sweet (*sélection des grains nobles*) wines are made, as with Riesling, in exceptional years.

Although the grape is also grown and the wine made in Germany, the German wines rarely approach the same quality as the Alsace wines. Elsewhere in Europe, it's a pleasant treat to find a unique and subtle version of this wine made in its original home, northeastern Italy. Here you discover wines that are less rich and more delicate in their distinct tapestry of flavors. The Gewürztraminers made in Central Europe resemble those of Italy.

In the New World, very well-made bottles now come from New Zealand's Gisborne, where I have sampled wines that are dead ringers for their Alsatian cousins and are made in both dry and off-dry styles. Efforts are being made in South America, and increasingly rare but better wines are being made in the United States, especially in Oregon and selected appellations within California, most notably Mendocino County and the Southern Central Coast's Edna Valley. A relatively recent arrival in South Africa, Gewürz is being made in Robertson and areas around Durbanville.

While I was writing this book, one of my Alsatian wine friends asked me to name the best American Gewürz I had ever had. I thought about it and replied that it came from Michigan, but as there's only one small winery that makes it, I won't tease you with a description here.

A table of principal wine-growing regions for Gewürztraminer appears on page 273.

VINTNER CHOICES

Ripe or unripe; skin contact; young or aged; wood or no wood;
dry, off-dry, or sweet; malolactic fermentation

As with Riesling, Gewürztraminer allows a vintner relatively few choices. Ensuring that the fruit is ripe on the vine and forward in taste is likely the most challenging. It's a slow-ripening grape, and, to maximize the flavor, vintners attempt to pick it as late in the harvest as possible; but with the weather changes of fall, waiting can be risky. The grape also shouldn't be overcropped, as it thereby loses its concentration and intensity.

The fruit itself is of a red, pink, or gray color rather than white, and the bulk of the flavor and taste is in the skins. For this reason, some producers leave the wine on the skins to extract the essential flavors. In contrast to what generally happens with this winemaking practice, the wines seem to age well, though Gewürztraminers that have undergone skin contact tend to be somewhat tannic (bitter and astringent). Why they age well is difficult to understand, as the grape generally produces wines of only moderate acid. The best ones alter in character as they age, putting forth more candied-fruit and dried-flower flavors. Whether you like your Gewürztraminer young or aged is a personal preference.

Somewhat surprisingly for a forward and flavorful wine, Gewürztraminer handles oak poorly, and, with a few notable exceptions, it is rarely aged in barrels. When it is, the casks used, as with Riesling, are large and old. The name suggests an association with sweetness, and though the Alsace style is dry (drier than most American Chardonnays, for that matter), there are a number of slightly sweet, off-dry examples made outside Europe. However, outside Europe such wines more often than not taste soapy and odd. As the wine is relatively low in acid to begin with, malolactic fermentation is usually aggressively avoided, though a few producers encourage it.

FLAVORS

Fruit: Apple, pear, peach, apricot, tangerine, lychee, orange or orange zest, passion fruit, pineapple, golden raisin, mango

Floral: Honeysuckle, tuberose, freesia, gardenia, jasmine, clove, cinnamon, anise, nutmeg, mace

Earth: Kerosene or fusel oil, smoke, mineral

Wood (if used): Vanilla, sweet spice

Other: Pepper, sauerkraut

WINE AND FOOD PAIRING

INGREDIENTS AND STYLES

Gewürztraminer can be a difficult wine to pair with food. People often think that the spiciness suggested in the name will make it a good match with all spicy dishes and cuisines. Nothing could be further from the truth. Gewürztraminer, being a late-ripening and relatively late-harvested grape, is ample in alcohol, and pairing such a "hot" wine with spicy foods can produce results that are far from refreshing or enjoyable. There is also a fable that it's the perfect wine to go with Chinese and other Asian cuisine. Although it can indeed go with many dishes (try an off-dry example with slightly spicy or sweet dishes, such as sweet and sour pork or hoisin-glazed ribs), the pairing is not a guaranteed success.

But if Gewürztraminer is choosy about what it pairs with, it compensates by pairing well with some unexpected and challenging foods. Classic, dry Gewürztraminer is best with rich dishes and can stand up to many a preparation that many other white wines can't share the table with. The traditional rich fowl are great: goose, duck, and turkey. Whether the bird is of the classic holiday roasted variety or something more daring like curried duck with lemon, honey, and ginger, Gewürz is quite content. White meats such as pork and veal are also excellent table companions for Gewürz, whether in the form of a classic Alsatian choucroute laden with pork chops, sausages, potatoes, and sauerkraut or a simple veal roast. Gewürz pairs well with crab and other sweet shellfish, including prawns and, depending on the treatment, scallops. Finally, many quiches and other egg-based tarts are exceptional with Gewürztraminer, making it one of the few wines that pair well with such a traditionally difficult match. Eggs are notoriously tough on wines.

Off-dry versions should be treated much in the same way as off-dry Rieslings: to match sweet dishes, show off sweet spices, or flirt with preparations that are higher in salt. Gewürz can be exceptional with many cheeses as well as less-sweet desserts.

Late-harvest or dessert styles of Gewürztraminer are best served alone, dribbled over some vanilla ice cream, or served with a compote or tart based on peach, pear, or lychee.

METHODS OF PREPARATION

Gewürztraminer, being bold, lends itself well to higher-impact cooking techniques. It holds its own against smoked, grilled, and even charred or blackened foods. Indeed, at times you need to use these potent cooking methods to stand up to the wine's extroverted personality. Even so, steaming and poaching (if the ingredients are well chosen) and sautéing can also work well with this grape.

PAIRING POINTERS

Gewürztraminer goes well:

· With aromatically spicy dishes. You need to be aware of the level of heat, but exotic cuisines that stress curry, ginger, clove, cinnamon, allspice, and cardamom are very happy tablemates.
· With strong cheeses. It is one of the few wines that can hold its own against aged and pungent cheese.
· With rich dishes. Fatty birds like goose and duck, luscious treatments of foie gras, and rich treatments of pork and ham are lovely.
· With smoked ingredients and foods grilled over aromatic woods (apple or almond rather than mesquite or hickory).
· With slightly fruity and sweet but not hot dishes: for instance, anything served with a fruit chutney, a tropical-fruit salsa, or pickled fruit (like peaches).
· With hard-to-match egg dishes such as quiche and frittata.

Gewürztraminer isn't good:

· With very spicy (capsaicin-driven) food. The combination of the spiciness of the food and the high alcohol content of the wine isn't enjoyable.
· With acidic dishes and ingredients. Avoid Gewürztraminer with green vegetables, tossed green salad, tomatoes, and other sharp-tasting ingredients or preparations.
· With dishes that are too sweet. While the wine matches nicely with mildly sweet preparations or those that imply sweetness, Gewürztraminer will taste harsh if accompanying anything that's too sweet (unless, of course, it's a sweeter style of wine).
· When matched with simple and delicate cuisines. The wine's generally too bold. If you are serving a subtle dish, opt for a less pungent interpretation of the wine, such as one from Italy.

CHEESE FONDUE

SERVES 4

SWISS-STYLE CHEESE FONDUE

1 pound Fontina Val d'Aosta or Gruyère cheese, or a combination of the two
1½ cups Gewürztraminer wine
1 teaspoon cornstarch, arrowroot, or potato starch
1 clove garlic, cut in half
Freshly ground black pepper (optional)
Grated nutmeg (optional)
Vegetable strips (such as fennel and carrots)
Toasted bread cubes or breadsticks

Remove the rind and dice the cheese.

In a small bowl, whisk together ¼ cup of the wine and the cornstarch. Rub the inside of the top of a double boiler with the garlic clove. Pour the remaining 1¼ cups wine into the top of the double boiler and add the garlic clove. When the wine is heated through, gradually add half the cheese, whisking constantly. When the cheese is melted and bubbly, whisk in the cornstarch mixture. Gradually add the rest of the cheese, whisking constantly until the cheese is melted. Season to taste with pepper and/or nutmeg, if desired.

Transfer to a fondue pot and place over a warmer. Serve with vegetables and bread.

ITALIAN-STYLE CHEESE FONDUE *(FONDUTA)*

12 ounces Fontina Val d'Aosta or Fontal cheese
1 cup milk
4 tablespoons (½ stick) unsalted butter
½ cup Gewürztraminer wine
1 teaspoon cornstarch dissolved in 2 tablespoons wine
2 egg yolks
½ teaspoon truffle oil or shavings of white truffle (optional)

Remove the rind and dice the cheese. In a large bowl, combine the cheese and milk and let soak overnight in the refrigerator or for 2 hours at room temperature.

In the top of a double boiler over simmering water, melt the butter. Add the cheese and milk mixture. Whisk well to combine, then continue to whisk, adding the wine and cornstarch mixture. Whisk in the egg yolks, 1 at a time. When the *fonduta* is smooth and creamy, after 6 to 8 minutes, stir in the truffle oil or truffle shavings, if desired. Transfer to a fondue pot and place over a warmer. Serve as above, with strips of fennel, carrots, and toasted bread or breadsticks.

· · · · ·

People love a meal when they can participate in the cooking process. Fondue is an ever-popular icebreaker at the table, as guests dip bread or crisp vegetables into the communal pot that holds the creamy, rich, and perfumed melted cheese. I've provided a Swiss version using cheese and wine and a version inspired by the Italian fonduta *that uses cheese, milk, and wine. Truffles are up to you.* —Joyce

Who would have thought that fondue would come back into vogue? A trip to Artisanal in Manhattan reminded me of how fun (and wine-friendly) this dish can be. Although many opt for Riesling and its higher acidity to accompany fondue, I prefer bright and fruit-forward Gewürztraminer, which has the texture and flavorful character to complement the cheese. While bread is a classic choice for dunking, flavorful white sausage, cooked pieces of potato, and even slightly sweeter carrots are lovely as well. For less ripe wines, I love pieces of fennel bulb, too. If you are using Fontina and making this dish as a fonduta, *stick with the New World versions of Gewürz; but if you add the truffles, which bring a touch of earthiness to the dish, you can easily go with a European bottling, especially one that's been aged a few years so that the* terroir *has developed.* —Evan

RECOMMENDED PRODUCERS
Floral, Fruit-Forward Gewürztraminers

EVERYDAY	PREMIUM
Foris (Rogue River Valley, Oregon)	Navarro (Mendocino County, California)
Husch (Mendocino County, California)	Claiborne & Churchill (Southern Central Coast, California)
Chateau St. Jean (Sonoma County, California)	Thomas Fogarty (Northern Central Coast, California)

FOR SPICY, OFF-DRY GEWÜRZTRAMINERS

SAVORY MEAT STRUDEL

2 STRUDELS SERVE 8 AS A MAIN COURSE OR 16 AS AN APPETIZER

½ cup dried currants or raisins

3 tablespoons butter

1 large onion, finely chopped

2 cloves garlic, minced

2 teaspoons chopped fresh thyme

½ teaspoon ground cinnamon

¼ teaspoon grated nutmeg

1 pound ground veal, or part veal and part pork

¼ cup chopped fresh flat-leaf parsley

¼ cup pine nuts, toasted

¼ cup dry breadcrumbs

1 egg

Salt and lots of freshly ground black pepper

8 tablespoons (1 stick) unsalted butter

½ pound phyllo (12 to 14 sheets)

Sour cream or crème fraîche

Chopped fresh chives

Cover the currants with hot water in a small bowl. Let stand for 30 minutes at room temperature until they soften and plump. Drain.

In a large sauté pan, melt the 3 tablespoons butter over medium heat. Add the onion and cook until soft, about 10 minutes. Add the garlic, thyme, cinnamon, and nutmeg and sauté to blend the flavors, 1 to 2 minutes. Add the ground meat and cook over medium-high heat, stirring often, until the meat is slightly browned. Remove the pan from the heat and stir in the currants, parsley, pine nuts, breadcrumbs, and egg. Season to taste with salt and plenty of pepper. Cover and chill the mixture.

To clarify the butter for even browning: Melt the 8 tablespoons butter in a small saucepan over low heat. Skim off the foam. Pour the clarified butter into a container, leaving behind the milky residue.

To assemble: Lightly brush a sheet of phyllo with the clarified butter, then top with another sheet. Butter again and repeat for a total of 6 layers. Place half the meat mixture in a strip along the long side, about 1 inch from the edge. Tuck in the ends and roll. Repeat with the remaining phyllo, clarified butter, and meat mixture. Place the strudels seam side down on a baking sheet. (These can be made ahead of time, covered loosely with foil, and refrigerated for up to 1 day or frozen for up to 1 month. Freeze before covering with foil to prevent the phyllo from sticking. The strudel can be baked frozen: remove the foil before baking and add 15 minutes to the cooking time.)

Preheat the oven to 350 degrees. Bake the strudels until golden brown, about 40 minutes. Cut the strudels on the diagonal with a sharp serrated knife. Serve with sour cream and chives.

$$\cdots\cdots$$

The sweet spices, currants, and rich meat enclosed in buttery phyllo in this strudel make for a fine first course or light lunch, if accompanied by a salad. This is a crunchy cross between a meat blintz and a knish. Either bake one strudel right away and freeze the second one, or serve both for a delightful appetizer at a party. Serve the strudel with sour cream or crème fraîche on the side. —Joyce

When your Gewürztraminer has a very traditional flavor profile, this strudel brings out the wine's true affinity for white meat. The richness of the strudel dough and its butter are the perfect platform for a richer, more unctuous wine, while the various sweet spices mirror the wine's flavors. And of course the sweetness of the currants resonates with the wine's off-dry character. If the wine seems less sweet or fruit-forward, which can happen in less ripe years, you may want to hold back on the currants. Wines that are more mature, on the other hand, play well to the pine nuts, and you may, after some experimentation, choose to add a few more of those. The crème fraîche or sour cream not only adds moisture and balance when served with the strudel but also accentuates the wine's rich texture. —Evan

RECOMMENDED PRODUCERS
Spicy, Off-Dry Gewürztraminers

EVERYDAY	PREMIUM
Columbia Crest (Greater Columbia Valley, Washington)	Domaine Weinbach (Alsace, France)
Weltevrede (Robertson, South Africa)	Brancott (Marlborough, New Zealand)
Hogue (Greater Columbia Valley, Washington)	Paul Blanck (Alsace, France)

SALMON WITH SPICED ONIONS AND CURRANTS

SERVES 4

½ cup dried currants
¼ cup cognac or brandy
¼ cup hot water
6 tablespoons olive oil or butter plus extra for buttering baking dishes
4 yellow onions, sliced into ¼-inch rings (about 6 cups)
½ teaspoon ground cinnamon
½ teaspoon grated nutmeg
½ teaspoon salt plus additional as needed
¼ teaspoon freshly ground black pepper plus additional as needed
4 6-ounce salmon fillets
½ cup fish or vegetable stock

Soak the currants in the cognac and hot water for 30 minutes until they soften and plump.

In a large sauté pan over medium heat, warm the 6 tablespoons oil or melt the butter. Reduce the heat to low, add the onions, and sauté until very tender and sweet, about 20 minutes. Add the cinnamon and nutmeg and currants with their liquid and cook to meld the flavors, about 5 minutes. Season with ½ teaspoon salt and ¼ teaspoon pepper. Set aside.

Preheat the oven to 450 degrees.

Butter individual gratin dishes and distribute the onion mixture evenly among them. Place the salmon fillets atop the onions. Sprinkle the fish with a little salt and pepper. Spoon the stock over the salmon and bake until the fish is done, 10 to 15 minutes, depending on the thickness of the fish.

VARIATION You can enclose the salmon and onion in parchment or foil packets. Cut out 4 heart-shaped pieces of parchment or foil large enough to enclose the fish when folded in half. (The packet should be at least 2 inches larger than the fish.) For each serving, place one-quarter of the onion mixture on one side of the heart, top with 1 salmon fillet, and sprinkle with salt and pepper. Fold over the top half of the heart and seal by crimping the edges. Bake at 450 degrees for 10 to 15 minutes.

· · · · ·

When onions are cooked for a long time they reveal their inherent sweetness. The sweet onions, fragrant spices, and brandied currants are a fine foil for the rich salmon here. For ease of serving, you may fully assemble the dish, cover with plastic, and refrigerate for up to 6 hours, then bake when needed. Leafy spinach is a good accompaniment, as it plays well with sweet spices; try a small side of sautéed spinach or mixed greens and rice. —Joyce

This is a personal favorite when I want to show off a terrific classic wine. Salmon with the aromatic spices and brandied currants is very successful with Gewürztraminer. Cook the onions slowly over low heat to bring out that earthy sweetness that the wine craves. Baking the fish in parchment or aluminum foil rather than in a pan preserves more of the onions' moisture and better accentuates the wine. If you find that spinach by itself is too bitter or sharp for the wine, toss in a few toasted nuts (pine nuts or slivered almonds) and a little lemon as a bridge. —Evan

RECOMMENDED PRODUCERS

Spicy, Bone-Dry, Fairly Austere Gewürztraminers

EVERYDAY	PREMIUM
Covey Run (Greater Columbia Valley, Washington)	Muré (Alsace, France)
Pierre Sparr (Alsace, France)	Zind Humbrecht (Alsace, France)
Jean-Baptiste Adam (Alsace, France)	Hugel (Alsace, France)

DUCK WITH ORANGE SAUCE

SERVES 4

1 5-pound duck, neck, feet, wings, and excess fat removed
Salt and freshly ground black pepper
3 whole oranges plus additional orange segments for garnish
4 tablespoons (½ stick) unsalted butter, room temperature,
plus 1 tablespoon for binding the sauce
3 tablespoons extra virgin olive oil
½ cup grappa
1 cup dry white wine
½ cup poultry broth, or more as needed
1½ teaspoons sugar, or more to taste
1 tablespoon flour

Preheat the oven to 350 degrees.

Wash and dry the duck. Sprinkle it with salt and pepper inside and out. Quarter 1 of the oranges, peeled or unpeeled, insert into the duck cavity, and skewer or sew closed. In a Dutch oven large enough to hold the duck, melt 4 tablespoons butter with 3 tablespoons oil over high heat. Add the duck and brown it, turning frequently, until it is colored on all sides, up to 25 minutes. Pour off the fat. Deglaze the pan with the grappa and add the wine. Cover the pot and transfer to the oven. Cook until the duck is tender, about 1½ hours.

Meanwhile, remove all the zest from 1 of the remaining oranges in long strips. Cut these into fine strips and blanch them in boiling water for 3 minutes. Strain and repeat this process once to rid the peel of bitterness. Strain and set aside.

Squeeze the juice of the remaining 2 oranges into a measuring cup to total about ³/₄ cup juice and set aside.

Remove the duck from the Dutch oven and place on a carving board. Skim the excess fat from the pan juices. Add ½ cup broth and the orange juice to the Dutch oven and bring to a boil over high heat. Boil the sauce until reduced to 1½ cups, 8 to 10 minutes. Reduce the heat to low. Stir in 1½ teaspoons sugar.

In a small bowl, stir the remaining 1 tablespoon butter and the flour to make a paste. Whisk bits of this paste in increments into the sauce to thicken it. Add the reserved zest and simmer to blend the flavors, about 5 minutes. Season the sauce to taste with salt, pepper, and additional sugar, if desired. Carve the duck into quarters, discarding the orange pieces from the interior. (For ease of serving, the duck can be carved into serving portions in advance and reheated in the sauce.) Place 1 duck quarter on each plate and spoon the sauce over the meat. Garnish with orange segments.

. . . . .

Most of us believe that duck with orange sauce is a French classic, but its origins are Italian. The recipe was brought to France by the Florentine cooks of Caterina de' Medici. Over time, French chefs modified the cooking technique and added the now traditional gastrique *of sugar-vinegar caramel to the* bigarade, *or sour orange sauce. This is the older version of the recipe, and it's still a winner. For a vibrant note of color, use blood oranges if they are available. A side dish of roasted butternut or acorn squash or braised fennel frames this dish perfectly. With ample side dishes, one duck can serve four, but if you are concerned about having enough duck, you may want to cook two. —Joyce*

This match was identified accidentally, when the only Gewürz I had on hand in my cellar was close to ten years old. Because the audience was friends and family, I figured if it didn't work, they'd cut me some slack. Well, to the contrary, we were all thrilled. While the duck's oily richness works for almost all Gewürztraminers, the orange sauce is what steers the dish toward the more mature wines. When they become older, many Gewürztraminers (both Old and New World styles) take on a candied-fruit (marmalade-like) and orange-zest character. This character is brought out by the sweet and sour sauce, and so the duck and the wine reaffirm each other's core personality. —Evan

RECOMMENDED PRODUCERS
Slightly Aged and Developed Gewürztraminers

EVERYDAY	PREMIUM
Amity (Willamette Valley, Oregon)	Andrew Rich (Willamette Valley, Oregon)
Canoe Ridge (Greater Columbia Valley, Washington)	Trimbach (Alsace, France)
Meridian (Southern Central Coast, California)	Léon Beyer (Alsace, France)

Sparkling Wine

Asian-Inspired Shrimp Salad

Zinfandel

Pasta with Artichokes, Pancetta, Mushrooms, and Peas

Sparkling Wine

Crab Salad in Endive Leaves

Sangiovese

Rustic Paella

Sauvignon Blanc
Baked Goat Cheese in a Walnut Crust with Greens and Apple

Riesling

Chinese Chicken Salad

Gewürztraminer
Duck with Orange Sauce

Merlot

Catalan Bean and Sausage Stew with Mint

Chardonnay

Grilled, Herb-Marinated Fish on a Bed of White Beans

Cabernet Sauvignon
Steak au Poivre

Pinot Gris
Butternut Squash Risotto with Gorgonzola Cheese

Viognier

Moroccan Lamb Tagine with Raisins, Almonds, and Honey

Pinot Noir

Salmon with Soy, Ginger, and Sake

Syrah

Korean Short Ribs

Sparkling Dessert Wine

Lemony Ricotta Soufflé Cake with Raspberry Sauce

Fortified Dessert Wine
Hazelnut Torte with Coffee Buttercream

VIOGNIER

Viognier (vee-own-*yay*) is a rare and idiosyncratic grape. Its flavors are unique, at once exotic and provocative. I once asked a vintner in Napa why we don't see more of this striking grape on store shelves and in restaurants. He chuckled and replied that it was a royal pain to make: it doesn't set a reliable or predictable crop; it ripens very slowly, which makes it susceptible to deer and birds consuming the harvest; and many winemakers don't really understand it. Oh. Is that all? Fortunately for wine lovers, enough winemakers around the globe remain steadfast in their desire to vinify this delicious grape into wine.

WINE-GROWING AREAS

This selection is a bit of a stretch for a book focusing on classic and commonly available wines. Viognier, by any measure, is not a high-volume player in the current wine market. Although it's been said that today more acreage is devoted to Viognier in the United States than in its native France, that area is dwarfed by the acres and acres of Chardonnay and even Gewürztraminer that are planted.

So why bother to make Viognier or write about it? Two reasons. First, it's a dynamite wine with food, and one that is increasingly showing up on the wine lists of restaurants across the country as well as in many retail stores. Second, it's very enjoyable in itself: Viognier has the captivating accessibility of a grape like Gewürztraminer, the aromatics of a great Riesling, and the round body and mouthfeel people adore in Chardonnay. In the years ahead, and with an ongoing commitment from producers worldwide, Viognier, I believe, will become a more important varietal in the American market. Only time will tell if it will become a fixture. Until then, I'll hedge.

Viognier is native to France, and specifically to the northern Rhône Valley. There is educated speculation that it may originally have come from Greece or somewhere else in southeastern Europe, but nothing definitive is known. However, even if it is not native to France's northern

Rhône, Viognier is the region's heart and soul—at least among white wines. The peach-skin-scented and subtly floral Viognier is the grape of the intriguing wines of Condrieu and Château Grillet, which have seduced many a winemaker into planting it elsewhere. Because these French appellations are small, increased demand in France has led to plantings of Viognier in the southeast (the Ardèche) and southwest (the Languedoc).

Across the Atlantic, Viognier has been planted and produced in California and, yes, Virginia! It is also now flourishing in Australia, in the Eden Valley, the Clare Valley, and South Australia. The single greatest difference between French Viogniers and those produced in the United States and Australia is the ripeness factor, which is much more reliable in the New World than in France. This is the reason bottles from the States can taste like a fruit basket, with explosive flavors, while those from France show more restraint and subtlety. With the increasing interest in Viognier worldwide, there are surely many plantings that we'll hear more about in the future, from other regions of Australia, other U.S. states, and South Africa.

A table of principal wine-growing regions for Viognier appears on page 274.

VINTNER CHOICES

Ripe or overripe; skin contact; lees stirring; wood or no wood;
dry or off-dry; malolactic fermentation; fresh or aged

With Viognier, less is more when it comes to winemaking interventions. The single most critical factor is ripeness. In order for the grape to sing, it must be ripe, but the extended ripening time leaves Viognier vulnerable to deer, birds, and other hungry vineyard predators. Often vintners have to net the vineyards to prevent crop loss. The aroma of a ripe Viognier vineyard is sweetly perfumed and intoxicating.

Increasingly, as with other aromatic grapes, like Gewürztraminer and Torrontés (a grape grown in Spain and Argentina), vintners are using limited prefermentation skin contact to extract more flavor. Although there are vocal proponents of oak-aged Viognier, it's generally thought that little or no use of oak is more compelling. Winemakers who do employ barrels generally use older wood so as not to overpower the delicious and succulent nature of the fruit. Of course, there are Chardonnay-style versions, and some producers age the wine partly in new oak to get a kiss of influence from new barrels. Other producers do choose to barrel-ferment (most often in older oak) and stir the lees for both texture and unique appeal. The use of malolactic fermentation is vigorously debated: some argue that it adds finesse, while others take the position that because the wine's acidity is already low, it should not be reduced further.

Although the French style of Viognier is well developed, New World producers are having to make style decisions as they go along. There has yet to emerge a clear-cut style in American

Viognier. The one point on which I have a firm opinion, regardless of style and origin, is bottle age. As with many whites, I prefer to drink Viognier when it is young—frankly, the younger the better. It's then that you are most captivated by the power and exuberance of the stone- and tree-fruit (golden apple and pear) flavors. Although aged Viognier can be interesting, stressing more of the developed nut, marmalade, and preserved-fruit notes, preferences become very subjective. The wines are still good, just different.

Virtually all Viognier is dry, but you sometimes see the rare, off-dry "Vin de Noël," a Christmas wine made in the Rhône that is balanced with a touch of sweetness and is really a treat. If it's available, splurge and buy it!

FLAVORS

Fruit: Lemon, lime, citrus zest, pear skin, peach or peach skin, nectarine, apricot, tangerine, marmalade, yellow plum, blood orange, golden apple

Floral: Citrus blossom, violet, narcissus, wildflower, honeysuckle, gardenia, acacia, tea leaf, cardamom, star anise

Earth: Mineral, stone, blond tobacco

Wood (oak): Vanilla, almond, nougat, toast

Other: Musk, sweet cream, honey, yogurt, pink peppercorn

WINE AND FOOD PAIRING

INGREDIENTS AND STYLES

Viognier is underrated in its ability to pair with food. A good example possesses the richness and creamy texture of Chardonnay, the balanced acidity of a well-made Sauvignon Blanc, and a flavor profile combining aspects of Gewürztraminer, Riesling, and Chardonnay. It's truly unique.

With young, unoaked Viognier, choose foods that suggest sweetness but are not really sweet, like a Moroccan tagine of chicken, preserved lemons, and cinnamon, or a yogurt-marinated, Indian-style kebab. If you prefer something less exotic, dishes such as long-braised chicken with forty cloves of garlic and trout stuffed with pine nuts and golden raisins work well. Any preparation which picks up on the fruit flavors and sweet spices of the wine will pair nicely. Other ingredients that work seamlessly with this grape include rich-textured, slow-cooked root vegetables (like squash, turnips, and carrots), pasta and grains (risotto and polenta), oily nuts (especially macadamias and cashews) and richer fish and white meats. Finally, Viognier goes well with holiday foods, especially goose, turkey, and honey-glazed ham (even with the pineapple and cherries!). So when I am asked to bring wine for holiday occasions, I often choose Viognier.

Viognier goes especially well with shellfish, as the texture and ripe fruit bring out the basic sweet flavors of quality scallops, crab, or lobster. And bring on the butter and cream, because this wine can both match them in texture and, with its balanced acidity, cut through their richness.

With aged versions, dishes which incorporate the aforementioned nuts, reconstituted dried fruit, and white meat, rather than seafood or fish, work best. And here's the most amazing discovery: Viognier is magic with a cheese course. Perhaps it is because, when ripe, the wine implies sweetness, like a dessert wine, or because Viognier has the right texture and acidity. I discovered this match by accident, and I am at a loss to explain it, but do try it sometime!

METHODS OF COOKING

Viognier does well with preparations and cooking techniques that bring out sweetness: slow roasting, caramelizing, smoking (which brings out a subtle, sweet edge), and even deep-fat frying and low-temperature sautéing in butter. Avoid heavy grilling or blackening, as it takes away from the wine's charm.

PAIRING POINTERS

Viognier goes well:

- With full-flavored and rich recipes. With its Chardonnay-like body, Viognier pairs seamlessly with thicker sauces and richly textured dishes.
- With combinations of fruit and sweet spice, including such items as Indian mango chutney, Chinese plum sauce, and a tangy fruit barbecue sauce.
- By itself. Viognier is a fun and different cocktail wine and one that can match well against salty-sweet appetizers and nosh foods: satays with peanut sauce, a cured-meat assortment, or even bar nuts!
- With almost all cheeses. When putting out a cheese platter, bring out the Viognier too.
- With curried anything! Whether it's Thai, Indian, Malaysian, or Caribbean, and as long as the dish isn't overly piquant, this wine pairs effortlessly.
- With smoked foods: fish, chicken, duck, and even cheese.
- With caramelized vegetables and starches. Viognier and roasted root vegetables, baked squash, polenta, and risotto can be mixed and matched into many winning combinations.
- With holiday fare, including turkey, ham, goose, and duck—and maybe even the ever-popular sweet potatoes with marshmallows!

Viognier isn't good:

- With lighter fare. The wine requires something to hang on to and match up with, or it will overpower the food.

- With foods that are very tart. Avoid serving it with green vegetables, fresh green herbs, olives, capers, endive, and other sharp ingredients.
- With sharp sauces. Stay away from vinaigrettes and other acid dressings.
- With fiery-hot dishes. Being fuller-bodied and more alcoholic, the wine can come off as very hot.
- With really fishy fish. Especially with a round and fruit-forward Viognier, avoid pungent fish such as sardines, anchovies, mackerel, or Chilean sea bass.

GINGER AND ORANGE FRIED CHICKEN

SERVES 6

12 small boneless, skinless chicken breast halves
2 cups buttermilk
3 tablespoons grated orange zest
2 tablespoons grated peeled fresh ginger
Salt and freshly ground black pepper
1½ cups all-purpose flour
2 tablespoons curry powder
1 teaspoon ground ginger
1 teaspoon salt
½ teaspoon freshly ground black pepper
Small pinch cayenne pepper (optional)
Canola oil for frying

Carefully cut away the tendons from the boneless chicken breasts and discard. Lightly pound the chicken breasts between sheets of plastic wrap to a uniform thickness.

In a large bowl, combine the buttermilk with the orange zest and fresh ginger, and season with salt and pepper. Add the chicken and refrigerate for 1 to 2 hours.

Combine the flour, curry powder, ground ginger, 1 teaspoon salt, ½ teaspoon pepper, and cayenne pepper, if desired, in a large bowl or a paper bag.

In a large, deep frying pan or skillet, pour the oil to a depth of 3 inches and heat to 365 degrees.

Remove the chicken breasts from the buttermilk and shake off the excess liquid. One at a time, dredge the pieces in the seasoned flour or place them in the paper bag and shake them to coat.

Fry until golden brown, turning once, 4 to 6 minutes per side. If the chicken is browning too quickly, lower the heat. Transfer the fried chicken to a plate lined with paper towels to drain. Serve warm.

VARIATION Cooking boneless chicken is fast and easy, but fried-chicken traditionalists will want to use chicken pieces on the bone, which can be picked up and eaten with fingers—the old-fashioned way. Purchase 2 small fryers and cut them each into 8 or 12 pieces. Marinate the chicken pieces up to 3 hours. Fry until the chicken is golden and cooked through, turning often, about 20 minutes.

. . . . .

Although frying chicken is a last-minute task, this chicken should marinate in the refrigerator for an hour or two. Buttermilk and ginger have a tenderizing effect, so be careful not to marinate the chicken too long or it will become mushy. The curried flour mixture can be assembled well ahead of time. This dish is sublime with a side of corn pudding and a sauté of sugar snap or snow peas. —Joyce

This recipe is so good with those explosively flavored fruit-basket wines, which have enough acidity to counter the richness of deep frying and the salt, while the fruit accents the sweetness imparted to the chicken by the frying and, more important, the buttermilk marinade and the orange zest. Ginger shows well with Viognier, and here is a sublime example of that pairing. The silky texture of the chicken created by the marinade is a seamless match in texture and weight with the fuller body of these ripe and generous wines. In the summer, try serving this dish with pickled peaches or apricots. —Evan

RECOMMENDED PRODUCERS

Bright, Fruit-Forward Viogniers

EVERYDAY	PREMIUM	SPLURGE
Callaway Coastal (multiple appellations, California)	Stags' Leap Winery (Napa Valley, California)	Newton (Napa Valley, California)
Pepperwood Grove (multiple appellations, California)	Sobon Estate (Sierra Foothills, California)	Joseph Phelps (Napa Valley, California)
Cline (Sonoma County, California)	Kunde (Sonoma County, California)	Cold Heaven (Southern Central Coast, California)

•
•

HALIBUT WITH ORANGE AND MINT SALSA VERDE

4 SERVINGS

SAUCE
¼ cup very finely diced red or sweet white onion
⅔ cup thinly sliced fresh mint leaves
2 tablespoons grated orange zest
⅓ cup mild olive oil
⅓ cup fresh orange juice
3 to 4 tablespoons lemon juice to taste
½ teaspoon salt

4 6-ounce halibut fillets
Salt and freshly ground black pepper
Olive oil, wine, or fish stock for cooking

For the sauce: In a medium bowl, whisk the onion, mint, orange zest, olive oil, orange juice, lemon juice, and salt to combine. (Can be prepared 2 to 3 hours ahead of time. Cover and refrigerate. Bring to room temperature before continuing.)

To bake the fish: Preheat the oven to 450 degrees. Sprinkle the fish with salt and pepper and place in an oiled baking dish. Bake until fish looks opaque when the point of a knife is inserted in the thickest part, 10 to 15 minutes.

To broil or grill the fish: Preheat the broiler or prepare a charcoal or gas grill. Brush the fish lightly with olive oil and sprinkle with salt and pepper. Broil or grill until the fish tests done, turning once, about 4 minutes per side.

To poach the fish: In a large, deep sauté pan with high sides, pour enough poaching liquid (white wine, fish stock, or water) to reach a depth of 2 inches. Bring the liquid to a boil. Reduce the heat so that the liquid is barely simmering. Add the fish fillets and poach, covered, until the fish tests done, about 7 minutes. Using a slotted spoon, carefully transfer the fish to a clean cloth towel to drain.

Transfer the cooked fish to serving plates. Stir the sauce, spoon it over the fish, and serve.

VARIATION You can add fine strips of fresh basil in place of some of the mint. Try the sauce with cooked shrimp or scallops, too.

. . . . .

Salsa verde is a classic Italian parsley-based sauce served with cooked fish, meat, or vegetables. This lively orange and mint sauce is a versatile variation on the classic. Instead of only tart lemon, the sweeter orange juice and zest are added, and sweet, fresh mint replaces parsley. The sauce is not heated but simply spooned over the fish, which may be baked, broiled, grilled, or poached. Alaskan halibut is the ideal fish for this dish, but salmon and sea bass are other options. The recipe makes enough sauce for both the fish and its vegetable accompaniments. The perfect side dishes are cooked asparagus, green beans, and beets, as they pair so well with citrus and mint. —Joyce

The orange and mint are the links between this fish dish and the wine. I recommend sticking to Old World interpretations of Viognier (some of which nevertheless come from the New World), because New World–style wines can sometimes be very ripe and display a distinctive orchard character that tastes sour. Fleshy fish are best, but this recipe can also work with Viognier if you use shellfish or poultry. If the wine seems really tart, combine some lemon juice with the orange in the sauce to bring up the acidity, or splash in a little wine to replace some of the citrus, and you'll create a natural liaison. —Evan

RECOMMENDED PRODUCERS
Earthy, Citrusy, Peach-Accented Viogniers

EVERYDAY	PREMIUM	SPLURGE
Laurent Miguel (Languedoc, France)	Georges Vernay (Rhône Valley, France)	Calera (Northern Central Coast, California)
Yalumba (multiple appellations, South Australia)	Arrowood (Sonoma County, California)	Domaine du Monteillet (Rhône Valley, France)
Bodegas Escorihuela (Mendoza, Argentina)	Incognito (Northern Central Valley, California)	Philippe Faury (Rhône Valley, France)

BRAZILIAN FISH AND SHELLFISH STEW

SERVES 4

¼ cup white wine

¼ teaspoon saffron threads, crushed

4 tablespoons (½ stick) unsalted butter

2 yellow onions, chopped

2 green bell peppers, seeded and chopped

2 to 3 jalapeño chiles or other hot peppers to taste, finely minced

6 cloves garlic, finely minced

1 tablespoon ground coriander

4 cups Fish Stock (see recipe page 105)

1½ cups drained canned tomatoes, chopped,
or 3 fresh ripe tomatoes, peeled, seeded, and diced

½ cup canned cream of coconut (such as Coco Lopez), or more to taste

8 tablespoons chopped fresh coriander (cilantro)

2 tablespoons lemon or lime juice, or more to taste

Salt and freshly ground black pepper

1½ pounds fish fillets (such as monkfish, snapper,
rock cod, or flounder), cut into 2-inch pieces

16 manila clams, scrubbed

16 shrimp, peeled and deveined

16 mussels, scrubbed and debearded

16 scallops, foot muscles removed

2 tablespoons toasted coconut (for garnish, optional)

Pour the wine into a small saucepan and bring it to a simmer. Remove the saucepan from the heat, add the saffron, and let steep 10 minutes.

Meanwhile, in a wide, deep pot, melt the butter over medium heat. Add the onions and cook until translucent, about 8 minutes. Add the bell peppers, jalapeños, garlic, and ground coriander, and sauté until softened and fragrant, about 5 minutes. Add the stock, tomatoes, ½ cup cream of coconut, 6 tablespoons of the fresh coriander, and the saffron infusion, and simmer to allow the flavors to blend, about 3 minutes. Stir in the 2 tablespoons lemon or lime juice, and season to taste with salt and pepper. Adjust sweet and sour balance by adding a bit more coconut cream or lemon juice, as needed. Add the fish and clams and simmer, covered, for 2 minutes. Add the shrimp and mussels, discarding any that do not close when tapped with a spoon, and simmer until the shrimp begin to turn pink and the mussels begin to open, about 2 minutes. Add the scallops and simmer until the clams and mussels are open and the scallops are opaque, about 2 minutes longer. (Discard any clams that haven't opened within 10 minutes.) Serve the stew over rice in individual bowls and garnish with the remaining 2 tablespoons chopped coriander and the coconut, if desired.

VARIATION To make a shellfish stock, replace the fish frames in the stock recipe on page 105 with the shells from 3 pounds of shrimp. Add 1 walnut-sized piece of peeled fresh ginger and 1 dried red pepper pod to the stock. Simmer 30 minutes, then strain, return stock to the pot, and cook until reduced by half.

· · · · ·

This recipe combines two Brazilian seafood classics: moqueca de peixe, *which is sautéed fish with coconut, tomatoes, garlic, lemon juice, coriander, and cayenne, and* mariscada, *a Brazilian bouillabaisse-style stew made with fish and shellfish and seasoned with coriander, onion, tomatoes, garlic, saffron, and cayenne. The sweet coconut cream offsets the tartness of the tomatoes and lemon and helps to balance the bitter flavors of the hot peppers, green peppers, saffron, coriander, and garlic. Serve with simple white rice, as this dish is sufficiently complex in taste. —Joyce*

Many excellent examples of Viognier are produced using judicious amounts of oak aging. While I may come off as being partisan toward unoaked versions, this recipe is really better with a little of the soft, toasty richness imparted by oak. The wine needs some weight (alcoholic body) in addition to the oak to stand up to this delicious broth-based stew. Once again, the use of ginger brings out the best of Viognier's fruit flavors. Do keep the jalapeño heat in check if your wine is high in alcohol, or it will make the wine taste unpleasant; but, at the same time, don't go too far the other way. —Evan

RECOMMENDED PRODUCERS
Rich, Partly Oak-Aged Viogniers

EVERYDAY	PREMIUM	SPLURGE
Echelon (Northern Central Valley, California)	Abacela (Umpqua Valley, Oregon)	Yves Cuilleron (Northern Rhône Valley, France)
Martine's Wines (Central Coast, California)	E. Guigal (Rhône Valley, France)	Alban (Southern Central Coast, California)
Château Routas (Southwest France)	Fairview (Coastal Region, South Africa)	

MOROCCAN LAMB TAGINE
WITH RAISINS, ALMONDS, AND HONEY

SERVES 6

3 pounds lamb shoulder, trimmed well and cut into 2½-inch pieces

1 teaspoon freshly ground black pepper

2 teaspoons ground cinnamon, or more to taste

1 teaspoon ground ginger

1 teaspoon ground cumin

1 teaspoon ground coriander

¼ teaspoon grated nutmeg

¼ teaspoon cayenne pepper

¼ teaspoon saffron threads, crushed

⅛ teaspoon ground cloves

½ cup water

1½ to 2 cups raisins

8 tablespoons (1 stick) unsalted butter, melted

2 onions, finely chopped

2 cloves garlic, finely minced

2 whole cinnamon sticks

1½ cups blanched whole almonds

½ cup dark honey, or to taste

Put the meat in a large nonaluminum container. In a small bowl, stir together the black pepper, 1 teaspoon of the ground cinnamon, ginger, cumin, ground coriander, nutmeg, cayenne pepper, saffron, and cloves to blend. Add ½ cup water and stir to form a paste. Rub half of this paste on the meat and refrigerate overnight. Cover and refrigerate the remaining spice paste.

Cover the raisins with hot water in a small bowl. Let stand for 30 minutes at room temperature until they soften and plump. Add the remaining spice paste to the raisins. Let stand for 1 hour for the raisins to absorb the seasonings.

Place the meat, butter, onions, garlic, and cinnamon sticks in a Dutch oven. Add enough water to just cover the meat. Bring to a gentle boil over medium heat, skim the scum from the surface, and then reduce the heat to low. Simmer, covered, until the meat is almost tender, about 1 hour 15 minutes. Check and stir occasionally, adding water as needed.

Add the raisins and any remaining soaking liquid, the almonds, ½ cup honey (or to taste), and the remaining 1 teaspoon ground cinnamon to the stew. Simmer, stirring often, until the sauce has thickened to a syrupy glaze, 15 to 30 minutes. Season to taste with additional cinnamon, if desired.

VARIATION Whole prunes, pitted or not, can be used instead of raisins.

. . . . .

You will understand the term sweetmeat *after you taste this voluptuous lamb stew, called a* tagine, *after the terra-cotta cooking vessel in which it is traditionally prepared. In Morocco, this lamb tagine is usually served along with couscous and two lighter tagines as part of a banquet meal. Lamb shoulder is better for stewing than the lean leg. The overnight marinating in the spice paste develops maximum flavor in the meat. —Joyce*

This stew is easy to prepare and impressive in both the simplicity of its ingredients and the complexity of its layers of flavor. Many of the characteristics that develop with Viognier as it matures are present in the recipe: honey, almonds, sweet spice (cinnamon), and dried fruit—in this case, raisins. I prefer the flavor of golden raisins (sultanas), though classic brown raisins work well, too, and the prunes make a tasty variation. As you might imagine, most similar North African tagines that combine sweet and savory flavors (lamb with apricots or quince, for example) would be equally successful with a mature and developed Viognier. —Evan

RECOMMENDED PRODUCERS
Aged, Mature Viogniers

EVERYDAY	PREMIUM	SPLURGE
Renwood (Sierra Foothills, California)	Alain Paret (Northern Rhône Valley, France)	Château Grillet (Northern Rhône Valley, France)
Yalumba (multiple appellations, South Australia)	Iron Horse (Sonoma County, California)	Domaine Chèze (Northern Rhône Valley, France)
Cline (Sonoma County, California)	Georges Vernay (Northern Rhône Valley, France)	E. Guigal (Northern Rhône Valley, France)

part three

THE RED JOURNEYS

CABERNET SAUVIGNON

In my experience, Cabernet Sauvignon (kah-behr-*nay* soh-veen-*yown*) is the grape people first become enamored with when exploring red wines. Considered by most as the red grape with the most distinguished pedigree, Cabernet Sauvignon is the principal component of the great French Bordeaux wines—for many the epitome of wine excellence. Cabernet is also noteworthy for having put Napa Valley on the international winemaking map, thanks to a controversial Paris blind tasting in 1976, in which a 1973 Stag's Leap Wine Cellars Cabernet placed above several great red Bordeaux wines. Wine drinkers, however, can be funny about this grape. I have known many a consumer to fall in love with Cabernet and then lose interest, turning to flirtations with other wines. However, almost all of them eventually come back to Cabernet, won over again by its seductive complexity and allure. Cabernet is indeed a wine of kings and, for many, the king of wines.

WINE-GROWING AREAS

Although there are some who claim that Cabernet Sauvignon may have initially appeared somewhere other than southwestern France (Spain's Rioja is often mentioned as a possible origin), most agree that the Bordeaux grape is the global model. It has now been proved to derive from a long-ago marriage of the Cabernet Franc, which is said to have come from Italy, and the local Sauvignon Blanc. The legendary wines of the Médoc peninsula (stretching along the left bank of the Gironde estuary from Saint-Estèphe in the north to the town of Bordeaux proper and the Graves region in the south) are those to which Cabernet owes its formidable reputation. Although credible examples of Cabernet-based wines are found throughout France's southwest, few, if any, rival the products of this area of Bordeaux (which are often referred to as clarets) for pedigree and complexity. A quick sniff of a glass of a great Médoc red reveals a torrent of complex and characteristic aromas, ranging from black currant and blackberry fruit to dusty earth, cigar-box, and graphite aromas.

In Italy, Cabernet has done well on its own in Piedmont and Tuscany, as well as blending majestically with Sangiovese in Tuscany to create a category of wines known as Super Tuscans.

Cabernet in Australia is explosive and complex, with strapping black fruit, ample body, and rich-textured tannins. Some of the world's most interesting Cabernet wines are coming from the renowned Australian wine regions of Coonawarra, the Barossa Valley, and Adelaide. Although stunning when pure, Cabernet has also proved to be quite compatible with Syrah (or Shiraz, as it's known down under) and makes for some exciting blended wines.

South America has historically provided a wealth of affordable Cabernets but recently has also been staking out territory in the premium arena. Better and better wines are coming from Chile's prominent Maipo Valley and the increasingly important Colchagua, Curicó, and Maule regions, dispelling the myth that the country is capable of producing only "smart-value" bottlings. However, many feel that the best Cabernets in South America emanate from Argentina and not Chile, in the emerging subregions of Mendoza's Uco Valley and those surrounding Mendoza proper. In addition to identifying which areas of the traditional Mendoza wine-growing region are best suited to Cabernet, Argentina's winemakers are experimenting with higher-altitude plantings, and the results have been exciting.

New Zealand Cabernet, after a rocky beginning, is finding its way in the warmer Hawkes Bay region, especially in the newly established Gimblett Gravels and the proven Havelock North area, and, farther north, outside Auckland on picturesque Waiheke Island. In South Africa, excellent wines are now being made throughout the Coastal Region, and some Cabernet is also being grown in Spain, mostly for blending with wines in the Ribera del Duero, but also for bottling on its own in Navarra.

In Central Europe, Romania and Bulgaria, though they have long-established Cabernet regions, are just beginning to produce quality wines. Farther east, some nice wines are coming out of Lebanon and Israel.

In the United States, California's Napa and Sonoma Valleys are historically and justifiably leaders in quality. Napa's international reputation owes much to the midvalley appellations of Rutherford and Oakville, which produce wines of ample weight, explosive black fruit, and copious but well-integrated tannins. A move to mountainside plantings in recent years has yielded tremendous results, with inky and firm berry-scented wines. Examples from areas such as Mount Veeder, Diamond Mountain, Spring Mountain, Howell Mountain, and Pritchard Hill are becoming must-haves among Cabernet aficionados. Sonoma County is known for making outstanding examples in both the Alexander Valley and Sonoma Mountain subappellations, where the wines are distinguished by anise and black-olive notes and softer tannins. Both Napa and Sonoma are looking over their shoulders at some extraordinarily tasty wines coming from farther north, in eastern Washington (the Walla Walla, Red Mountain, and Tri-City areas). And while Cabernet Sauvignon wines from other states are still fighting for media attention, some well-made Cabernets are coming out of Texas's Hill Country, Long Island's North Fork, and, increasingly, Virginia.

A table of principal wine-growing regions for Cabernet Sauvignon appears on pages 275–77.

VINTNER CHOICES

Fermentation temperature; length of postfermentation maceration; wood or no wood; type, size, and age of wood; stainless-steel or barrel fermentation; 100 percent varietal or blended; tannin management; micro-oxygenation; selections and clones

The vintner choices in red wine production are fairly consistent across grape types, as we will see in the other red wine journeys. As with all red wines, Cabernet Sauvignon's personality comes from its skins. And, as with other red wine grapes, when Cabernet grapes are crushed, the juice is clear, but as fermentation begins, the color, flavor, and tannins are extracted from the skins. Warm and vigorous fermentations, followed by a period of macerating the wine with its skins, are the best approach for this grape. The maceration period varies, but most vintners set it somewhere between one and three weeks.

The style of wine is often dictated by the geographical region and the quality of its grapes. Cabernet wines range from inexpensive, unoaked examples that are quite suitable for everyday drinking to the top-tier versions reverently aged in Bordeaux (and elsewhere) in select French oak barrels that cost $700 a pop. The choices made about wood aging have a very significant effect on the wine. For instance, although older barrels impart significantly less oak flavor to a wine than newer ones do, they permit wines to develop through very gradual oxidation; the wood is breathable and allows for the extremely gentle incorporation of air into the wine (oxidation). The size of the barrels is also critical. Small oak barrels are not only attractive but (remember geometry class) increase the surface area where wood and wine come into contact. A large, upright wood tank has a smaller wine-to-wood ratio and will have less flavor impact. Most of the wood used is oak, though some credible wines are aged in chestnut (in Portugal and Italy) and even in large, old redwood casks. Vintners can impart oak flavors in other ways, too: for example, by submerging wood staves into the wine (a practice called inner staving) or by macerating large bags of oak chips in the wine (known as "tea bagging"). Both of these methods, though they are being refined over time, produce far less subtle results than barrel aging, and the oak flavors are less well integrated into the wine.

Cabernet can be pure (that's to say, 100 percent Cabernet Sauvignon) or blended with related grapes (primarily Merlot and Cabernet Franc). These blends result in different styles of wine. Increasing the proportions of other grapes can soften the impact of Cabernet's potentially domineering character. In the United States, wines that list Cabernet on the label, as with all varietal wines, must contain at least 75 percent Cabernet fruit.

Tannin management is the vintner's practice of working with the tannin, minimizing or maximizing its presence in the wine. Tannins can be maximized through letting the wine spend extended time on the grape skins (which also adds color) both before and after fermentation. They can be minimized by cutting back on these steps and through a process called fining (in which a substance is added which attracts the tannins, binds with them, and precipitates them out) or very gentle filtration. To soften hard tannins, vintners are increasingly turning to a process called micro-oxygenation to soften the wine while bringing out the bright character of the fruit and adding rich mouthfeel. This method, which is similar to putting an aerator in a fish tank, percolates small, measured amounts of oxygen into the wine during and after fermentation in the tank. The technique has proved so effective that it's now often practiced with other grapes, including Merlot and Syrah.

The choice of clones and selections (as discussed in the Chardonnay section) plays an important role.

FLAVORS

Fruit and vegetable: Blackberry, black raspberry, black currant (cassis), plum, blueberry, black or red cherry, bell pepper, black or green olive, fennel, rhubarb, tomato leaf, cola nut, sugar beet

Floral: Eucalyptus, laurel, mint, thyme, sage, rosemary, black tea, sarsaparilla, violet, cigar box

Earth: Dusty earth, humus, mushroom, truffle, graphite (pencil box), cedar, tobacco, mineral

Wood (oak): Dill weed, nutmeg, coconut, coffee bean, mocha, chocolate, cocoa, molasses, vanilla, brown sugar, caramel, walnut, cinnamon, maple, rum raisin, sawdust or cut wood, char or ash, toast

Other: Leather, soy, tar

WINE AND FOOD PAIRING

INGREDIENTS AND STYLES

Cabernet's bold personality demands attention and, while universally admired, is not always easy to match with a meal. In contrast to Chardonnay, which can easily be masked by a dish which is too bold, Cabernet Sauvignon can crush almost anything light and delicate, potentially spoiling many possibilities for epicurean happiness.

Cabernet's expressive individuality carries plenty of tannin. This, combined with its higher alcohol content (12 to 14 percent or sometimes even more) and a good lacing of oak, means that recipes must be selected carefully around the wine. Most of us drink Cabernet young, when it's chock-full of everything—oak, tannin, and alcohol. Tannin needs a counterbalance (fat or protein), and the higher alcohol level demands more ample food. That usually means choosing a dish with considerable character; add to that the requirement of something that pairs well with oak, and your choices are limited. Steaks, chops, and other red meat are classics for a reason—especially when grilled, because the acrid flavors of charring mirror the bitter edge supplied by the tannins. Recent novelty meats such as ostrich and buffalo are also prime candidates for pairing with Cabernet, as are more pungent fowl, such as squab, wild pheasant, and wild duck. Hearty sauces (with dark mushrooms, wine reductions, peppers, and so on) are fine here. Black pepper is also a nice foil to tannin, so *steak au poivre* is a slam dunk!

The need to tame the tannins with high-fat foods would seem to suggest that many cheeses should work. Alas, the "big wine goes with big cheese" theory fails more often than it succeeds. Cabernet is best when served with cheeses that range from mild to moderate in flavor, which pair with the wine rather than compete with it (think Saint-Nectaire, Brie, *young* Camembert, raclette, Monterey Jack, or fresh mozzarella). Head for the hills if someone offers up Roquefort or any other blue-veined wedges. Another fallacy is that pasta and risotto are excellent in taming tannins. Starch does not cut tannin, although it has body and texture that meld with the weight of Cabernet Sauvignon. Fat does lessen tannin, so you can be liberal in your use of butter and most dairy products.

Characteristic of the wines of Bordeaux are the readily apparent mineral, earth, tobacco, and cedar or cigar-box flavors, which set these wines apart from the well-made Cabernet-based wines of California's Napa Valley or Australia's Coonawarra region. Bordeaux reds allow increased play with fresh herbs, wild or dried mushrooms, and sharp vegetables (such as eggplant, zucchini, chard, and escarole).

Not all Cabernet-based wines are big and tannic, however, so when you opt for a softer, lighter-bodied wine, dishes featuring lighter fowl (especially chicken, Cornish game hens, and quail) or meatier fish (say, shark or swordfish) become options.

COOKING METHODS

Cabernet's tannins almost always lean toward bitter and sharp. Because grilling and charring add similar bitter elements to food, it's no surprise that such treatments make for successful pairings. Playing to the oak is also a good rule of thumb: again, grilling works, along with smoking and plank roasting. The texture of fuller-bodied Cabernet Sauvignons demands thicker dishes, so rich stews, daubes, and other long-braised, viscous dishes are naturals.

One of the great pleasures of Cabernet-based wines is the graceful way they develop: the flavors unravel and the tannins calm down. With a mature Cabernet, it's best to keep the food simple and really allow the wine to show. Feature straightforward dishes of suitable weight and style. I love a simple beef stew, an uncomplicated pot roast, or a plainly grilled veal or lamb chop to frame a developed Cabernet (one that has aged for at least eight years and perhaps for decades).

Cabernet Sauvignon works well:

· With red meats. There's a good reason this pairing is a classic. For a twist on the obvious, select an older wine to accompany rarer cuts and, conversely, a wine that's youthful and juicy to go with longer-cooked meat or stews.

· With grilled foods. Grilling adds a bitter component to the food and creates a great stage for Cabernet's tannins.

· With bitter foods. From mustard greens to radicchio, from braised escarole to endive or roasted eggplant, bitter items pair well with Cabernet's tannins.

· With foods or treatments that pick up on the wine's oak character. Grilling, smoking, and plank roasting mirror oak's characteristics and its impact on wine. The incorporation of toasted or roasted nuts or a charred soy-honey glaze on meat will echo similar tastes in the wine.

· At countering fat. Creamy, buttery, or otherwise fat-laden dishes that coat the mouth with a light film of texture will be lovely with a chewy Cabernet.

· With black pepper. On steak, as a crust for tuna, or simply added generously but judiciously to a dish, pepper will tame Cabernet's tannic bite. This combination works best with younger wines.

· With earthy and herbal elements. In particular, wines that stress similar flavors (those from Bordeaux, Washington State, and New Zealand) are complemented by fresh herbs and dark mushrooms.

Cabernet doesn't work well:

· With delicate and subtle dishes. Its personality is just too bold. Think of placing a blowhard in the same room as a wallflower: it's a recipe for failure.

· With strong cheeses. Counterintuitively, the stronger the cheese, the less successful the match. Opt for milder cheeses that won't fight with the wine for attention.

· With most fish. Meatier and less oily fish are generally the best matches (ahi tuna, swordfish, shark).

· With spicy-hot foods. The capsaicins create a storm by ratcheting up the perception of the wine's alcohol while accentuating the bitter and astringent nature of the tannins.

· With dishes that have no fat or protein (such as plain risotto or crudités). These may well accentuate the wine's bitterness.

· With most chocolate. Really. Never mind what you've heard. While bitter and semisweet chocolate can work well with a ripe American or Australian Cabernet (in a not-too-sweet mole sauce for example), most chocolate is simply too sweet for any dry red wine, and it never pairs well with the austere wines of Bordeaux.

STEAK AU POIVRE

SERVES 4

4 filets of beef, each about 1½ inches thick
2 teaspoons kosher salt, plus salt for pan
2 or 3 tablespoons coarsely cracked black pepper
½ cup dry white wine
¼ cup brandy or cognac
1 tablespoon Dijon mustard
2 teaspoons Worcestershire sauce
3 tablespoons unsalted butter
1 tablespoon oil
½ cup heavy cream (optional)

Rub each filet with about ½ teaspoon salt. Using the heel of your hand, press the cracked pepper onto both sides of each steak. Let the steaks stand at room temperature for at least 30 minutes and up to 1 hour.

In a small bowl, whisk the wine, brandy, mustard, and Worcestershire sauce to blend.

Sprinkle salt over the bottom of a large heavy skillet (just enough to film the bottom lightly). Place over high heat. Add the butter and oil and heat until melted. Add the steaks and sear on both sides. Reduce the heat to medium and cook the steaks to the desired degree of doneness, turning once, 3 to 4 minutes per side for rare. Transfer the steaks to a warm platter.

Deglaze the skillet with the wine mixture and boil until reduced by half. Whisk in the cream if a smoother sauce is desired. Spoon the sauce over the steaks and serve.

. . . . .

Of all the cuts of steak, filet is the most neutral in flavor—some might even say bland. It is, however, a perfect foil for an assertive sauce. This recipe is a cross between two classics: French steak au poivre *and American steak Diane. Because the filet does not have much fat or marbling, it does not compete with the cream in the sauce. Serve with spinach and fried or roast potatoes. —Joyce*

Sometimes it's best to go with the obvious. The hearty sauce, infused with mustard, cognac, and Worcestershire sauce, is earthy and powerful, providing an appropriately strong yet straightforward stage for the wine's flavor. The black pepper neutralizes the perception of the wine's tannins, and the bright fruit of the wine shines through to play off the meat. This dish works best with younger wines. If you're serving a more mature bottle, you may want to cut back on the black pepper, which, in the presence of less tannin, may only serve to pop the alcohol. —Evan

RECOMMENDED PRODUCERS
Earthy, Black-Currant-Accented Cabernet Sauvignons

EVERYDAY	PREMIUM	SPLURGE
Château La Cardonne (Bordeaux, France)	Château Phélan-Ségur (Bordeaux, France)	Château Cos d'Estournel (Bordeaux, France)
Château Larose-Trintaudon (Bordeaux, France)	Château du Tertre (Bordeaux, France)	Château Lynch-Bages (Bordeaux, France)
Château Camensac (Bordeaux, France)	Kanonkop (Coastal Region, South Africa)	Château Gruaud-Larose (Bordeaux, France)

SPANISH LAMB RAGOUT WITH ROASTED SWEET PEPPERS

SERVES 6

4 whole red bell peppers
3 pounds lamb shoulder, fat and sinew trimmed, cut into 2-inch cubes,
or 6 small lamb shanks

MARINADE
1 tablespoon sweet paprika or pimentón
de la Vera (Spanish smoked paprika)
2 teaspoons ground cumin
1 bay leaf, crumbled
½ cup dry red wine
¼ cup extra virgin olive oil

½ cup mild olive oil, or more as needed
Salt and freshly ground black pepper
2 yellow onions, chopped
2 tablespoons finely minced garlic
2 tablespoons sweet paprika or pimentón de la Vera
2 teaspoons ground cumin
½ cup dry red wine
1½ cups meat stock
5 tablespoons tomato paste
¼ cup chopped fresh flat-leaf parsley
1 cup oil-cured black olives

Place the bell peppers under the broiler or over a direct flame on a grill or stovetop. With tongs, turn the peppers a few times until they are charred almost black on all sides. Place in a plastic container or plastic bag and let stand for 30 minutes. Scrape away all the charred peel, discard the seeds and thick ribs, and cut the peppers into wide strips. Set aside. (Can be prepared up to 4 days ahead of time. To store, toss the peppers with olive oil to coat and refrigerate.)

Place the lamb in a large nonaluminum container.

For the marinade: In a medium bowl, stir together 1 tablespoon sweet paprika, 2 teaspoons cumin, and the bay leaf. Whisk in ½ cup wine and ¼ cup oil. Pour over the meat. Cover with plastic wrap and marinate overnight in the refrigerator.

Bring the marinated lamb to room temperature. Remove the lamb from the marinade and pat dry.

In a large sauté pan, heat ¼ cup of the olive oil over high heat. Sprinkle the lamb with salt and pepper and cook it in batches until brown, 8 to 10 minutes, adding more oil as needed. Using a slotted spoon, transfer the lamb to a large pot. Pour off the fat from the sauté pan and wipe out any burned bits. Add the remaining ¼ cup oil to the pan and set over medium heat. Add the onions and sauté until they are translucent and tender, about 10 minutes. Add the garlic, 2 tablespoons paprika, and 2 teaspoons cumin and cook to blend the flavors, about 2 minutes longer. Season the onion mixture to taste with salt and pepper and add to the lamb in the pot. Deglaze the pan with ½ cup wine and add the pan juices to the lamb. In a medium bowl, whisk the stock and tomato paste to combine. Add the stock and tomato paste to the pot and bring to a gentle boil. Reduce the heat to low and cover the pan. Simmer gently until the lamb is tender, about 1 hour 30 minutes. Add the roasted pepper strips. Simmer to blend the flavors, about 15 minutes longer. Season to taste with salt and pepper. Garnish the stew with chopped parsley and olives.

· · · · ·

Meat and sweet peppers are a traditional combination all over the Mediterranean. In Spain, the mixture of sweet paprika and sweet peppers, contrasted with pungent seasonings and rich meat, is called al chilindrón. In Portugal, sweet red peppers are ground into a paste with garlic and salt and rubbed on meat or poultry before cooking. And in Turkey, sweet red peppers are combined with tomatoes or hot peppers for another savory spice mixture. This stew can be made the day before and reheated gently. Serve with small roasted potatoes and green beans with tomatoes and mint or fresh coriander. —Joyce

Roasted peppers are a great pairing with oaky wines. The sweet, smoky elements brought out when the peppers are charred mirror the flavors imparted by the barrel. While many people automatically pair beef with Cabernet, lamb is equally tasty, and this preparation is at once complex in its mélange of flavors and simple in the way it frames the dish. If the Cabernet is on the dry side, you may want to cut back on the tomato paste. Conversely, if the wine is riper or sweeter, increase the amount of tomato paste, which will add sweetness to the stew. —Evan

RECOMMENDED PRODUCERS

Rich, Oaky Cabernet Sauvignons with Jammy Fruit

EVERYDAY	PREMIUM	SPLURGE
Wolf Blass (multiple appellations, South Australia)	Geyser Peak (Sonoma County, California)	Shafer (Napa Valley, California)
Gallo of Sonoma (Sonoma County, California)	Provenance (Napa Valley, California)	Miner Family (Napa Valley, California)
Estancia (Sonoma/Central Coast, California)	Silverado Vineyards (Napa Valley, California)	Joseph Phelps (Napa Valley, California)

LAMB STEAKS WITH GREEK-INSPIRED TOMATO SAUCE

SERVES 4

MARINADE
½ cup dry red wine
3 tablespoons olive oil
2 teaspoons dried oregano
Freshly ground black pepper
Pinch ground cinnamon

4 ¾-inch-thick lamb steaks (8 to 10 ounces per steak),
or 12 lamb loin chops (about 6 ounces per chop)

¼ cup olive oil
1 bunch green onions (including tender green tops), chopped
4 teaspoons minced garlic
1 teaspoon cinnamon
1 teaspoon dried oregano
2 cups canned tomato sauce
1 cup meat stock or dry red wine
Salt and freshly ground black pepper
Honey or sugar to taste
3 tablespoons chopped fresh flat-leaf parsley

For the marinade: In a medium bowl, whisk together the wine, olive oil, oregano, a few grinds of black pepper, and a pinch of cinnamon. Place the lamb in a single layer in a large nonaluminum baking dish. Pour the marinade over the lamb. Marinate overnight in the refrigerator or for 1 to 2 hours at room temperature. If refrigerated, bring to room temperature before continuing.

For the sauce: Heat the ¼ cup olive oil in a sauté pan over medium heat. Add the green onions and sauté until they are soft, about 5 minutes. Add the garlic, cinnamon, and oregano and cook, stirring occasionally, until tender, about 5 minutes. Add the tomato sauce and stock or wine, bring the mixture to a gentle boil, and then quickly reduce the heat to low. Simmer to blend the flavors, about 8 minutes. Season the sauce with salt and pepper. Add honey or sugar to taste if the tomato sauce is excessively acidic.

Preheat the broiler. Remove the lamb steaks from the marinade and pat them dry. Broil the steaks to desired doneness, turning once, about 4 minutes per side for medium rare. Transfer to dinner plates and spoon the sauce over the top. Garnish with parsley.

VARIATION Instead of broiling the lamb, pat the lamb steaks dry and sauté in 2 tablespoons oil in a heavy skillet over medium heat. Cook to desired doneness, turning once, 4 to 5 minutes per side for medium rare. Transfer the steaks to a plate, deglaze the skillet with ¼ cup stock or wine, and add the hot tomato sauce. Return the steaks to the skillet to coat with the sauce. Transfer to dinner plates and top with parsley.

You may also try using 1½ cup chopped yellow, red, or white onion instead of green onions.

· · · · ·

Tomatoes, cinnamon, and oregano are a signature flavor combination in Greece. This recipe plays with the acidity of tomatoes, the sweetness of cinnamon, the earthiness of oregano, and the rich, meaty taste of lamb. Lamb steaks, cut across the leg, are easier to eat than the bonier loin chops. Serve with roast potatoes and sautéed zucchini or eggplant, a vegetable much beloved by the Greeks. —Joyce

This recipe is a study in bridging Old World and New World flavors. Here the elements of oregano, green onions, garlic, and parsley open up the dish for a wine that stresses more herbal flavors, while the cinnamon, tomato, and honey mandate a warmer-climate wine with ripe fruit. This dish, interestingly, works with both older and younger wines and manages tannins well; you can adjust the acidity of the sauce to match the wine. If you have a very tannic wine, ensure that the tomato sauce is not too acidic, and perhaps counter that sharpness with a little extra honey—not so much that it makes the dish sweet, but enough to counter the acidity. —Evan

RECOMMENDED PRODUCERS
Herbal, Olive-Accented Cabernet Sauvignons

EVERYDAY	PREMIUM	SPLURGE
Viña Santa Rita (Central Valley, Chile)	Woodward Canyon (Greater Columbia Valley, Washington)	Catena Zapata (Mendoza, Argentina)
Jacob's Creek (multiple appellations, South Australia)	Forefathers (Sonoma County, California)	Liparita (Napa Valley, California)
Columbia Crest (Greater Columbia Valley, Washington)	Ridge (Northern Central Coast, California)	Dominus (Napa Valley, California)

COFFEE- AND PEPPER-RUBBED RIB ROAST

SERVES 6 TO 8

1 8-pound rib roast (3 to 4 ribs)
3 large cloves garlic, slivered
3 tablespoons soy sauce
2 tablespoons Dijon mustard
1 tablespoon coarsely ground black pepper
1 tablespoon freshly ground coffee
4 tablespoons olive oil

Using a small sharp knife, make slits at intervals in the meat. Insert slivers of garlic into the slits. Place the meat in a roasting pan.

In a small bowl, whisk together the soy sauce and mustard. Whisk in the pepper and coffee and then gradually beat in the olive oil. Spread this mixture all over the roast. Let the roast stand at room temperature for at least 1 and up to 2 hours.

Preheat the oven to 450 degrees. Cook the roast 15 minutes, then reduce the heat to 350 degrees. Roast to desired doneness, about 1 hour 30 minutes longer, until a meat thermometer reads 115 degrees for very rare. (The internal temperature will rise about 10 degrees as the meat stands, bringing it to rare.) Remove from the oven and let stand 15 to 20 minutes before carving.

· · · · ·

In these days of celebrity chefs and complex gourmet cooking, it may seem terribly old-fashioned to serve roast beef. Let me assure you that your guests will love it because they never make it at home. Plus you will get great leftovers. The coffee and pepper rub provides a deep, earthy flavor that harmonizes beautifully with the tannin in the wine pairing. This doesn't need a sauce, as the meat is so rich and can be served with just its juices. Serve with potatoes and the vegetable of your choice. —Joyce

A cop-out? Well, in all of my years of matching wine and food, I have yet to discover a pairing that can show off a complex, mature Cabernet better than a simple rib roast. This dish is all about showcasing the wine—plain and simple. The rarer the better, in my opinion, but that's personal, as many diners are not enamored of rare meat. Fear not, as the wine will work with all degrees of doneness: blue (very, very rare), rare, medium, and, yes, even well done. The caramelized elements of the glaze (especially the coffee and soy) create a flavorful crust, and the oven roasting brings out sweet charred elements that match well with the wine. —Evan

RECOMMENDED PRODUCERS
Aged, Developed Cabernet Sauvignons

EVERYDAY	PREMIUM	SPLURGE
Concha y Toro (Central Valley, Chile)	L'Ecole No. 41 (Walla Walla Valley, Washington)	Cakebread Cellars (Napa Valley, California)
Mitchelton (Victoria, Australia)	Joseph Phelps (Napa Valley, California)	Leonetti (Walla Walla Valley, Washington)
Château Citran (Bordeaux, France)	Château Sociando Mallet (Bordeaux, France)	Château Ducru-Beaucaillou (Bordeaux, France)

MERLOT

It was not long ago that Merlot (merh-*loh*), one of America's most popular red wines, was barely a blip on the radar screen. Though long important to Bordeaux, Merlot has been appearing as a distinct varietal on American store shelves and wine lists for less than forty years! A few different factors have contributed to its relatively recent popularity. First, it's easy to pronounce—and, laugh as you may, that's a big deal. Second, Merlot is often rounder, plummier, more fruit-forward, and plusher in tannins than many of its counterparts, so it makes for easier and, for many wine drinkers, more pleasant drinking. In fact, the smoothness of Merlot is frequently used in blends to soften and round out the edges of its more astringent relative, Cabernet Sauvignon.

WINE-GROWING AREAS

As with Cabernet Sauvignon, Merlot's native home is southwest France, again in the Bordeaux region. However, Merlot is most prodigious in cooler climates, and it originally thrived on the eastern "right bank" of the Bordeaux region, in Pomerol and its surrounding areas. That's not to say no quality Merlot is grown in the Médoc ("left bank"); the great wines of Saint-Estèphe attest to its pedigree there. In fact, there's more Merlot planted in the Médoc today than any other grape (including the great Cabernet Sauvignon). But Pomerol and the wines of the right bank represent the classic Merlot paradigm.

Merlot from Bordeaux is expressive, juicy, and redolent of blueberry, boysenberry, and ripe cherry fruit, framed by accents of cool fresh herbs and minerally earth, and balanced by velvety-smooth tannins.

In order to quench the ever-growing American thirst for Merlot, which peaked in the 1990s, the French spread their wings and expanded the Merlot growing regions, and now abundant and tasty Merlot is found in the Languedoc and other parts of southwest France. It is less complex and can be distinctly more herbaceous, but it's unmistakably Merlot.

Merlot is a very happy and well-traveled expatriate and has settled down in many places outside France. It is found throughout Italy's northeast, where it makes an herbal-scented, light, easy-drinking wine. Northern Italian Merlots can be lean or austere, and, while not great for quaffing alone or too abundantly, they go splendidly with the local cuisines.

South America has earned a great reputation for Merlot, notably in Chile. Intriguingly, though, many of the plantings of grapes that were thought to be Merlot have been found on closer inspection to be a different grape that also came from Bordeaux, the less-heralded Carmenère. Merlot (along with Carmenère) thrives in the Maipo Valley, Colchagua, Curicó, and, increasingly, in Casablanca, a region more often associated with Chardonnay. In Argentina, Merlot has done quite well in Mendoza and especially well in the higher-elevation vineyards of the Uco Valley's Tupungato, where the wines have ripe fruit, balanced acidity, and extraordinary structure.

Merlot's ability to flourish in cooler climates has attracted much interest in New Zealand where, after a shaky beginning, it is being successfully vinified in a distinctively Bordelais style in Hawkes Bay, in both the Te Mata and the Gimblett Gravels areas.

Sporadic and indeed hit-and-miss efforts have been attempted in Australia, Spain, and South Africa, all of which are relative newcomers to the varietal. Some long-established Central European countries like Bulgaria (and to a lesser degree Moldova) are providing some solid wines at reasonable prices.

In the United States, the coastal regions of Napa, Sonoma, and Monterey in California have overwhelmingly led the way. Excellent examples of Merlot, chock-full of ripe blackberry and black raspberry flavors, can be found in Napa's Carneros, Mount Veeder, Oakville, and Rutherford appellations. In adjacent Sonoma County, the other side of Carneros, Dry Creek Valley, and the Alexander Valley are notable for the black cherry, tea-leaf, and plum notes in their Merlot. Farther north, there are world-class and stunning wines from Washington State, east of the Cascade Mountains, where the long days and cool nights provide a near-perfect environment. The recent focus on smaller subappellations such as the Rattlesnake Hills and Red Mountain have really brought into focus the qualities of this special area. Wines from eastern Washington share a New World fruit character while resembling their counterparts in Bordeaux in tannins, acidity, and texture.

Other American wine-producing regions that have had success with Merlot include the North Fork region of Long Island in New York State, Virginia's Shenandoah Valley, and Oregon's Rogue River Valley.

A table of principal wine-growing regions for Merlot appears on pages 278–79.

*Type, size and age of wood; wood or no wood; 100 percent varietal or
blended; barrel fermentation; tannin management; micro-oxygenation;
selections and clones; Cabernet Sauvignon–style vinification*

Vintner choices in the production of Merlot are roughly the same as those for Cabernet Sauvignon (as regards choice of wood and so forth). The fact that Merlot is a cooler-climate grape, however, dictates certain harvest decisions, including timing: judging when to pick Merlot grapes for optimal ripeness can be tricky. Like a spice in a dish, Merlot is used for blending with Cabernet Sauvignon for its flavors, palate-softening qualities, and other textural contributions. Other winemakers add balanced amounts of Cabernet to their Merlot to gain structure and additional complexity. Tannin management and micro-oxygenation treatments are important: these decisions determine whether the grape is made into a Cabernet Sauvignon–style wine (a Cabernet wannabe).

Consumers are often puzzled because they have been led to believe and trust that Merlot-based wines are soft, supple, and easy to drink. And some are. But selecting a random bottle of Merlot and expecting an easy and approachable wine is at best a crapshoot and at worst a big mistake. There are three distinctive styles of Merlot. The first is soft, easy, and quite smooth. Next is a middle-of-the-road style, like the first style but with a bit more oomph. The third consists of wines which are big, brawny, and stylistically very similar to Cabernet. They can be awfully good, but if that's not what you're expecting or you don't like that style of red wine, you may be disappointed. So it is essential before shopping to ask your retailer or read up a little to get some sense of the stylistic variations among different appellations and producers.

FLAVORS

Fruit and vegetable: Blackberry, mulberry, boysenberry, black currant (cassis), plum, blueberry, black or red cherry, ollalieberry, bell pepper, black or green olive, fennel, rhubarb, tomato leaf, cola nut

Floral: Leaves, eucalyptus, oregano, laurel, mint, thyme, sage, rosemary, pine, green or black tea, sarsaparilla, tobacco or cigar box

Earth: Dusty earth, humus, mushroom, truffle, graphite (pencil box), cedar, tobacco

Wood (oak): Dill weed, nutmeg, coconut, coffee bean, mocha, chocolate, toast, cocoa, molasses, walnut, maple, vanilla, brown sugar, caramel, sawdust or cut wood, smoke

Other: Leather, musk, tar

INGREDIENTS AND STYLES

Merlot lies somewhere between Pinot Noir and Cabernet Sauvignon in its wine and food affinity. Ample, Cabernet-style Merlot wines should be considered as Cabernet Sauvignons and matched accordingly. Those which are truly soft and easy on the palate can be treated the same way as Pinot Noir, especially with respect to compatibility with fish. I love the flexibility of Merlot with salmon, for example.

The intrigue of Merlot lies in its signature array of flavors: green, herbal, earthy, and mushroom. I enjoy Merlot with dishes containing olives (a ragout of lamb with black olives and fresh thyme), mushrooms (just about anything!), and herbal treatments of meat (either marinades or sauces). Vegetables that can be hard on Cabernet, including fennel, eggplant, radicchio, chard, and broccoli, can pair well with Merlot's green character. Ensure that the Merlot is not fat and sweet or too heavily oaked to make those vegetable-based matches sing. Opting for a leaner, European-style example (French or Italian) will stack the deck in your favor.

Merlot's early ripening gives it lighter weight and higher acidity than Cabernet Sauvignon, which in turn give it greater flexibility at the table. In addition to the standard red-meat pairings, for which Merlot and Cabernet are both excellent, Merlot is a wonderful partner for tuna, salmon, and even certain treatments of prawns or scallops (for example, wrapped in roasted or grilled bacon or prosciutto). As with Cabernet, for aged and developed bottles of Merlot, simpler recipes, which allow the juiciness of the dish to fill in any cracks left by the maturing of the wine, work best.

COOKING METHODS

Merlot goes beautifully with grilled and charred foods, so feel free to light up the Weber! As with Cabernet, smoking and plank roasting will highlight the oakier components of an oak-aged wine. Marinades with sharper flavors that will be echoed in a dish (yogurt, tart herbs such as tarragon and thyme, or not-too-sweet fruit extracts like pomegranate) are a great platform for Merlot because of their higher acidity levels.

PAIRING POINTERS

Merlot goes well:

- With an array of sour or sharp ingredients: mild citrus, green vegetables, raw or slightly cooked onion and garlic, and tomatoes.
- With mushrooms and fresh herbs: even more than Cabernet Sauvignon, Merlot is at home with these earthy ingredients.

- With some fish and shellfish. Salmon, prawns, tuna, and scallops can all be magic with Merlot, especially if prepared with some meat, such as pancetta, prosciutto, or Spanish *jamón*.
- With a wide array of dishes. Because of the multitude of styles, Merlot offers great flexibility at the table.
- With berry fruits. Any recipe prepared with fresh or reconstituted dried cherries, cranberries, prunes, or dark raisins can be sublime, as these ingredients resonate with core flavors in the wine.
- With grilled or smoked items. Incorporate fresh herbs into the heat source to pick up on the same elements in the wine. It's amazing what a branch of rosemary can add to a fire!

Merlot isn't good:
- When the wine style doesn't fit the food. The downside of Merlot's diversity is that occasionally the wrong style can be selected for a dish. Match food weights with wine intensities.
- With strong cheeses. While its higher acidity and less ample body make it a more flexible option than Cabernet, Merlot still shouldn't be matched with strongly flavored or blue-veined cheeses.
- With delicate and subtle dishes. Like Cabernet, most Merlot-based wines are just too bold for lighter dishes.
- With very spicy or fiery foods. Capsaicins increase the perception of the alcohol in the wine while accentuating the bitter and astringent nature of the tannins.
- With dishes that have no fat, protein, or texture, such as delicately flavored risotto, pastas, or steamed vegetables. These absences can again make the wine seem harsher.

ROAST CORNISH HENS STUFFED WITH PORK AND PRUNES

SERVES 4

1¼ cups pitted prunes, halved

1 cup Armagnac or other brandy

8 tablespoons (1 stick) unsalted butter

2 small yellow onions, diced

4 small stalks celery, chopped

8 plump cloves garlic, minced, plus additional for seasoned butter

2 tablespoons olive oil

½ pound lean ground pork

2 teaspoons chopped fresh thyme, plus additional for seasoned butter

1 teaspoon freshly grated nutmeg, plus additional for seasoned butter

Salt and freshly ground black pepper

4 1-pound Cornish hens

Soak the prunes in the Armagnac for 1 hour, until they soften and plump.

In a large sauté pan, melt 4 tablespoons of the butter over medium heat. Add the onions and cook until they are translucent, about 8 minutes. Add the celery and 8 minced cloves garlic and cook until fragrant, about 3 minutes longer. Set aside.

Heat the olive oil in a large sauté pan over medium heat and add the ground pork. Cook the pork, stirring often, until it is cooked through and no longer pink, about 10 minutes. Add the celery and onion mixture, the prunes and their soaking liquid, 2 teaspoons thyme, and 1 teaspoon nutmeg. Season the stuffing to taste with salt and pepper.

Preheat the oven to 500 degrees.

Melt the remaining 4 tablespoons butter in a small saucepan. Season the butter to taste with additional salt, pepper, garlic, thyme, and nutmeg. Set aside.

Stuff the birds with the pork and prune mixture and sew or skewer closed. Sprinkle them with salt and pepper. Place them on a rack in a roasting pan. Roast 15 minutes, then reduce the oven temperature to 400 degrees and cook until the birds are cooked through and the juices run clear, about 30 minutes longer. Use the seasoned butter to baste the birds a few times during the cooking.

To serve, remove the thread that enclosed the stuffing. Cut the birds in half lengthwise to reveal the stuffing. Arrange 2 halves facing up on each plate.

VARIATION Use this stuffing for 1 large bird. For a 5-pound chicken, increase the total roasting time to about 1 hour 30 minutes.

. . . . .

In the French region of Gascony, cooks love to combine prunes with Armagnac. Armagnac has become quite an expensive import, so feel free to use a more reasonably priced good brandy instead. The brandy perfumes the stuffing and adds richness of flavor. Serving individual birds such as Cornish hens or poussins (small young chickens) at the table is always a festive presentation, but you can use this stuffing for one large bird as well. Serve with roast potatoes and spinach, chard, or green beans. —Joyce

Merlots exploding with rich fruit show well with some fruit in a recipe. In addition to aiding your digestion, prunes are very helpful in bringing out the flavors in the wine while adding textural richness and moistness; this is one reason you find them incorporated into so many fat-free muffins. The fresh thyme is a built-in link to the wine's herbal notes, while the pork and poultry are natural tablemates with red wine. Interestingly, the wine's fruit and the prunes meld so well that the balance of the red wine's character comes out expressively without dominating the less-than-bold character of fowl and white meat. —Evan

RECOMMENDED PRODUCERS
Plummy, Juicy, Fruit-Forward Merlots

EVERYDAY	PREMIUM	SPLURGE
Viña Carmen (Central Valley, Chile)	Provenance (Napa Valley, California)	Pride Mountain (Napa Valley, California)
Delicato (multiple appellations, California)	Franciscan (Napa Valley, California)	Beringer (Napa Valley, California)
Clos du Bois (Sonoma County, California)	Sterling (Napa Valley, California)	Markham (Napa Valley, California)

TUNA WITH ROSEMARY AND CITRUS TAPENADE

SERVES 4

TAPENADE

¼ cup chopped Kalamata olives

¼ cup chopped green picholine olives

1½ tablespoons chopped fresh rosemary

1 tablespoon grated orange zest

2 teaspoons finely minced garlic

½ teaspoon freshly ground black pepper

1 tablespoon fresh lemon juice

2 tablespoons orange juice

½ cup extra virgin olive oil

4 6-ounce tuna fillets (each ¾ to 1 inch thick)

1 tablespoon olive oil, or as needed

Salt and freshly ground black pepper

For the olive tapenade: In a medium bowl, whisk the olives, rosemary, orange zest, garlic, and ½ teaspoon pepper to combine. Whisk in the lemon juice, orange juice, and ½ cup olive oil. (Can be made up to 2 days ahead of time. Cover with plastic wrap and refrigerate. Bring to room temperature before cooking the tuna.)

Preheat the broiler or prepare a charcoal or gas grill.

Brush the fish with 1 tablespoon olive oil and sprinkle with salt and pepper. Cook the fish until browned on both sides, turning once, 3 to 4 minutes per side. Transfer to dinner plates. Rewhisk the sauce and spoon it over the fish.

VARIATION For greater pungency, rub the fish with a paste of finely minced garlic, rosemary, lemon juice, and olive oil and refrigerate for 1 hour before cooking.

. . . . .

Briny olives and bitter rosemary are combined with orange zest and fragrant olive oil for a slightly assertive sauce to accompany a meaty fish such as tuna. The olive tapenade may be made well ahead of time and brought to room temperature just before you start cooking. You can broil the fish or grill it over a charcoal fire; grilling adds another dimension of flavor. Potatoes, green beans, beets, carrots, and fennel are easy accompaniments. If you want to push the taste envelope with a more aggressive vegetable such as broccoli, cauliflower, or eggplant, you will need a neutral mediator like potato to make peace among these assertive flavors. —Joyce

I am a strong advocate of pairing Merlot and fish when the recipe merits it. This dish is designed specifically to showcase a leaner and more herbal style of wine. The high acidity of this style of Merlot works well with some citrus, while the two styles of olives, the garlic, and the rosemary create a tapestry of wine-friendly flavors and textures that make a slightly more herbal Merlot shine. If you can't find tuna, this dish works equally well with swordfish, shark, and even tilapia. If your wine's less tart, play down the lemon juice while perhaps creating an orange- and lemon-zest mix instead of using exclusively orange.
—Evan

RECOMMENDED PRODUCERS
More Austere, Herb and Bell Pepper–Accented Merlots

EVERYDAY	PREMIUM
Fleur du Cap (Coastal Region, South Africa)	Livio Felluga (Friuli–Venezia Giulia, Italy)
Volpe Pasini (Friuli–Venezia Giulia, Italy)	Thelema (Coastal Region, South Africa)
Bodega Norton (Mendoza, Argentina)	Alpha Domus (Hawkes Bay, New Zealand)

CATALAN BEAN AND SAUSAGE STEW WITH MINT

SERVES 4

BEANS
2 cups dried white beans or dried favas
1 onion, chopped
2 whole cloves garlic, peeled
1 bay leaf
2 teaspoons salt, or more to taste
Freshly ground black pepper

4 chorizo, botifarra, or other fresh spicy sausages
(about 1 pound, not encased in plastic)
2 tablespoons olive oil
¼ pound salt pork or bacon, diced
1 onion, chopped
3 cloves garlic, minced
3 tomatoes, peeled, seeded, and chopped,
or 1½ cups canned chopped tomatoes, drained
1 tablespoon sweet paprika or pimentón de la Vera
½ cup meat stock or water, or more as needed
½ cup dry white wine
3 tablespoons chopped fresh mint plus additional for garnish
Salt and freshly ground black pepper

Overnight method: Place the beans in a large pot. Fill the pot with enough cold water to cover and soak the beans overnight in the refrigerator.

Quick-soak method: If you need beans in a hurry, and you don't want to use canned, use this method. In a large pot, combine the beans with 2 quarts of water and bring to a boil. Boil for 2 minutes, then remove from the heat, cover the pot, and let the beans stand for 1 hour.

Drain and rinse the beans. Return them to the pot. Add enough cold water to cover the beans by 2 inches, then add 1 chopped onion, 2 garlic cloves, and the bay leaf and bring to a boil. Reduce the heat to low, add salt, and simmer until the beans are tender, about 40 minutes. Season to taste with 2 teaspoons salt and pepper to taste. Set aside.

Place the sausages in a large skillet and prick them with a fork in a few places. Add water to a depth of ¼ inch and cook the sausages until the water has evaporated and the sausages are browned, about 10 minutes. Cool. Transfer the sausages to a cutting board and slice into 1½-inch pieces. (Leave them whole if they are small.)

In a large Dutch oven, heat the olive oil over medium-high heat. Add the salt pork or bacon and sauté until crispy, 5 to 8 minutes. Using a slotted spoon, transfer the meat to a plate, leaving the drippings in the Dutch oven. Add 1 chopped onion to the drippings and cook over medium heat until the onion is tender, 8 to 10 minutes. Add the minced garlic, tomatoes, and paprika to the onions and cook 3 minutes longer. Add the stock, wine, sausages, cooked bacon or pork, and 3 tablespoons chopped mint and simmer to blend the flavors, about 10 minutes. Add the cooked beans and simmer, covered, until heated through, about 10 minutes. If the stew seems dry, add additional stock. Season the stew to taste with salt and pepper. Sprinkle with additional mint as a garnish and serve.

· · · · ·

In this rustic Spanish stew from the province of Catalonia, the beans are a neutral foil for rich and full-flavored sausages. Mint adds sweetness and a bit of lightness to the mixture. As with most stews, for maximum flavor development, this dish is best prepared ahead of time and then reheated. A traditional accompaniment would be a side of cooked greens such as chard, collard greens, or spinach. —Joyce

Although many of the wines that fit this category are clearly French, the dish is decidedly Spanish. When the pairing worked so well, I decided to call it a happy E.U. match! The waxy texture of the beans is a great platform for the wine, while the rustic nature of the chorizo is set off well by this style of Merlot. A fruitier wine might have a harder time pairing with the other elements, including the salt pork or bacon, the tomatoes, and the cooked-down wine. These last two ratchet up the dish's acidity just enough to render a more fruit-forward wine "hot" and potentially unpleasant. The mint is the quintessential link between the wine and the stew. —Evan

RECOMMENDED PRODUCERS
Minty, Earthy Merlots

EVERYDAY	PREMIUM	SPLURGE
Concha y Toro (Central Valley, Chile)	Barnard Griffin (Greater Columbia Valley, Washington)	Northstar (Greater Columbia Valley, Washington)
Columbia Crest (Greater Columbia Valley, Washington)	Château La Grave à Pomerol (Bordeaux, France)	Clos L'Église (Bordeaux, France)
Bogle (multiple appellations, California)	Château de Sales (Bordeaux, France)	Château La Conseillante (Bordeaux, France)

MEDITERRANEAN VEGETABLE RAGOUT
ON A BED OF POLENTA

SERVES 4

2 medium eggplants, peeled and cut into 1-inch cubes
Salt
1 scant cup olive oil, or as needed
2 red onions, chopped
4 cloves garlic, minced
2 red or green bell peppers, seeded and diced
3 zucchini, sliced into ½-inch pieces
½ pound cremini or white mushrooms, left whole if small,
halved or quartered if large
3 large or 4 medium tomatoes, peeled, seeded, and diced
Freshly ground black pepper
¼ cup chopped fresh basil
Basic Polenta (see recipe below)

Place the eggplant pieces in a colander and sprinkle with salt. Let stand for 30 minutes. Wipe off the salt with paper towels.

In a large nonstick frying pan, heat 3 tablespoons of the olive oil over medium-high heat and sauté half the eggplant until tender, 6 to 8 minutes. Using a slotted spoon, transfer the cooked eggplant to a large bowl. Add 3 more tablespoons olive oil, sauté the remaining eggplant until tender, and add to the bowl. Add 2 more tablespoons oil to the pan and add the onions. Sauté until soft and pale gold, about 15 minutes. Add the garlic and cook until fragrant, about 2 minutes longer. Transfer to the bowl with the eggplant.

Add 3 more tablespoons oil to the pan and add the bell peppers and zucchini. Sauté until the vegetables are soft, 5 to 8 minutes. Using a slotted spoon, transfer to the bowl with the eggplant and onion mixture.

Add 2 to 3 more tablespoons oil to the pan and add the mushrooms. Sauté the mushrooms over medium-high heat until soft, about 5 minutes. Add all the cooked vegetables from the bowl to the mushrooms in the pan. Stir in the diced tomatoes, reduce heat to low, and cook until well blended and the tomatoes are softened and melted, about 15 minutes. Season to taste with salt and pepper and stir in the basil. (Can be made up to 2 days ahead of time. Cover and refrigerate. Reheat gently before serving.) Serve over a bed of polenta.

BASIC POLENTA

4 cups cold water
2 teaspoons salt
1 cup medium- or coarse-grind cornmeal (not instant)
4 tablespoons (½ stick) unsalted butter
3 tablespoons grated Parmesan cheese

Most recipes for polenta say to bring salted water to a boil and add the cornmeal in a thin stream, stirring constantly to prevent lumps, then reduce the heat to low and simmer slowly, stirring every 5 minutes or so, until the polenta is cooked, about 25 to 45 minutes. However, I have found the following method to be foolproof, resulting in lump-free polenta every time. In a large saucepan, whisk together the cold water, salt, and cornmeal. Bring to a gradual boil over medium heat, whisking occasionally. When it reaches a boil, immediately reduce the heat to low and simmer, stirring occasionally with a wooden spoon, until the polenta is creamy and not grainy on the tongue, about 30 minutes. Stir in the butter and Parmesan until melted. Serve warm.

Cooked polenta can be kept soft and liquid in the pot just by adding hot water in increments. The longer it is kept hot, the more water it will take.

VARIATION If you don't want soft polenta, pour it onto an oiled, rimmed baking sheet and refrigerate until set, at least 2 hours and up to 2 days. To serve, cut it into strips, and bake, fry, or grill the pieces.

On the package of Golden Pheasant Polenta is a technique that takes longer but requires virtually no stirring. Combine the cornmeal, water, salt, and melted butter, pour into a well-buttered deep baking dish, and place in a 350-degree oven for 45 minutes. Stir and add salt to taste. Bake 10 more minutes, until the polenta is cooked.

. . . . .

Although this could be called ratatouille, the combination of eggplant, peppers, onions, tomatoes, zucchini, and mushrooms is served all over the Mediterranean—not just in France. The herbs may vary, and the vegetables may be grilled, roasted, or sautéed. Of course, the polenta adds an Italian accent to this filling meatless meal. —Joyce

This delicious stew will please both vegetarians and nonvegetarians and is spot-on with a mature Merlot, regardless of origin. The cornucopia of nature showcased in this dish is friendly with Merlot, especially the eggplant, peppers, and zucchini. Tomatoes always increase sharpness, and, since the wine may well have lost a little acidity during its time in the bottle, that's not at all bad. If the wine has become very round and smooth, you might want to cook the vegetables a little longer, as smoother-textured veggies are preferable with a mellower wine. The polenta's comforting richness completes the match and adds some substance for those craving more than simply vegetables. —Evan

RECOMMENDED PRODUCERS
Aged, Mature Merlots

EVERYDAY	PREMIUM	SPLURGE
Miguel Torres (Central Valley, Chile)	Chateau Ste. Michelle (Greater Columbia Valley, Washington)	Leonetti (Walla Walla Valley, Washington)
Hogue (Greater Columbia Valley, Washington)	Shafer (Napa Valley, California)	Duckhorn (Napa Valley, California)
Cape Indaba (Coastal Region, South Africa)	Château Borgneuf (Bordeaux, France)	Château Trotanoy (Bordeaux, France)

PINOT NOIR

Pinot Noir (*pee*-noh *nwahr*) can inspire the classic love-hate relationship. The most entrancing table wine I have ever enjoyed was a Pinot Noir. Yet the most disappointing wine I ever tasted was also a Pinot Noir. Sampling the possibilities of this incredibly captivating and fickle grape can make you feel like Goldilocks in the Three Bears' house, always searching for the choice that's just right. The challenge may be rooted in Pinot's precise needs—perfect climate, just the right amount of oak treatment to add complexity, and precise tannin management to ensure a silky and pleasing mouthfeel. When Pinot Noir does strike that exact balance, nothing is better. Alas, that's far from a sure bet. Pinot Noir is the most evocative, provocative, and mysterious varietal grown. The best efforts at Pinot Noir (regardless of origin) are lush, exotic, spicy, and sexy. The worst are green, stalky, and bitter. But when it's good, it can be very, very good. The darling of sommeliers, Pinot Noir is, in my opinion, *the* most food-friendly red wine. I look at it as a white wine in red wine clothing, because it's soft on tannin, long on acidity, and chock-full of fruit and food-related flavors. It's been claimed that almost one out of every ten bottles sold in American fine-dining restaurants is Pinot Noir. Read on and understand why.

WINE-GROWING AREAS

One of the oldest grapes on the planet, Pinot Noir originated in France, although there are stellar examples produced in other parts of the globe with temperate to cool climates. As with Chardonnay, Pinot Noir, as a still wine, finds its spiritual grounding in Burgundy's Côte d'Or, where a fine Vosne-Romanée, Clos de la Roche, or Echézeaux can bring tears to the eyes. The awesome combination of red cherry, lavender, smoky or sweet oak, and a hint of what the French call *animal* can simply be nirvana. Also like Chardonnay, Pinot Noir is a mainstay in the production of Champagne and sparkling wines around the world, contributing body and complexity as well as abundant fruit and an intrinsic spiciness.

A great red Burgundy can make you cry, and vintners around the world unite in the pursuit of the winemaker's Holy Grail, a fine Pinot Noir. There are a few blessed spots where it's been successful.

Outside the shrine of the Côte d'Or, France makes fine Pinot Noir in the Loire Valley (as both a red and rosé), in Champagne (both for bottling as a still wine and for adding color to rosé bubblies), and in Alsace, where the examples range from rosé to light red.

In Germany, Pinot Noir is called Spätburgunder. In the southern Pfalz region, more and better wines are being made as vintners learn how to coax the wine's character out. They are increasingly using small oak barrels to add pedigree to a varietal that was pleasant but historically lacking in complexity. Italy's north-central area of Franciacorta (a part of Lombardy), where the climate is just right for the grape, makes fine still and sparkling wines from what is known there as Pinot Nero. Less readily available but nevertheless well-made examples can be found in Central Europe and in small amounts in Spain.

Down under is another area for Pinot discovery. Australia was long thought to be too warm for this cool-climate grape, and indeed the initial efforts there were quite ghastly. However, over time, as with Australian Riesling, finding the right microclimates has resulted in lovely wines with clear and vibrant tart red fruit, complex spice flavors, and adequate weight and body. Seek out those from the Adelaide Hills and the Yarra Valley to find out what Australian winemakers are capable of!

New Zealand, many feel, will be the source of the next stellar Pinot Noirs, and I support that conviction. Given the relative youth of its wine industry and the incredibly successful wines that New Zealand vintners have produced from very young vines, it's easy to understand why this country's Pinot Noirs make many Burgundians nervous. Though several appellations are making excellent Pinot Noir, the wines that come closest to the Burgundy style emanate from the South Island's Central Otago, Waipara, and Marlborough regions and are worth the extra effort to find. The North Island's Martinborough appellation, though small, is bottling similarly wonderful wines. Pinot Noir wines from South Africa, while still relatively rare, are also encouraging, and they come, as one would guess, from newer, cool-climate areas such as Mossel Bay and Walker Bay.

In America, you can find stellar examples of Pinot Noir grown in California's Napa and Sonoma areas. In Napa, Carneros is the spot. Its wines have a signature jammy, strawberry flavor and are clean and spicy, with notes of orange peel and pine forest. In my opinion, Sonoma County is a stronger Pinot area, with several noteworthy regions, including the larger Sonoma Coast (where the wines have explosive black cherry and exotic sandalwood aromas), the Russian River Valley (with dark-fruited, sensual, succulent, and fleshy wines), and the small Green Valley (producing velvety-supple wines with black cherry and spice). Farther north is the Anderson Valley in Mendocino, which makes outstanding, juicy Pinot Noirs, and down in the southern part of the Central Coast appellation, in Santa Ynez, Santa Barbara, and Santa Maria, you find extraordinary bottles jammed full of wonderful strawberry and raspberry fruit and seductive herbal notes. Recently the Santa Lucia Highlands close to Monterey have been coming on strong as well. Modern California efforts are exceptional, and I'd put them up against fine Burgundy any day.

You can't conclude a Pinot Noir discussion in North America without spending some time exploring and enjoying the complex and delicious cherry-scented wines of Oregon's Willamette Valley, specifically the subregions of Red Hill, Dundee, and Yamhill. And, as you might predict, Pinot Noir does well in the Okanagan Valley, farther north in Canada's British Columbia, where the wines are getting better all the time.

A table of principal wine-growing regions for Pinot Noir appears on pages 280–81.

VINTNER CHOICES

Still or sparkling; red or rosé; old or new wood; age, size, and type of wood; char treatment of oak; barrel fermentation; whole-cluster fermentation; clones and selections; vinification techniques (bleeding, prefermentation cold soaking, fining, and filtration); tannin management

The vintner and the viticulture team encounter many forks in the road to a good Pinot Noir. First, as with Chardonnay, the winemaker needs to decide whether the grapes are destined to make bubbly or still wine. That choice precipitates a whole lot of questions and subsequent decisions. Pinot Noir lends itself to a lovely rosé still wine (often called *vin gris*) which can be quite enjoyable for summer drinking. Here the grape skins are removed from the wine as soon as the desired blush color is achieved, and the wine continues to ferment dry, resulting in a deliciously spicy and refreshing rosé wine. But because the red wine market is more active than the blush market, most producers opt for making the regal red type, with all its attendant challenges.

Having discussed oak at length in the Cabernet section, I'll simply say that the same issues (regarding fining and such) apply to Pinot, although many vintners would add that Pinot Noir is more vulnerable to having too much oak, so restraint and prudence are needed in matching the oak regimen (age and toast levels in particular) to the wine. Barrel fermentation in oak (once applied only to white wines) is being increasingly practiced in reds, including Pinot Noir, as it adds texture and suppleness to the wine. Other tricks include the use of whole clusters of grapes (as opposed to only skins and pulp), warmer fermentation temperatures (90 degrees Fahrenheit or even higher is quite normal for Pinot Noir, compared with 53–64 degrees for white wines and 77–86 degrees for other reds), and prefermentation "cold soaks" to extract better color, flavor, and texture. Measured use of fining and filtration to clarify the wine is essential, with many a winemaker preferring to allow gravity to do most of the fining and then filtering the wines minimally, if at all, for stability and clarity. As with other red wines, tannin management is critical with Pinot Noir. Much of the charm of a great Pinot Noir is based on its evident but transparently supple and soft tannic structure.

Finally, as with Chardonnay, Pinot Noir is almost never blended with other grapes, so achieving complexity depends on the use of different clones and selections. As it happens, Pinot Noir has a propensity for mutating in the vineyard, producing grapes of widely differing character that result in progressively more refined and complex wines.

FLAVORS

Fruit and vegetable: Red and black cherry, raspberry, strawberry, prune, plum, pomegranate, citrus, blackberry, red currant, beet, fennel, olive

Floral: Lavender, jasmine, violet, mint, menthol, eucalyptus, tea leaf

Earth: Mushroom, truffle, mineral, humus, damp or dry leaves

Wood (oak): Coffee, allspice, coriander, ginger, clove, cinnamon, cocoa, mocha, espresso, smoke, caramel, burnt sugar, walnut, roasted pecan, vanilla, coconut, toast, sandalwood

Other: Meaty *(animal),* soy, feral or farmyard, charcuterie

WINE AND FOOD PAIRING

INGREDIENTS AND STYLES

My friend Jancis Robinson once described Pinot Noir as "liquid chicken": find one that everyone enjoys, and all your troubles are solved. I have never forgotten that comment, as it's such a spot-on observation. Pinot Noir really is a white wine in red wine clothing. It expresses itself best in cooler climates and has zesty, aromatic fruit, high acidity, and moderate alcohol—characteristics found in most white wines. However, it possesses a distinctively "red" flavor personality devoid of big red wine's ample tannins. So you can have the best of both worlds and the world's easiest red wine to match with food. I am speaking specifically of the red wines rather than the vin gris or rosé styles, which, like most great dry blush wines, should be treated as light white wines when pairing with food; they can be brilliant with fish, fowl, white meats, grains and pasta, and the summer's bounty of produce.

There are very few foods Pinot Noir doesn't pair well with, although extreme levels of spicy heat in a dish will blow out this delicate wine. Additionally, recipes that are very rich or bold can easily overpower the wine, and, since it's generally expensive, you might not want to chance it.

Lamb and Pinot Noir are time-honored partners, and the dizzying array of natural herb and spice flavors inherent to Pinot Noir let you play around with a variety of marinades, crusts, and sauces. Pinot also pairs delightfully with beef, less well with venison. I love Pinot Noir with less strong fish, especially salmon, swordfish, and tuna. They can be simply grilled or seared in a white-hot pan and minimally jazzed up.

Pinot Noir is sublime with poultry, and indeed the classic coq au vin is said to have originated in Burgundy. Quail, game birds (especially squab), and poussin are perfect tablemates. And don't overlook offal: Pinot is great with liver, kidneys, and sweetbreads. Pasta, pizza, and risotto can match up well, but keep them simple. Pinot's ample acidity does enable it to stand up to most tomato-based sauces, which are inherently sharp.

Earthier styles (especially from Burgundy and New Zealand) can be truly sublime with more pungent tastes, including game: wild (rather than farmed) venison or pheasant, wild goose, hare, and, of course, aged lamb.

Cheese and Pinot Noir are a famous couple, as Pinot stands up to many cheese styles: aged and fresh, hard and creamy. As with many reds, you are best off avoiding blue-veined cheeses, but don't automatically avoid all pungent examples; play around. A word of warning, though: one of the worst wine and food combinations in my book is Burgundy's native and strongly favored Époisses served with . . . red Burgundy!

For particularly difficult pairing challenges—in a restaurant or in a finicky household where each person wants to eat something different—Pinot Noir is the great equalizer at the table, content to accompany fish, fowl, sweetbreads, and salmon.

COOKING METHODS

As with all reds, be aware of the oak. If it is strong, play off it with smoked, grilled, peppered, and charred treatments. Slow roasting or braising, during which the ingredients pick up texture, can be lovely if the Pinot Noir has a round texture. Avoid too much cream, butter, or fat, which can dominate Pinot's subtlety.

If the Pinot Noir is older, prepare simpler recipes to show it off: a basic leg of lamb, roast loin of veal, or that age-old classic, coq au vin.

PAIRING POINTERS

Pinot Noir goes well:

- With just about everything. Its combination of red-wine and white-wine qualities gives it incredible flexibility with many different ingredients and preparations.
- With dishes that pick up on its inherently spicy flavors. Use a good Pinot Noir to pair with a dish containing coriander, cumin, cinnamon, ginger, or any one of the spices found in the wine.
- With foods that are smoked, grilled, or lightly charred, especially if you're serving a smoky and more oak-driven style of wine.
- With many fish. Tuna and swordfish are prime candidates. Indeed, the quintessential local pair-

ing in Oregon is northwest salmon and Oregon Pinot Noir. If you don't try this combination when you're there, they won't let you out!

- With vegetables and earthier flavors. Especially when you're serving an earthier-style bottle, Pinot Noir shows well with cooked greens, squash, and fennel, and with lentils, onion, garlic, cooked brown mushrooms, and Dijon mustard.
- With a multitude of Asian cuisines. Indian, Chinese, Japanese, Singaporean, and Korean foods all pair well. Dishes that have sweet-salt flavor combinations and texture are great: Peking duck, tea-smoked crispy or tandoori chicken, or Hoisin- and soy-glazed pork roast.
- With many room-temperature cold cuts: mild cheeses, a plate of charcuterie, and sliced ham or turkey are easy to enjoy with a glass of Pinot Noir. It's a great picnic wine, especially if served slightly chilled.

Pinot Noir isn't good:
- With stronger seafood and fish. Avoid mussels, sea bass, anchovies, sardines, and mackerel.
- With overly rich sauces and dishes. The wine is just too delicate to stand up to copious quantities of cream, butter, and thick, mayonnaise-based sauces.
- With fiery heat. Anything that burns the lips will burn out the Pinot Noir.
- With recipes that are too bold. Pinot Noir is all about subtlety, and a dish that commands too much attention can easily drown it out.
- With almost all strong-flavored cheeses. As with most red wines, the best cheeses to serve with Pinot Noir are mild and creamy: Teleme, Taleggio, Brie, and so forth. But Pinot can work with stronger cheeses, too, so do play around.

PORK LOIN GLAZED WITH POMEGRANATE AND ORANGE

SERVES 6

1 3-pound boneless pork roast, or 2 1½-pound pork tenderloins

SPICE PASTE
¼ cup fresh orange juice
2 tablespoons soy sauce
2 tablespoons grated peeled fresh ginger
2 tablespoons pomegranate syrup or pomegranate molasses
2 tablespoons hot mustard
Grated zest of 1 orange
2 teaspoons finely minced garlic

BASTING SAUCE
⅓ cup fresh orange juice
3 tablespoons honey
3 tablespoons pomegranate syrup or pomegranate molasses
2 tablespoons soy sauce
2 tablespoons reserved spice paste

Place the pork in a large nonaluminum container.

For the spice paste: In a bowl, stir together the orange juice, soy sauce, ginger, pomegranate syrup, hot mustard, orange zest, and garlic. Reserve 2 tablespoons paste for the sauce. Rub the remaining spice paste onto the meat. Cover and marinate in the refrigerator at least 6 hours or overnight. Let the meat stand at room temperature for 30 minutes before cooking.

For the basting sauce: In a bowl, whisk the orange juice, honey, pomegranate syrup, soy sauce, and reserved 2 tablespoons spice paste to blend. Set aside ¼ cup sauce to spoon on at the end.

Preheat the broiler or prepare a charcoal or gas grill. Broil or grill the pork, not too close to the heat source, basting with the sauce and turning a few times for even cooking, until an instant-read thermometer registers 140 degrees, 20 to 30 minutes for 1 large loin, or 5 to 8 minutes per side for tenderloins.

Transfer the meat to a carving board and let stand for 10 minutes. Slice thinly. Spoon the reserved basting sauce over the meat.

VARIATION Try roasting this pork loin instead of grilling or broiling it. Preheat the oven to 400 degrees and place the pork in a roasting pan. Roast until an instant-read thermometer registers 140 degrees, about 40 minutes, basting often with half of the basting sauce. Spoon the remaining half of the basting sauce over the meat before serving.

· · · · ·

To make the glaze for this pork loin, use pomegranate syrup (sometimes called pomegranate molasses), which is available in markets that specialize in Middle Eastern foods. Or reduce fresh or bottled pomegranate juice over high heat to a syrupy consistency. The pomegranate marinade balances the inherent sweet and tart fruit flavors with saltiness from the soy and the bitter elements of mustard and ginger. For maximum flavor, marinate the mild and sweet pork in the spice paste overnight. This dish is good hot or cold and is ideal for a large party or buffet, as the recipe doubles nicely. Serve with rice (or a blend of wild rice and white rice) and sugar snap peas or asparagus. —Joyce

As a general rule, Middle Eastern cuisine works well with both Pinot Noir and Syrah, but this dish cries out for Pinot Noir. Pinot is noteworthy for the tart, red qualities of its fruit, and this recipe's use of pomegranate, a flavor I often find in Pinot, and orange, which resonates with the wine's acidity, brings these partners together. Ginger, mustard, and soy are friends with Pinot Noir, and this recipe combines all three. The richness of this pork roast nudges my preference toward the fruit-forward styles of the New World, but a riper Old World Burgundy could hold its own, too. Finally, roasting caramelizes the exterior of the pork and mirrors the flavors of barrel aging's sweet, toasted oak. —Evan

RECOMMENDED PRODUCERS
Ripe, Fruit-Forward Pinot Noirs

EVERYDAY	PREMIUM	SPLURGE
Navarro (Mendocino County, California)	Te Kairanga (Wairarapa, New Zealand)	Patz & Hall (Sonoma County, California)
Brancott (Marlborough, New Zealand)	Ponzi (Willamette Valley, Oregon)	Felton Road (Central Otago, New Zealand)
Firesteed (Willamette Valley, Oregon)	Saintsbury (Napa Valley, California)	Argyle (Willamette Valley, Oregon)

STUFFED ROASTED SQUAB

SERVES 2 TO 4

2 squabs, including giblets

Oil for baking pan

2 sweet Italian sausages, casings removed, crumbled

½ to ¾ cup fresh breadcrumbs

2 tablespoons grated pecorino or Parmesan cheese

2 tablespoons chopped fresh flat-leaf parsley

2 tablespoons unsalted butter, room temperature

½ teaspoon salt, or more to taste

¼ teaspoon freshly ground black pepper, or more to taste

1 egg, beaten to blend

4 thin slices pancetta or prosciutto with some fat

2 tablespoons chopped fresh rosemary

4 to 5 sage leaves, chopped

Extra virgin olive oil

1 cup sweet wine such as *vin santo* or sherry, or more as needed

Preheat the oven to 400 degrees. Wash the birds and pat dry. Oil a baking pan large enough to hold the birds comfortably.

Chop the squab hearts and livers. In a bowl, combine the giblets with the crumbled sausage. Stir in ½ cup breadcrumbs, cheese, and parsley. Then stir in the butter, ½ teaspoon salt, ¼ teaspoon pepper, and the egg to bind the stuffing. Add more breadcrumbs if the mixture is too wet. Spoon the stuffing into the birds and sew closed.

Sprinkle each bird with additional salt and pepper and wrap in pancetta or prosciutto. Place them in the prepared pan. Sprinkle the birds with chopped rosemary and sage. Drizzle with extra virgin olive oil.

Roast the birds for 45 minutes, basting with the wine, then remove the pancetta and continue to cook until the birds are golden, 10 minutes longer.

Transfer the birds to a cutting board and remove the thread that enclosed the stuffing. Cut the birds in half lengthwise to reveal the stuffing. Arrange the halves on warm dinner plates and drizzle with the pan juices.

. . . . .

Squab, or young pigeon, is the favored game bird in the Italian region of Umbria. The most popular method of cooking it is on the spit, after marinating the birds in red wine and sage. As squabs are rather small and not too meaty, except in the breast, you probably need one bird per person as a main course. Compared to chicken, farm-raised squab is rather expensive. So if you are on a budget, I suggest you offer a filling first course and then half a bird per person. —Joyce

Though Italian in origin, this squab recipe works so well with French Pinot Noir that it could easily defect. The bird's stuffing contains many Pinot-friendly elements that allow it to pair well with Burgundy's more austere interpretations—the pecorino (sharpness), sausage and giblets (the meaty character), and parsley (a note of greenness). The sage and rosemary in the marinade have an indirect, subtle impact but nevertheless echo the more herbal character of an Old World wine. Finally, the foundation of this match, the squab, has a pungent and earthy flavor that is enhanced by the pancetta. The recipe would also work with Cornish hen or poussin. —Evan

RECOMMENDED PRODUCERS
Earthy, Slightly Lean Pinot Noirs

EVERYDAY	PREMIUM	SPLURGE
Tollot Beaut (Burgundy, France)	Domaine Faiveley (Burgundy, France)	Méo-Camuzet (Burgundy, France)
Jean-Claude Boisset (Burgundy, France)	Antonin Guyon (Burgundy, France)	Domaine Georges Roumier (Burgundy, France)
Bouchard Père et Fils (Burgundy, France)	Louis Jadot (Burgundy, France)	Jean Grivot (Burgundy, France)

SALMON WITH SOY, GINGER, AND SAKE

SERVES 4

⅔ cup chicken stock
⅓ cup sake
3 tablespoons soy sauce
1 tablespoon grated peeled fresh ginger, or more to taste
1 teaspoon finely minced garlic
2 to 3 tablespoons unsalted butter (optional)

4 6-ounce salmon fillets
Olive oil
Salt and freshly ground black pepper

In a medium saucepan, combine the stock, sake, soy sauce, 1 tablespoon ginger, and garlic over medium heat. Bring to a boil and simmer until reduced by half, 8 to 10 minutes. Season with additional ginger, if desired. Whisk in the butter, if desired. (This sauce can be made up to 5 days ahead of time, but whisk in the butter just before serving. Cover and refrigerate. Bring to a simmer before continuing.)

Brush the fish fillets lightly with oil. Sprinkle with salt and pepper.

Preheat the broiler or prepare a charcoal or gas grill. Cook the salmon, turning once and basting with some of the sauce, until the fish looks almost opaque when the point of a knife is inserted into the thickest part, 3 to 4 minutes per side. (Salmon can be served medium rather than well done.) Bring the remaining sauce to a simmer and pour over the cooked fish just before serving.

VARIATION The salmon can be baked instead of broiled or grilled. Preheat the oven to 450 degrees and place the fish in an oiled baking dish. Bake, basting once with the sauce, until the fish looks almost opaque when the point of a knife is inserted into the thickest part, 8 to 10 minutes.

The delicious Japanese-inspired marinade used for this salmon is not as sweet as teriyaki, but it is quite fragrant. Salty and bitter flavors are mellowed by the richness of the fish and a bit of butter. Serve this dish with steamed rice and sautéed spinach or baby bok choy. Or, for a touch of sweetness, serve sugar snap peas or snow peas. —Joyce

Many of the best Pinot Noirs use balanced but copious amounts of oak. If not specifically addressed, this ample oak can dominate the food. Playing to it without overdoing it is a tricky balancing act. This salmon dish pulls it off. Salmon and Pinot are delicious partners, and the Asian combination of sake, soy, and ginger pulls the dish together. It's most successful when you grill the fish, preferably over charcoal, and when you reduce the sauce to an almost syrupy consistency. —Evan

RECOMMENDED PRODUCERS
Oaky, Smoky, Ample Pinot Noirs

EVERYDAY	PREMIUM	SPLURGE
Sebastiani (Sonoma County, California)	Wild Horse (Southern Central Coast, California)	Foley (Southern Central Coast, California)
Estancia (Sonoma/Central Coast, California)	La Crema (Sonoma County, California)	Archery Summit (Willamette Valley, Oregon)
Kenwood (Sonoma County, California)	Cristom (Willamette Valley, Oregon)	Siduri (multiple appellations, California)

LAMB SHISH KEBABS

SERVES 4

MARINADE
1 onion, grated

1 tablespoon minced garlic

2 teaspoons dried oregano or chopped fresh thyme

1 teaspoon freshly ground black pepper

1 teaspoon ground cinnamon

1 teaspoon ground cumin

Pinch hot pepper such as Aleppo pepper, cayenne,

hot paprika, or hot pimentón de la Vera (optional)

½ cup extra virgin olive oil

Salt to taste

2 pounds tender lamb, preferably from the leg, well trimmed and
cut across the grain into 1½-inch cubes

VEGETABLES
1 red onion, cut into squares or quarter-round slices

2 red or green bell peppers, seeded and cut into squares

4 small tomatoes, halved, or 8 to 12 whole cherry tomatoes

Olive oil for brushing vegetables

Salt and freshly ground black pepper

For the marinade: In a bowl, stir together the onion, garlic, oregano, black pepper, cinnamon, cumin, and hot pepper, if desired. Whisk in the olive oil and season the marinade to taste with salt. Reserve 2 tablespoons marinade for basting; cover and refrigerate. Pour the remaining marinade into a large nonaluminum container. Add the meat cubes to the marinade and toss to coat. Cover and refrigerate overnight.

Preheat the broiler or prepare a charcoal or gas grill. Thread the meat onto skewers, interspersing the lamb with the onion pieces and pepper squares, or threading the onion and peppers on separate skewers, as desired, leaving a little space between the items for even cooking. Thread the tomatoes on separate skewers. Brush the vegetables with olive oil and sprinkle with salt and pepper.

Broil or grill the lamb kebabs, turning the skewers and basting with the reserved marinade, until the meat is evenly cooked but remains pink in the center, 8 to 12 minutes total. Broil or grill the vegetables, turning once, until tender, about 5 minutes.

The aroma of grilling lamb pervades the cities of the eastern Mediterranean. If you are in Turkey, order sis kebap; in Greece, souvlaki; in Morocco, qodban. For this savory brochette, use tender lamb cut from the leg. (The marinade also works well on lamb loin, lamb chops, or a boned, butterflied leg of lamb.) Sometimes the meat is arranged on skewers along with onion slices, cubed peppers, mushrooms, or cherry tomatoes. In a perfect world they would all be cooked at the same time, leaving the vegetables juicy and the meat perfectly done. In real life the timing is more tricky. Peppers and onions are fairly hardy and don't fall apart or fall off the skewer. Occasionally the mushrooms may be overcooked or a bit underdone, depending on size. However, little tomatoes can explode or fall off the skewer and into the fire or your lap. So for perfectly grilled tomatoes, put them on a separate skewer and baste them with the olive oil. Serve kebabs with warmed pita bread or with rice or bulgar pilaf. —Joyce

Older wines really should be allowed to show without having to compete with elaborate dishes for attention. But Pinot's exotic nature is brought out by the subtle use of spicy seasoning. The savory simplicity of this dish makes a perfect backdrop for a developed Pinot Noir. There's a lovely mirroring of spiciness in the food and the wine, and the grilled vegetables bring out elements of oak and earthiness. I recommend keeping the meat rare or, at most, pink in the middle to ensure that it's juicy enough to "pop" the wine's developed and mature fruit character. —Evan

RECOMMENDED PRODUCERS

Aged, Developed Pinot Noirs

EVERYDAY	PREMIUM	SPLURGE
Edna Valley (Southern Central Coast, California)	Morgan (Northern Central Coast, California)	Ken Wright (Willamette Valley, Oregon)
Meridian (Southern Central Coast, California)	Elk Cove (Willamette Valley, Oregon)	Domaine Dujac (Burgundy, France)
Joseph Drouhin (Burgundy, France)	Etude (Napa Valley, California)	Gary Farrell (Sonoma County, California)

SANGIOVESE

Ask most consumers about Sangiovese (san-jo-*vay*-zay) and they are left open-mouthed. But if you ask what they know about Chianti, that's a totally different story. Or is it?

Sangiovese is the primary grape of Chianti, which is not a wine, as is commonly thought, but rather the best-known subregion in Italy's Tuscany. Sangiovese's immediate family includes the equally well-regarded clones of Brunello, the Sangiovese selection of Brunello di Montalcino, and Prugnolo Gentile, the selection that constitutes Vino Nobile di Montepulciano. Over the years, Tuscans engaged in lots of winemaking experiments, closely following the wine laws when they believed in them and quietly "fixing" them when they didn't. Wine consumers have been the beneficiaries of this experimentation, which has led to dramatic improvements in the wines, none more surprising than with Sangiovese.

Long gone are the days when Sangiovese meant tart and inexpensive Chianti in straw-covered *fiasco* bottles dangling off plastic grape arbors. The past twenty-plus years have seen a revolution with this varietal, and today the finest bottles of Sangiovese fetch sums rivaling those of the world's greatest red wines.

WINE-GROWING AREAS

Sangiovese is indigenous to central Italy and at its finest in Tuscany. Here it manifests itself in a variety of styles, from the balanced, enjoyably quaffable wines of basic Chianti to the pedigreed and massive wines of Montalcino and the rich and more rustic wines of Montepulciano. Tuscany is, of course, the home of the "Super Tuscan" wines, which are either pure assemblages of the best Sangiovese from specific estates or blends of Sangiovese with other classic grapes, predominantly (if not entirely) Cabernet Sauvignon. Sangiovese in Chianti and its subregions, including Chianti Classico, Chianti Rufina, and Chianti Montespertoli, is a grand expression of this varietal: medium to medium-full in body and singing with tart cherry and raspberry fruit, earthy truffle and tar notes, and nuances of coffee, leather, and spice. Wines from the area around

Montalcino, made from its distinctive clone of Brunello, are fuller in texture, with concentrated flavors of black cherry, plum, mocha, and a sweet dusty-earth character.

The largest concentration of Sangiovese vines outside Italy is in Argentina, primarily in Mendoza, although few of those wines are currently sold in the American market. They are frequently well made but vinified in a style that is most appreciated by Argentine consumers. So while they can be enjoyable, I believe there's a reason more of them are not exported: they simply do not have the same palate profile that many global wine consumers have come to expect from the grape. For those who want to pay tribute to Argentina's strong Italian heritage, try Bonarda, which is increasingly being exported.

In the past two decades, Sangiovese has made its way semisuccessfully to California, specifically to the north coast of California, clustered in Napa and Sonoma Counties. The vines seem to have taken a long time to become established. That said, some Sangiovese vines have a very long history. Many vintners in the Golden State are of Italian ancestry, especially in Sonoma County, where we find the majority of these older vines. However, most of the California Sangiovese plantings are recent, and it may be too early to judge the real potential of this grape in California, as vintners are still learning the best combinations of clones and sites, and the vines need time to mature. In California, as in Tuscany, you find the grape treated in different ways: vinified pure, blended as in the Super Tuscan models, and oak-aged according to varying regimens. Other American states, notably Washington, are dabbling with this varietal and having some success, though at the time of this book's publication, Sangiovese still accounts for only a very small percentage of the vineyard plantings there.

A table of principal wine-growing regions for Sangiovese appears on page 282.

VINTNER CHOICES
*Selections and clones; wood or no wood; age, size,
and type of wood; blended or pure; interpretation*

This grape is a straight shooter. Some of the most complex decision making happens before the fruit reaches the winery.

There are many clones and selections of Sangiovese, and they make for significant differences in the personality and flavor of the wine. The clone of Sangiovese in the Chianti district is vastly different from the Sangiovese Grosso of Montalcino or the Prugnolo Gentile clone of Montepulciano. The Italian oenologist Ezio Rivella once told me that there are several dozen official and scores more of unofficial selections of Sangiovese planted in Tuscany, each with distinct and unique characteristics. And, he added humbly, they are still trying to match clones with the optimal sites *there!* So you can imagine the challenges for those who have taken the grape overseas.

Many Sangiovese and Sangiovese-based wines stand up well to wood. As with other grapes, it's common for winemakers to use a judicious combination of older and newer barrels to try to hit the "sweet spot" for oak. The fashion of moving from a barrel regimen balancing old and new wood to one driven by new and small *barriques* has resulted in strong oak influences that the fruit just can't handle, and the wines consequently taste overoaked. Oaking, more than any other factor in winemaking, depends on fruit pedigree. If the grapes aren't of high quality and flavor concentration, the use of exclusively new oak is likely to overwhelm the wine.

Part of the magic of Sangiovese is how well it blends with other grapes. It can be sublime with Cabernet Sauvignon, Merlot, Syrah, and even Pinot Noir. The key here is recognizing when the Sangiovese stops being enhanced by other grapes and starts being overpowered. This is tricky: at times a mere 4 to 5 percent Cabernet Sauvignon added to Sangiovese may be enough to mask the Sangiovese fruit character and produce a wine that tastes distinctly like a Cabernet. Blending decisions have to be made wine by wine, and winemakers participate in dozens of trials before selecting their final assemblage.

Sangiovese can produce many styles of wine. Aside from the fruit itself, the choice of philosophy or interpretation will steer many production decisions. Is the goal to produce a light, quaffable, basic Chianti style? A more massive Brunello di Montalcino–like wine? A more in-between interpretation, like the wines of Carmignano? Or a blend that will produce a "Super Tuscan"—and, if so, blended with what and how much? So many choices!

FLAVORS

Fruit and vegetable: Cherry (red, black, or sour), raspberry, red plum, cherry tomato, prune, chard

Floral: Rose, chamomile, dried floral (potpourri), marjoram, thyme, caper, tea leaf

Earth: Truffle, mushroom, smoke, earth

Wood (oak): Cinnamon, vanilla, pepper, toasted grain, coffee, mocha, nut, cedar, cola nut

Other: Tar, leather

WINE AND FOOD PAIRING

INGREDIENTS AND STYLES

Sangiovese is one of the wine world's great gifts to the table. It's moderate in alcohol, carries with it a sharp backbone of acidity, and, by and large, has very balanced levels of tannin. This basic profile allows it to marry well with many dishes. The pairing of Chianti with tomato-based pasta and pizza sauces is a cliché for a good reason: even without much attention, it is almost always successful, as the tomato's acidic nature can stand up to that of the wine. Additionally, Sangiovese's medium body and weight give it tremendous flexibility. "Local" dishes such as *bistecca alla fiorentina*—a steak marinated in light olive oil with black pepper—pair well with Sangiovese, as do the aforementioned tomato-based pastas and pizzas, and risotto. Dishes as straightforward as meat loaf and roast chicken take on new life. With its balanced acidity, Sangiovese is great with many tuna, swordfish, and shark preparations, especially those with Italian or Provençale tomato-based sauces. Many preparations of offal (calf's liver and sweetbreads), sausage, and charcuterie also match nicely. Recipes that pair meat or poultry and fruit (especially those with tart flavors, such as sour cherry, orange, tangerine, and fresh tomatoes—yes, tomatoes are a fruit) are quite good with the California fruit-forward interpretations. And green vegetables or herbal additions will show nicely with earthier and classic Italian wines. Think fresh basil, roasted fennel, roasted and stuffed peppers or tomatoes, and even grilled asparagus.

When Cabernet Sauvignon or other grapes are blended with Sangiovese, the wine's profile changes. Blends almost always have more body and alcohol, and the flavors inherent to the other varietals (usually Cabernet or Merlot) come forward. Match these wines with dishes that are more traditional matches for big red wines, but with a bit of a kick. The zip from the Sangiovese seems to accommodate an array of herbs and spices that might otherwise appear odd or off with a pure Cabernet Sauvignon. More powerful pure Sangiovese wines, like Brunello di Montalcino or many of the Super Tuscan genre, should be treated in the same way.

COOKING METHODS

High acidity coupled with body means that you can serve Sangiovese with those rich, slow braises which a Pinot Noir may not be forceful enough to accompany. Most wines with some oak treatment can handle a light char-grilled or smoked dish. Nearly all roasts (roasted meat and vegetables alike) are well suited to this grape. Deglazing the cooking pan with sharp liquids (wine or a combination of wine and lemon) works well to produce pan juices or a sauce to accompany Sangiovese; the same practice can also work with Pinot Noir.

Aging Sangiovese brings out more of the mushroom, truffle, and spice notes, while the classic red and black cherry flavors taste drier and less plump than in the wine's youth. As with other mature wines, I enjoy rare to medium-rare meats whose juiciness will fill in the flavor gaps left by the aging of the wine. Sangiovese can also be delightful with many cheeses, especially harder but mild varieties.

PAIRING POINTERS

Sangiovese goes well:

· With tomato-based sauces. Isn't it nice to know that the time-honored combination of pizza and red-sauced pastas with Chianti gets a gastronomic stamp of approval?

- With fresh herbs. Whether it's basil accompanying the tomatoes in a caprese salad or fresh chopped thyme or sage on a dish, Sangiovese's inherent herbal edge enables these matches to sing.
- With richer, thicker soups. Try a Sangiovese with a puréed bean soup, traditional minestrone, or the increasingly popular "bread soup," Italian *ribollita*.
- With many mushrooms. Truffles, morels, porcini, and any other stronger mushrooms are lovely with this grape. Wild mushrooms are sublime.
- With a variety of cheeses. Sangiovese's rustic personality and racy acidity allow it to pair with a wider array of cheeses than most other red wines do. Milder blue-veined cheeses, like Gorgonzola and Cambozola, pair very well.

Sangiovese isn't good:
- With high levels of fiery spice and heat. Most Sangiovese-based wines will have their balance distorted and thrown off.
- With a lot of seafood. Outside the realm of "red-friendly" fish (tuna, swordfish, and salmon), Sangiovese is not a sure bet with shellfish and fish.
- When you select the wrong one. They come in different personalities, which vary in their food affinities. Many of the "Super Tuscan" blends (with a high percentage of Cabernet) should be treated like a more ample, tannic Cabernet Sauvignon rather than like a Sangiovese.

ITALIAN MEATBALL AND VEGETABLE SOUP

SERVES 4

MEATBALLS

½ pound ground beef or veal

½ cup fresh breadcrumbs, soaked in water and squeezed dry

¼ cup grated onion (optional)

1 egg, beaten to blend

3 tablespoons grated Parmesan cheese (optional)

3 tablespoons chopped fresh flat-leaf parsley

1 teaspoon salt

½ teaspoon freshly ground black pepper

6 tablespoons extra virgin olive oil

¼ pound finely chopped pancetta

3 spring onions, chopped, or 1 large onion, chopped

2 carrots, peeled and chopped

2 ribs celery, chopped

6 cups meat or poultry broth

2 cups fresh or canned diced plum tomatoes, drained

2 bunches spinach, stemmed, washed, drained, and cut into ½-inch strips

1½ pounds fresh favas, shelled (about 1¼ cups), blanched, and peeled

1 pound English peas, shelled (about 1 cup), blanched

1½ cups pasta shells cooked al dente (optional)

Salt and freshly ground black pepper

8 slices rustic bread, toasted (optional)

¼ cup grated Parmesan or grana cheese

For the meatballs: In a large bowl, combine the beef, breadcrumbs, grated onion (if desired), egg, grated cheese (if desired), parsley, salt, and pepper and mix well. Form a tiny meatball the size of a hazelnut. Poach or fry this sample, taste, and adjust the seasoning. Line a baking sheet with waxed paper. Form the rest of the meat into meatballs, about 1 inch in diameter, and place them on the prepared sheet. Cover loosely with waxed paper and set aside.

In a large saucepan or soup pot, heat 2 tablespoons of the oil over medium heat. Add the pancetta and sauté until browned, about 8 minutes. Remove with a slotted spoon and set aside. Add the spring onions, carrots, and celery to the drippings in the saucepan and sauté until the onions are softened, 8 to 10 minutes. Return the pancetta to the saucepan. Add the broth and tomatoes and bring to a gentle boil. Reduce the heat to low, cover the pan, and simmer 30 minutes. Add the meatballs to the soup and simmer 10 minutes longer. Add the spinach, favas, peas, and cooked pasta, if desired, and simmer 10 minutes longer.

Season the soup to taste with salt and pepper. If you did not add the pasta, arrange the toasted bread in warm soup bowls. Ladle the hot soup over the bread and top with grated cheese.

· · · · ·

This substantial soup is really a meal in a bowl. To round out the combination of savory meatballs and vegetables, choose either cooked pasta or grilled bread to add to the soup at the end. —Joyce

I love meatballs—and who doesn't? This dish showcases the tasty simplicity of those meatballs with clean, straightforward flavors: broth, peas, onions, and tomatoes. You don't want or need a "big" wine for this dish; in fact, you need just the opposite. If the wine is too big and complex, the subtlety is lost from both wine and food. A balanced to tart level of acidity in the wine is critical. If it's too low, you'll definitely need the pasta accompaniment to add enough texture for a rounder wine to grab onto. Broth, often a pairing challenge, is matched here with the wine's acidity, so if your wine doesn't have the sharpness, bring on the noodles. —Evan

RECOMMENDED PRODUCERS
Easy-Drinking, Fruit-Forward Sangioveses

EVERYDAY	PREMIUM	SPLURGE
Valley of the Moon (Sonoma County, California)	Fontodi (Tuscany, Italy)	Monsanto (Tuscany, Italy)
Monte Antico (Tuscany, Italy)	Castello di Querceto (Tuscany, Italy)	La Massa (Tuscany, Italy)
Cecchi (Tuscany, Italy)	Atlas Peak (Napa Valley, California)	Frescobaldi (Tuscany, Italy)

ROAST LEG OF LAMB WITH OLIVES AND ORANGE

SERVES 6

OLIVE PASTE
1 cup pitted chopped Niçoise or Kalamata olives
2 tablespoons finely minced garlic
2 tablespoons grated orange zest
2 tablespoons chopped fresh sage
2 tablespoons finely chopped anchovy
½ teaspoon freshly ground black pepper

1 6-pound boned leg of lamb
2 cloves garlic, slivered
2 to 4 tablespoons olive oil
1 cup dry red wine
1 cup lamb or meat broth (optional)

In a food processor, combine the olives, garlic, orange zest, sage, anchovy, and pepper and process to make a paste. Reserve 2 tablespoons of the paste to make a sauce for the roast later on, if desired.

Unroll the boned leg of lamb and flatten it with the side of a cleaver. Cut away excess gristle and spread the olive paste on the lamb, then roll up. Using kitchen twine, tie the lamb closed at 1- or 2-inch intervals. With the tip of a sharp knife, cut a few slits in the lamb leg and insert the garlic slivers.

Preheat the oven to 400 degrees.

In a large sauté pan over high heat, add enough olive oil to film the bottom lightly. When hot, add the lamb and brown well on all sides, turning frequently, 8 to 10 minutes. Transfer to a roasting pan and add the red wine to the pan.

Roast the lamb, basting occasionally with the wine, until an instant-read thermometer inserted into the thickest part registers 120 degrees, 45 minutes to 1 hour for rare meat, depending on the diameter of the roast. For medium meat, roast to 130 degrees, about 8 to 10 minutes longer. (Remember that the meat will continue to cook after it is removed from the oven.)

Remove the roast from the oven and transfer it to a cutting board. Let it rest for at least 10 minutes before slicing.

To make a sauce, bring the broth to a boil and whisk in the 2 tablespoons reserved olive paste. Slice the lamb and serve with the pan juices and sauce, if desired.

. . . . .

Sage, garlic, anchovy, and olives marinated with orange are traditional seasonings in the Italian region of Umbria. These flavors are quite harmonious when paired with lamb. Don't let the anchovy scare you. It adds a subtle saltiness that is better than salt and really picks up the other flavors. The olives add their own saltiness, tempered by the bittersweet tartness of the orange zest. Sage and garlic add an earthy component. This leg of lamb is excellent with creamy mashed potatoes. Green beans, chard, or carrots are a nice complement. —Joyce

This pairing is a good bet because it matches a local dish with a local wine. Lamb sings alongside Sangiovese, and here it's set off beautifully through the use of orange and olive, two flavors that complement Sangiovese. The earthy, rustic elements of the coating paste are brought to the forefront by the wine. Although you don't need a true Brunello to have a successful match, the wine does need to have some weight and breadth to it. If anything, opt for a "Super Tuscan" rather than a lighter interpretation of the varietal. —Evan

RECOMMENDED PRODUCERS
Ample, Rich, Spicy Sangioveses

EVERYDAY	PREMIUM	SPLURGE
Fattoria le Pupille (Tuscany, Italy)	Banfi (Tuscany, Italy)	Silvio Nardi (Tuscany, Italy)
Col d'Orcia (Tuscany, Italy)	Altamura (Napa Valley, California)	Caparzo (Tuscany, Italy)
Lamole di Lamole (Tuscany, Italy)	Fortius (Tuscany, Italy)	Poggio Antico (Tuscany, Italy)

OSSO BUCO WITH MUSHROOMS AND TOMATOES

SERVES 4

3 tablespoons olive oil
4 veal shanks, 1 to 1½ pounds each
6 tablespoons unsalted butter
2 onions, diced
1½ cups hot beef broth
1 cup dry Marsala or dry red wine
6 tablespoons tomato paste
1 ounce dry porcini, soaked in hot water to cover for 30 minutes
1 pound cremini mushrooms, stemmed and sliced or quartered
Salt and freshly ground black pepper

In a heavy skillet, heat the oil over medium-high heat. Add the veal shanks and cook, turning frequently, until browned on all sides, 6 to 8 minutes. Using a slotted spoon, transfer the shanks to a Dutch oven.

In a sauté pan, melt 3 tablespoons of butter over medium heat. Add the onions and sauté until they are translucent, about 8 minutes. Add the onions to the veal shanks.

In a large bowl, whisk the broth, Marsala, and tomato paste to blend. Add to the veal and onions in the Dutch oven. Bring to a gentle boil, reduce the heat to low, and cover. Braise the veal shanks 1 hour.

Meanwhile, prepare the mushroom mixture. Strain the porcini mushrooms through a cheese-cloth-lined strainer placed over a bowl, reserving the porcini soaking liquid. Chop the porcini. In a large sauté pan, melt the remaining 3 tablespoons butter over high heat and add the cremini mushrooms. Sauté the mushrooms until the juices are released, about 5 minutes. Stir the porcini and the reserved soaking liquid into the sautéed mushrooms. After the veal has cooked for 1 hour, add the mushroom mixture to the veal and continue braising until the veal is tender, 30 minutes to 1 hour longer, depending on the size of the shanks. Season to taste with salt and pepper and serve.

VARIATION You can also braise the veal shanks in a 350-degree oven.

· · · · ·

The classic osso buco alla Milanese *with lemon, garlic, and parsley* gremolata *is a familiar and much-loved dish, but try this recipe for a delicious change of pace. The porcini and sautéed cremini mushrooms add a deep, earthy flavor. You may also use chanterelles, fresh porcini, or morels to accentuate the woodland notes. Serve with mashed potatoes, risotto, or polenta for an immensely satisfying dinner. —Joyce*

This match is another pairing of locals and so perhaps is safe and obvious, but having a keen sense of the obvious is not always bad. Osso buco is rich, and the wine needs richness to meld with the ample texture and mouth-coating sumptuousness that comes with the slow braising of the shanks. Mushrooms add another dimension of flavor and texture and open the door for the components of the Cabernet family of grapes. Brown mushrooms or chanterelles or other white mushrooms can add to the mix. Yet richness without acidity would be over the top: the acidity in the wine will set off both the wine and the dish, so opt for a wine that's mostly Sangiovese, and not obviously dominated by Cabernet Sauvignon or Merlot. While this recipe is delicious over or alongside mashed potatoes or polenta, I enjoy the additional textural elements risotto adds; but that is, of course, a personal preference. —Evan

RECOMMENDED PRODUCERS
Blended Sangioveses

EVERYDAY	PREMIUM	SPLURGE
Banfi (Tuscany, Italy)	Ferrari-Carano (Sonoma County, California)	Luce della Vite (Tuscany, Italy)
Fonterutoli (Tuscany, Italy)	Cabreo (Tuscany, Italy)	Tenuta San Guido (Tuscany, Italy)
Falesco (Umbria, Italy)	Sette Ponti (Tuscany, Italy)	Querciabella (Tuscany, Italy)

RUSTIC PAELLA

SERVES 4

1 tablespoon finely minced garlic

1 tablespoon dried oregano

2 teaspoons coarsely ground black pepper

1 teaspoon salt

3 tablespoons red wine vinegar

5 tablespoons extra virgin olive oil

4 small chicken thighs

4 small chicken breast halves

¼ cup white wine or water

½ teaspoon saffron threads, crushed

5 tablespoons olive oil, or more as needed

1 large onion, chopped

3 cups peeled, seeded, and diced tomatoes (canned are fine)

1 tablespoon minced garlic

2 teaspoons sweet paprika or pimentón
de la Vera (Spanish smoked paprika)

2 cups Spanish short-grain rice such as Bomba or Calasparra

5 cups chicken broth, or more as needed

1 cup cooked peas, lima beans, chickpeas, or white beans

24 large shrimp, shelled and deveined (optional)

3 dozen clams or mussels, scrubbed and mussels debearded

White wine or water for steaming clams

In a small bowl, stir the garlic, oregano, pepper, and salt to combine. Add the vinegar and stir to form a paste. Whisk in the 5 tablespoons olive oil. Rub the marinade on the chicken and place in a nonaluminum container. Cover the container and marinate overnight in the refrigerator.

Pour the ¼ cup wine into a small saucepan and bring it to a simmer. Remove the saucepan from the heat, add the saffron, and let steep 10 minutes.

Meanwhile, in a large skillet, heat 3 tablespoons of the olive oil over high heat. Add the chicken pieces in batches and sauté until browned on all sides, 8 to 10 minutes. Add more oil as needed. Using tongs, transfer the chicken to a plate. Wipe the skillet clean of any burned bits. Add the remaining 2 tablespoons oil to the skillet and warm over medium heat. Add the onion and sauté until soft, about 10 minutes. Add the tomatoes, 1 tablespoon garlic, and paprika and cook 5 minutes longer. Add the rice, reduce heat to low, and stir until opaque, about 3 minutes. Raise the heat, add the 5 cups of broth and the saffron infusion, and bring to a gentle boil. Reduce heat and simmer uncovered for 10 minutes. Add the chicken and cook until the liquid is absorbed and the chicken is cooked through, about 5 minutes longer. Add the peas and the shrimp, if using, and cook until the shrimp is pink, adding more broth if necessary, about 5 minutes longer. Cover to keep warm.

Discard any open clams and any mussels that do not close when tapped with a spoon. In a large pot, pour the wine or water to a depth of 1 inch. Add the clams and mussels. Place over medium-high heat, cover, and steam until the shellfish open, 3 to 5 minutes. (They won't all open at once, so keep checking.) As they open, use a slotted spoon to transfer them to the paella. Continue steaming until all have opened. (Clams can be stubborn; after 5 minutes, turn off the heat and cover the pan. Discard any clams that haven't opened within 10 minutes.) Let the paella stand for 10 minutes before serving.

VARIATION Instead of making the paella entirely on the stovetop, you may complete it in the oven. Add the peas and clams when the chicken is added, and place the pan in a 325-degree oven until the liquids are mostly absorbed, about 15 minutes.

· · · · ·

When most cooks think about making paella, they stop to think again, because they believe that it takes time and money to make a showstopper. However, it need not be an elaborate and expensive dish. Some of the very best paellas are the simplest, combining just rice, chicken, and mussels, with a few added beans or peas. Of course, you're free to add chunks of diced ham or chorizo. But it's amazing how satisfying this simple, rustic paella can be. For deeper flavor, the chicken should be marinated overnight. —Joyce

I didn't originally intend to include this pairing, but you can't ignore what works. In hindsight it makes sense. Sangiovese shares all of the elements that enable the paella's classic match with Spain's Tempranillo, the red grape used for Rioja and many other Spanish reds: tart red fruit (to lend acidity), medium weight (supplying a moderate level of alcohol), moderate tannins, and ample but balanced use of oak. Paella's a wonderful dish to show off Sangioveses. Here the Sangiovese is framed by the influence of the sharp but exotic saffron, the paprika, and the oregano. If you find the clams and mussels to be a little too strong in flavor, temper them by scooping them up with rice rather than popping them into your mouth solo; follow immediately with a sip of wine. —Evan

RECOMMENDED PRODUCERS

Excellent All-Around Sangioveses

EVERYDAY	PREMIUM	SPLURGE
Bodega Norton (Mendoza, Argentina)	Caparzo (Tuscany, Italy)	Il Poggione (Tuscany, Italy)
Le Corti (Tuscany, Italy)	Avignonesi (Tuscany, Italy)	Fattoria del Felsina (Tuscany, Italy)
Antinori (Tuscany, Italy)	Volpaia (Tuscany, Italy)	Altesino (Tuscany, Italy

SYRAH

The most important grape of France's northern Rhône Valley and the red varietal that drives the wine industry of Australia (where it is known as Shiraz), Syrah (see-*rah*) has rapidly become one of the most talked-about and widely enjoyed of all red wines. The synergy between the growing demand for Syrah and the producers' mounting excitement is spurring the production of some excellent wines. No longer the domain of the cognoscenti, Syrah and Syrah-based wines have become more and more popular at home and in restaurants. Is this because it quenches a thirst for big red wines? Or because of the accessibility of its natural bold flavors? Or maybe because Syrah is a very food-friendly grape that is well suited to many popular dishes? Whatever the reason, Syrah is a keeper and a wine whose impact will no doubt persist for a long, long time.

WINE-GROWING AREAS

The origin of Syrah was something of a mystery until recently. It was originally thought to have had its roots in Persia and Mesopotamia or even Cyprus, but the renowned grape geneticist Carole Meredith, of the University of California at Davis, helped prove that its humble beginnings were actually French: long ago two uninspiring grapes, the white Mondeuse Blanche and the red Dureza, likely cross-pollinated to create this hybrid.

Syrah's pedigree is evident in France, where you find the notable Côte Rôtie, Cornas, and Hermitage wines, bottlings that are close to 100 percent Syrah and packed with intense dark fruit and distinctive smoky leather, bacon, or meat characters, and Syrah's unmistakable cracked-pepper accents. In the southern Rhône, Syrah is playing an increasingly important role in the blended wines of Châteauneuf du Pape and the ubiquitous Côtes du Rhône. In the blend, Syrah's ample structure and unique flavor marry with the predominant Grenache grape to make for a wine reminiscent of a jammy, spicy Zinfandel. More Syrah and Syrah-based wines are being produced in areas surrounding the Rhône (particularly the Languedoc and the Ardèche). Plantings of Syrah in France trail those of Cabernet Sauvignon by only a few thousand acres and may well surpass them one day. Wines from these other regions of southern France by and large offer both good value and great flavor.

Australia has had tremendous success with Syrah (or Shiraz). It is the most widely planted grape down under. Whether as a pure varietal from McLaren Vale or the Barossa Valley or blended with Cabernet Sauvignon elsewhere in Australia, Australian Shiraz can rank among the world's top examples. Here the Syrah is more fruit-forward, with jammy, brambly, and berry flavors, a minty accent, and a smooth, mouth-filling texture. With these qualities and the ample body provided by the warmer climate, Australian Shiraz provides a second model that rivals the French style.

Syrah is also grown and produced in Italy's Tuscany and in smaller but increasing quantities in Spain. Both countries produce the wine as a proprietary varietal (that is, with proprietary names given by individual vintners), but Syrah is also now frequently being employed as a blending grape, and it brings a lot to those blends.

In the United States, the home of the most significant plantings outside France and Australia, Syrah shouldn't be confused with Petite Sirah, which is in fact made from an ancient Rhône grape called Duriff that is field-blended with a few other grapes. California-style Syrah resembles a cross between Australian wines and some Rhône wines and can be scrumptious. Once thought of as an amusing change from other grapes, Syrah is now the leading grape in the Paso Robles area of the Southern Central Coast region, where it seems to have found a real niche. Look for wines produced from older vines and smaller crop yields of Syrah from that area as well as those from the Sierra Foothills.

Washington State and South Africa are newer but very exciting players in the world of Syrah. Washington's efforts have been made in small lots emanating from the eastern part of the state and showing characteristics that appear to combine the best of France and California. And although South Africa's efforts began only in the late 1990s, initial bottles coming from Stellenbosch and Paarl have proved noteworthy. Finally, Syrah from Argentina's San Juan province is rich and powerful, while wines from Mendoza increasingly resemble Syrah from Washington State and the northern Rhône. Chile, too, shows great promise, especially in the areas of Aconcagua and the Maipo Valley.

A table of principal wine-growing regions for Syrah appears on pages 283–84.

VINTNER CHOICES
Wood or no wood; age, type, and size of wood; tannin management;
barrel fermentation; micro-oxygenation; 100 percent varietal or blended; style

With Syrah, vintners have to address the ubiquitous red wine issues of tannin management, micro-oxygenation, and oak. Like Zinfandel, Syrah can't take large doses of new oak. Despite its enormous flavor and personality, if too much oak is used, the wood is essentially all you can taste. In fact, many producers (especially those in France) don't expose their wines to any new oak, preferring to let the inherent Syrah personality dictate the character of the wine. Other winemakers introduce a little new wood into each vintage. The Aussies developed and introduced red wine barrel fermentation (not just aging) with their very successful use of the technique in Shiraz production, and it's now more and more commonly practiced outside Australia. Texture and tannin management have led to experiments with micro-oxygenation, and various regimens of postfermentation skin contact have been useful in managing what can be a coarse tannic structure.

Ultimately, though, the style choice and blending are the factors that most influence the character of the wine. Is the winemaker aiming to make a 100 percent pure Syrah wine? a classic Rhône blend of Syrah and Grenache? an Aussie-style Cabernet Sauvignon–Syrah blend? Or is the goal to create a proprietary assemblage of which Syrah is an integral component? Syrah, despite its massiveness, is very malleable and, blended with other grapes in the correct proportions, adds complexity without demanding center stage.

FLAVORS

Fruit and vegetable: Boysenberry, black cherry, blackberry, black currant (cassis), black raspberry, black plum, prune, fennel, black olive, bell pepper, citrus (orange), mulberry, stewed fruit, fruitcake

Floral: Violet, tea leaf, mint, eucalyptus, menthol

Earth: Dust, graphite, mushroom, charcoal, truffle

Wood (oak): Cinnamon, clove, chocolate, cocoa, smoke or char, vanilla, coconut, toast, coffee

Other: Peppercorn (white and black), sausage (roasted meat), bacon, soy, leather, animal

WINE AND FOOD PAIRING

INGREDIENTS AND STYLES

With Syrah, style is a significant factor in determining how to match the wine with food. For classic French Syrah-based wines, I prefer red meat in almost any form (grilled, stewed, smoked, or roasted), stews, and other stick-to-the-ribs fare. Play off the implicit peppery character of the wine by incorporating spices and peppers into marinades, glazes, sauces, and accompanying side dishes or condiments. Almost all Syrah and Syrah-based wines are generous in alcohol, so don't serve subtle recipes that will be buried. Dishes with coarse texture work well with Syrah: polenta, black beans, and even a sauce made with whole-grain mustard all offer a nice rough scrape against this ample wine.

New World Syrah and Syrah-based wines, such as those from Australia and California, packed with generous black and red fruit, are very good with meat and fowl alike. Roasts of pork and venison, especially when accented by a choice condiment, can play off the wine's fruit: try serving a fruit chutney or spiced tomato conserve alongside. Ample examples of regional cuisine, such as French cassoulet, Greek moussaka, or good old American chili (rich but not too spicy hot), are natural partners with Syrah. If the wine is softer and less alcoholic, a robust fish stew, such as a spicy bouillabaisse or cioppino, will reward the adventurous. If you are looking for a wine to go with your Texas barbecue, look no further. Syrah is also a natural with many styles of cheese, especially those crusted with black pepper or herbs.

COOKING METHODS

Grilling always shows off Syrah and Syrah blends, and if there's a hint of mint or green herb (bay leaf, thyme, or rosemary) in the wine, try and play off it in the dish. Smoked ingredients pair well with lightly oak-aged examples of Syrah, especially those from California or Washington. Slow braises and stews make a great stage for showing off a more concentrated bottle.

Syrah becomes more like Cabernet as it matures and should be treated as such when you're matching it with food.

PAIRING POINTERS

Syrah goes well:

- With grilled foods. A char-grilled steak, a peppercorn-crusted tuna, or even assorted grilled vegetables such as eggplant, zucchini, and tomatoes pair well.
- With thicker and fuller preparations. The weight and body of Syrah and Syrah-based wines make them natural partners for thick stews and one-dish meals.
- With pungent and wild flavors. Squab, wild boar, and other strong-flavored foods are tamed and happy when served with most Syrahs.
- With herbs. Whether they are coating a cheese, sprinkled onto a dish, used as an accent for a marinade, or simply adding flavor to the grill's coals, fresh herbs are a winner with Syrah—especially French-style, earthier, and herbal examples.
- With barbecue. No matter what the style (from Texas, the Carolinas, or Saint Louis), Syrah is a great accompaniment.

Syrah isn't good:

- With most fish. Though some salmon and tuna preparations and fish stews pair well with lighter styles of Syrah, it's generally too much for most seafood recipes and can be thrown out of balance by stronger fish.

- With very hot and fiery recipes. With Syrah's high alcohol level, any increase on the Scoville scale will increase the perception of alcohol in the Syrah and leave you reaching for a beer.
- With sour foods. Sharp vinegar bases and tart vegetables (such as escarole and leeks) can be tough to pair with a Syrah unless you're working with a leaner and more austere example.
- With really mild cheeses. With Syrah, pungency in the cheese is a plus. Although, again, blue-veined cheeses are difficult to match with the wine, Syrah pairs well with harder strong cheeses: aged Dutch Gouda, Parmesan, aged goat cheese, and dry jack. Avoid soft and mild cheeses or those that are runny and strong-smelling, like Époisses or aged Camembert.

MOROCCAN LAMB BARBECUE

SERVES 6

CHARMOULA
1 large onion, grated

4 cloves garlic, finely minced

2 teaspoons ground cumin

1 teaspoon sweet paprika

1 teaspoon salt

1 teaspoon freshly ground black pepper

½ teaspoon cayenne pepper

½ teaspoon ground cinnamon

½ teaspoon ground ginger

¼ cup chopped flat-leaf parsley

¼ cup chopped fresh coriander (cilantro)

¼ cup fresh lemon juice

½ cup olive oil

1 6-pound leg of lamb (weight with bone), boned and butterflied, or 12 loin lamb chops, or 2½ pounds boneless leg of lamb, trimmed and cut into 1½-inch cubes

6 tablespoons olive oil or unsalted butter, melted, plus 1 tablespoon oil for coating the lamb

In a bowl, combine the onion, garlic, spices, herbs, lemon juice, and ½ cup olive oil to make the *charmoula,* or spice mix. Reserve one-quarter of the charmoula in a small bowl for basting; cover and refrigerate.

Trim all excess fat and sinew from the lamb. Place the lamb in a large nonaluminum container and rub it with the remaining charmoula. Cover and refrigerate overnight.

Bring the meat to room temperature. Remove the meat from the marinade. Preheat the broiler or prepare a charcoal or gas grill.

Add 6 tablespoons olive oil or melted butter to the reserved charmoula in the bowl and whisk to blend well.

For leg of lamb, brush with the 1 tablespoon oil and broil or grill, turning once and basting with the charmoula mixture, until an instant-read thermometer inserted into the thickest part reads 120 degrees for rare (8 to 10 minutes per side), 130 degrees for medium (10 to 15 minutes per side), or 140 degrees for well done (15 to 18 minutes per side). For lamb chops, allow 4 to 6 minutes per side, depending on the thickness of the chops. For kebabs, thread cubes of lamb on skewers and broil or grill about 4 minutes per side for medium rare.

VARIATION You can also roast a leg of lamb in the oven. For a boneless leg of lamb, rub the inside all over with half of the charmoula, then roll the meat and tie it with kitchen twine. Place in a large nonaluminum container and rub the remaining half of the charmoula over the outside of the lamb. Cover and refrigerate overnight.

Sear the lamb in 2 to 4 tablespoons oil in a hot ovenproof skillet until colored on all sides. Finish cooking in a 350-degree oven until an instant-read thermometer inserted into the thickest part reads 120 degrees for rare (45 minutes to 1 hour), 130 degrees for medium (about 10 minutes longer), or 140 degrees for well done (about 10 additional minutes).

· · · · ·

This is a variation on the Moroccan mechoui, *which is typically prepared with a whole lamb that is spit-roasted over a charcoal or wood fire. The traditional spice paste, called a* charmoula, *works equally well on leg of lamb, lamb kebabs, or lamb chops. Just marinate the meat in the refrigerator overnight and bring it to room temperature a few hours before cooking. Serve the lamb with couscous and some grilled vegetables, such as eggplant, zucchini, or peppers. —Joyce*

North African food has a real affinity for Syrah, especially wines of the spicy and meaty style. Lamb is more pungent than most other red meats, and Syrahs always show well with it. In this dish, the affinity is enhanced by the spices in the marinade, which share the flavors in the wine. The rustic character of this dish is a real winner, and if you grill the lamb you'll be rewarded by the charred, smokier traits that cooking over charcoal or wood introduces. Even if you only grill the exterior and then finish roasting the meat in the oven, grilling will do more than pan searing to bring out the complexity of the wine. —Evan

RECOMMENDED PRODUCERS
Smoky, Peppery, Meaty Syrahs

EVERYDAY	PREMIUM	SPLURGE
Boekenhoutskloof (Coastal Region, South Africa)	Domaine de Bonsérine (Rhône Valley, France)	E. Guigal (Rhône Valley, France)
Cave de Tain l'Hermitage (Rhône Valley, France)	Qupé (Southern Central Coast, California)	Jean-Luc Colombo (Rhône Valley, France)
Andrew Murray (Southern Central Coast, California)	P. Jaboulet (Rhône Valley, France)	Delas Frères (Rhône Valley, France)

FOR JAMMY, FRUIT-FORWARD SYRAHS (AUSTRALIAN-STYLE)

DUCK WITH SAUSAGE AND LENTILS

SERVES 4

DUCK

1 tablespoon minced garlic

1½ teaspoons toasted fennel seeds, ground

1 tablespoon rosemary, chopped

1 teaspoon salt

½ teaspoon freshly ground black pepper

1 5-pound duck, neck, feet, wings, and excess fat removed

2 sprigs fresh rosemary

LENTILS

2 cups green or brown lentils (preferably Italian or French)

4½ cups water

1 teaspoon salt

1½ pounds mild Italian sausage with fennel

2 tablespoons olive oil

2 onions, finely chopped

2 carrots, finely chopped

2 ribs celery, finely chopped

2 tablespoons chopped garlic

1 tablespoon finely chopped rosemary

1 tablespoon toasted fennel seeds, ground

1 cup dry red wine (such as Syrah)

1 cup beef, poultry, or duck stock

Salt and lots of freshly ground black pepper

Preheat the oven to 450 degrees. With a mortar and pestle, make a paste of the garlic, ground fennel seeds, chopped rosemary, salt, and pepper. Spread the paste over the duck, inside and out. Insert the rosemary sprigs inside the cavity. Prick the duck all over with the tines of a fork so that the fat can drain away. Place the duck on a rack set in a roasting pan. Roast the duck until cooked through and tender, about 1 hour. When the duck is cool enough to handle, cut into serving portions or remove all of the meat from the bones in largish pieces.

Meanwhile, prepare the lentils: In a heavy saucepan, combine the lentils and the water and bring to a boil. Reduce the heat to low, add the salt, cover the pan, and simmer until the lentils are tender but firm to the bite, 30 to 40 minutes for green lentils and 15 to 40 minutes for brown lentils, depending on their age. (Keep testing for doneness; mushy lentils are fine for soup, but not as a dish on their own.)

Prick the sausages in a few spots with a sharp knife. In a large sauté pan, warm the olive oil over high heat. Add the sausages and cook until browned, 5 to 7 minutes. Remove from the pan and set aside. Add the onions, carrots, and celery to the pan and sauté until softened, about 10 minutes. Add the garlic, rosemary, and ground fennel seeds, reduce the heat to low, and cook until the vegetables are tender, about 5 minutes longer.

Final assembly: In a large, heavy saucepan or stew pot, combine the duck, lentils, sausages, vegetables, wine, and stock and cook over medium heat until the pan juices have thickened, about 20 minutes. Season the sauce to taste with salt and a generous amount of black pepper. Serve hot.

VARIATION Try hot sausage instead of mild.

· · · · ·

The combination of rich duck, earthy lentils, and aromatic vegetables is a Mediterranean classic. The pungent seasonings here are Italian and are reminiscent of the seasonings for the classic porchetta, *or roast suckling pig. Garlic, bitter rosemary, and musky toasted fennel are the classic flavor trio, assertive enough to stand up to the richness of the duck and sausage. This is an ideal dish for entertaining because all of the parts can be cooked in advance and the dish easily assembled and simmered to completion. —Joyce*

As much as I enjoy lamb with Syrah, I may like duck even more. This substantial preparation is a perfect stage for generous and fleshy wines. The sausage and lentils bring out the basic rustic traits of the wine, while the sweetness of the meat calls out for a fruit-forward style. If you find that the Syrah has that minty edge found in some Aussie examples, by all means use green Puy-style lentils. Otherwise, I prefer the warm personality of brown lentils as well as their creamier texture, which shows well against the smoother, full body that is common in this style of Syrah. —Evan

RECOMMENDED PRODUCERS
Jammy, Fruit-Forward Syrahs

EVERYDAY	PREMIUM	SPLURGE
BV Coastal Estates (multiple appellations, California)	Penley (Coonawarra, South Australia)	Pax (Sonoma County, California)
Rosemount (multiple appellations, South Australia)	St. Hallett (Adelaide, South Australia)	Clarendon Hills (Barossa Valley, South Australia)
Jim Barry (Clare Valley, South Australia)	Io (Southern Central Coast, California)	Henschke (Eden Valley, South Australia)

PORK CHILI VERDE

SERVES 6

SPICE RUB
2 teaspoons oregano
1½ teaspoons ground coriander
1½ teaspoons ground cumin
¼ teaspoon cayenne pepper
¼ teaspoon ground cinnamon

3 pounds pork shoulder or butt, cut into 1½- to 2-inch cubes
4 tablespoons vegetable oil or lard, or more as needed
Salt and freshly ground black pepper
2 onions, chopped
4 cloves garlic, minced
1 7-ounce can whole or diced roasted green chiles
1 14-ounce can plum or fire-roasted tomatoes
2 10-ounce cans Mexican green tomatillos, drained
¼ cup chopped fresh coriander (cilantro) plus additional for garnish
1 cup meat or poultry stock
1 to 2 tablespoons red or white wine vinegar (optional)
Sour cream (optional)

In a small bowl, combine the oregano, coriander, cumin, cayenne, and cinnamon.

Place the pork in a large nonaluminum container and rub with the spice mixture. Cover and marinate overnight in the refrigerator or for 1 to 2 hours at room temperature.

Heat 2 tablespoons of the oil in a large sauté pan over high heat. Add the meat in batches, sprinkling with salt and pepper, and cook until brown, adding oil as needed, 8 to 10 minutes per batch. Set aside the browned meat.

In a stew pot or Dutch oven, heat 2 tablespoons oil over medium heat and add the onions. Sauté the onions until softened, about 10 minutes. Add the garlic and sauté for 2 minutes longer. Add the reserved pork to the onion mixture.

In a blender or food processor, puree the green chiles, tomatoes, tomatillos, and fresh coriander. Stir this puree and the meat stock into the pork and onions. Bring the mixture to a gentle boil, reduce the heat to low, and cover the pot. Simmer until the pork is tender, 1½ to 2 hours.

Add salt, pepper, and vinegar (if desired) to taste. Sprinkle with additional chopped coriander and a dollop of sour cream, if desired. Serve warm.

VARIATION Add pieces of parboiled chayote squash or sautéed strips of red or green peppers to the pork during the last 20 minutes of cooking. You can also prepare this stew with beef instead of pork.

. . . . .

This Mexican pork stew is complex in taste but a breeze to assemble. It is a balancing act of flavors: the sweetness of the pork tinged with a pinch of cinnamon; the tartness of tomatillos, tomatoes, and vinegar; the earthiness of coriander, cumin, and cilantro; and the mild heat of roasted chiles and a touch of cayenne. I like to use the fire-roasted tomatoes from Muir Glen, but you can use any brand of canned red tomato you like. Serve this with warm corn tortillas and/or rice. —Joyce

I've had a lot of experience in matching wines with chili verde, as it's a favorite with my kids. My original thinking was that the fuller-flavored wines would work best, but, to match the sharpness that comes with the tomatillos and tomatoes, it works better to choose a wine of slightly higher acidity. A wine that displays that common mint or eucalyptus character is particularly well suited to this dish, as the tomatillos and cilantro add a piquant green character. At my house, most of us add a healthy dollop of sour cream to the stew, which further reinforces the need for a wine that's full-bodied yet still maintains an acidic edge; sour cream can make some wines taste a little metallic. —Evan

RECOMMENDED PRODUCERS
Minty, Slightly Austere, Fruit-Forward Syrahs

EVERYDAY	PREMIUM	SPLURGE
Viña Doña Paula (Mendoza, Argentina)	d'Arenberg (McLaren Vale, Australia)	Cayuse (Walla Walla Valley, Washington)
Columbia Crest (Greater Columbia Valley, Washington)	Lincourt (Southern Central Coast, California)	L'École No. 41 (Greater Columbia Valley, Washington)
Brown Brothers (Victoria, Australia)	Viña Montes (Central Valley, Chile)	Alban (Southern Central Coast, California)

KOREAN SHORT RIBS

SERVES 4

3 pounds meaty English short ribs, each rib about 3 inches long
¼ cup sugar
¼ cup toasted sesame oil
½ cup soy sauce
2 green onions, minced
4 cloves garlic, minced
¼ cup sesame seeds, toasted and ground
2 tablespoons flour
1 teaspoon red pepper flakes
½ teaspoon ground ginger

Using a sharp knife, score the meat deeply every half inch, but do not detach the meat from the bones. Rub all over and into the cuts with the sugar and sesame oil. Place the meat in a large nonaluminum container. Let stand for 30 minutes at room temperature.

In a small bowl, combine the soy sauce, green onions, garlic, sesame seeds, flour, red pepper flakes, and ginger. Rub this mixture all over the ribs and into the cuts. Let stand at room temperature for 1 additional hour. (Or marinate the ribs for up to 4 hours in the refrigerator, but bring them to room temperature before grilling.)

Preheat the broiler or prepare a charcoal or gas grill. Broil or grill the ribs until tender, turning frequently, 4 to 5 minutes per side, or about 20 minutes in all.

VARIATION This marinade would also work well for skirt steak or flank steak.

Sweet, pungent, hot, and salty—everything you could want in a marinade for rich and meaty beef short ribs. These ribs are to be eaten with your fingers, so have lots of napkins on hand. The fastidious can cut the meat off the bones and eat it with a knife and fork. Serve with steamed rice and sautéed spinach topped with toasted sesame seeds. —Joyce

Never in a million years would I have thought this match out on a purely intellectual level. The dish is rich and the sweetness can echo the wine, but it didn't seem to cry out for Syrah. When I was doing some work in Seoul, this classic dish was served, and Syrah was the best choice available. Wow! I learned that though a younger Syrah can also work admirably, a more developed and mature wine adds intriguing flavor layers to the already complex mix of sesame, soy, sugar, and onion and the caramelized flavors of the sugar and meat developed by high-temperature cooking. Keep the red pepper in check, but don't be afraid: this match works well, though you may want to pass on the kimchi. —Evan

RECOMMENDED PRODUCERS
Aged, Developed Syrahs

EVERYDAY	PREMIUM	SPLURGE
Kirralaa (multiple appellations, South Australia)	Wolf Blass (multiple appellations, South Australia)	Jade Mountain (Napa Valley, California)
Jacob's Creek (multiple appellations, South Australia)	Eberle (Southern Central Coast, California)	Penfolds (multiple appellations, South Australia)
McDowell (Lake County, California)	Alain Graillot (Northern Rhône Valley, France)	Michel Chapoutier (Rhône Valley, France)

ZINFANDEL

I'm crazy about Zinfandel (*tzin*-fan-del), for several reasons. First, I am a proud flag waver for what is essentially America's own grape. Next, I am always captivated by the wine's approachable charm on top of its potency and rusticity. Finally, the explosive brambly qualities that fill the mouth with a cornucopia of raspberries, blackberries, dark cherries, and plums are absolutely delicious.

Given that Zinfandel is not as popular as Cabernet Sauvignon or Merlot, I've met an amazing number of wine drinkers over the years who claim that the first bottle of wine they ever tried was a Zinfandel. It's equally amazing to hear how many of them didn't know it was a red wine, as they are only familiar with the oft-maligned blush version that consumers know as white Zinfandel.

The grape has a history of moving in and out of fashion, which creates a quandary for producers, who need to decide whether to commit the time, energy, winery space, and financial resources required to make a good Zinfandel. The grape has had all sorts of historical ups and downs and is made in a dizzying array of styles and interpretations. This roller-coaster ride may be the reason why it's remained an object of veneration to some and completely puzzling to others.

WINE-GROWING AREAS

As with Syrah, Zinfandel's origins have been the subject of a lively wine discussion that now and again has turned argumentative. The question was finally put to rest when Carole Meredith, who also solved the Syrah puzzle, demonstrated beyond a shadow of a doubt that the Zinfandel grape can be traced back to a Croatian varietal called Crljenak, found on the Dalmatian coast. Studies have also shown conclusively that Zinfandel is genetically very similar to the Primitivo grape found in many parts of southern Italy, but it didn't originate there.

Notwithstanding its mysterious origins (wine experts are still unsure how the grape first arrived in America), most wine connoisseurs concur that no other part of the world produces Zinfandels of the caliber found in California. In fact, that belief, in concert with Zinfandel's being one of the first grapes to be planted in any quantity in the Golden State, has led many a wine drinker to assume that the varietal is California's own.

In California, Zinfandel has not only flourished but also established regional styles. Wines from the Napa Valley brim with the young, exuberant black and purple berry fruits that consumers love. In Sonoma's Dry Creek Valley, home of some of the state's oldest vines, Zinfandel is characterized by a deep jammy and briary fruit character and an underlying peppery and spicy perfume. Up in the Sierra Foothills, Zins have a distinct mineral quality, with an inky anise flavor and an almost iodine-like intensity that is enthralling. Those from the vineyards surrounding the Southern Central Coast's Paso Robles and the Northern Central Valley's Lodi subappellations have a warm and ripe dark-cherry personality and a pleasant herbal spiciness. California Zinfandel, regardless of origin, is not for the faint of heart: almost all these Zins are high in both tannins and alcohol. Although there are smatterings of Zin in Washington and undoubtedly parcels in other states, California drives the Zin engine in the United States.

But Zinfandel is not a solely American phenomenon. Primitivo is increasingly available from the south of Italy, either as a 100 percent varietal (as in the stunning Primitivo di Manduria) or blended with other local red grapes. These wines have the same implicit rustic character as their American counterparts, but with an underlying rusticity and flavor palate that screams, "I'm Italian!"

Regarding the rest of Europe, I haven't had the pleasure of tasting many Zinfandels from Slovenia, Croatia, or elsewhere in Central Europe, but I am told by connoisseurs whose mouths I respect that these wines are clearly of the same quality as the Italian Zins. With increased financial investment and continuing winemaking improvements, these bottles will be seen with greater frequency outside Central Europe.

I have tried examples from Western Australia and South Africa, and I believe that this grape has a very bright future in both countries. Finally I have been told of a few "suitcase clones" of Zinfandel in warmer parts of France!* Yes, Zinfandel in France.

A table of principal wine-growing regions for Zinfandel appears on page 285.

---

* *Suitcase clones* (or *Samsonite clones*) is winespeak for grapes propagated from cuttings smuggled into a country in a grower's suitcase. While it is illegal in most countries to import vines this way, and the risk of spreading disease and viruses is real, some wines made from these contraband selections have been delightful and complex, and they are extremely difficult for the agricultural quarantine officers to trace.

*Wood or no wood; age, size, and type of wood; use of barrel fermentation; vinification
or style (white, nouveau, claret, or monster); old or young vines; selections and clones;
ripe or overripe fruit; tannin management; 100 percent varietal or blend*

At this point in the book the fundamental winemaking choices for red wines should be very familiar. With Zinfandel, some winemakers have found that partial barrel fermenting results in attractive flavors and texture.

As with other red grapes, the amount of oak is important. Despite its forthright and powerful character, Zinfandel, like Syrah, can be buried under an abundance of oak.

With Zinfandel, the greatest frustration for most consumers is understanding the range of styles. It takes patience and practice to learn which winemaking approaches, bottlings, and producers you like best and which styles best accompany which foods.

As with Merlot, a Zinfandel label can be somewhat misleading. First off, there is white Zinfandel, one of America's most popular wines, which is rosé-style, blush in color, and off-dry in sweetness. Although these wines may cause a connoisseur's lip to curl, and they are typically produced for the mass market (with no premium or "splurge" interpretations available), they can be delightfully refreshing and are sometimes just right for the occasion and the meal. But they aren't anything like red Zinfandel. As with Merlot, too, there are three distinctive styles of red Zinfandel. First are wines that are grapey, jammy, and juicy, much like a Beaujolais Nouveau in personality, with softer tannins and moderate alcohol. Then you have "tweeners," the middle ground between the coarse, rustic charm of good old-fashioned Zin and a refined Cabernet Sauvignon or Merlot; these are often referred to as "claret-style," as they resemble Cabernet Sauvignon or Bordeaux. They are medium- to full-bodied with corresponding tannins. Finally, there are the classic Zinfandels, which are monster trucks in a bottle! These are huge wines, rustic and minimally processed, generous in alcohol, and bursting with peppery, ripe fruit. While they are not, in my opinion, complex per se, they provide great enjoyment: they are oozing with syrupy fruit and packed full of flavor. Again, play around to get to know the different styles of Zinfandel.

Older vines always make more concentrated and complex wines. This rule is more important for reds than whites, and indisputable for Zinfandel. So when reading labels in the store or perusing the wine list, look for references to older vines. Such wines generally come from California's Sonoma County (especially Dry Creek and Russian River), San Luis Obispo, Napa Valley, Amador County, Lodi, and the higher elevations around Mendocino (specifically the Mendocino Ridge subappellation). Note that as with the term *reserve,* there is no legal definition for old vines, but the term generally means that the fruit comes from vines that are at least thirty years old; many are fifty to seventy-five years old, and some even older.

Tannin management is essential with Zinfandel, as the grape can yield very bitter wines. And while ripe fruit and more generous levels of alcohol are hallmarks of a great Zinfandel, a wine can be too ripe (prune-flavored or port-like) and too alcoholic (unpleasant to drink and not food-friendly). Although I personally believe vine age, regions, and appellation are more important than clones and selections in determining the characteristics of a Zin, there are clear-cut differences between newer and older clones, often referred to as "mother clones."

While most Zinfandels are 100 percent pure, the grape can be blended with a small percentage of other grapes like Syrah, Petite Sirah, and even Cabernet Sauvignon to add complexity. And it's not unusual to add Zin judiciously to those varietals to add body, spice, and weight.

FLAVORS

Fruit and vegetable: Blackberry, raspberry, jam, red or black cherry, blueberry, plum, watermelon, bramble berry, fruitcake, summer pudding, compote, port, prune, raisin, pie fruit, rhubarb, bell pepper, olive

Floral: Green herbs, fennel seed, coriander, dill, lavender, black tea leaf, eucalyptus, mint

Earth: Damp earth, mineral, dust, humus

Wood (oak): Clove, nutmeg, allspice, chocolate, cocoa, coffee, mocha, char, smoke, toast, coconut

Other: Black pepper, soy

WINE AND FOOD PAIRING

INGREDIENTS AND STYLES

The style of Zinfandel is critical to matching it with food, and, depending on whether the selection of the wine or of the dish comes first, there are options galore. I'd recommend treating white Zinfandel as you would an off-dry white Riesling. The Zin has less acidity and more alcohol, so adjust seasonings accordingly to create the best possible matches. Enjoy white Zinfandel with ketchup-slathered burgers, aromatic curries, spicy Asian fare, and sweet barbecue sauce.

The nouveau (or Beaujolais) style of red Zin will also go fine with those burgers and barbecue, but also savor it with prosciutto, sausages, and other charcuterie. Moderate levels of aromatic heat can be tempered by a succulent nouveau style of Zin as well. In this case, chilling the Zinfandel to bring out the fruit flavors can be very enjoyable—especially in warm weather.

A more elegant, claret-style Zinfandel can be treated like a fruity Merlot or medium-weight Cabernet or Syrah. With the pedal-to-the-metal monster Zinfandels, opt for dishes like rich pastas, hearty pizza, grilled sausages, stick-to-the-ribs stews, and robust preparations of red meat or game. Chewy Zinfandel is not friendly with most fish or shellfish, although it can pair nicely with various styles of creamy and mature cheese—especially if you have a wine with ripe, concentrated fruit and an almost port-like sweetness.

Speaking of sweet, Zin's fruit-forward nature enables it to match up with less sugary, gooey chocolate desserts and those that stress nuts and coconut. A rich, port-like Zin and a plate of chocolate-covered almonds or coconut macaroons is heaven. Make certain, though, that any accompanying dessert is more bitter than sweet to really make the combination satisfying.

METHODS OF COOKING

Zin loves a grill. Zin loves barbecue. Zin loves slow-smoked dishes and rich braises. Low-impact techniques such as poaching and steaming don't work at all with Zinfandel unless you're serving the blush and off-dry type: steamed dim sum and white Zin can be great.

White Zin doesn't benefit from age—at all. Buy it and drink it. Aged red Zinfandel is very different from young red Zinfandel and, from a food standpoint, is best treated like a mature Cabernet or Merlot. I am not a great advocate of older Zins, but I have had several terrific examples, and they have matched to cuisines of all types. So, while many might argue that the charm of Zin is young fruit, I'd recommend cellaring a few bottles and making that decision on your own!

PAIRING POINTERS

Zinfandel goes well:

- With rich and robust recipes. But this is not an absolute rule. Gauge the body of the Zin and match the weight of the food to that of the wine. Since most Zins range between medium- and full-bodied, the dishes served should likely also be fuller.
- With strong-flavored foods. Zinfandel is a perfect choice for many Mexican dishes and is equally at home with many Indian, Pakistani, and North African preparations. Again, this rule is not an absolute: a hearty Zin might overwhelm the more delicate dishes from these cuisines.
- With barbecue. Yum. All styles. And when the barbecue style leans toward the sweet (as in Texas), a zippy, off-dry white Zin may be even better than the red stuff.
- With a range of cheeses. Cheeses with some sharpness (Cheddar, Teleme, aged Gouda) are great with the fruit-forward styles of Zinfandel, while creamy and blue-veined cheeses can pair nicely with Zins that have a port-like character and a hint of real sweetness.
- With game and roasted red meats. The more concentrated or densely flavored Zins, packed with fruit and rich textures, are great with venison, roast lamb, and grilled steak. Accompany the dish with a fruit-based sauce (cherries or berries) or a fruit-driven marinade (tamarind or pomegranate).
- With slightly spicy foods. This recommendation is very specific to juicy and young Zinfandels

that can handle being chilled and have vivid fruit and minimal tannins. Many Southwestern dishes and mildly hot Asian preparations are lovely with a lightly chilled red Zin, as are sandwiches, cold cuts, burgers, and most other picnic fare.

Zinfandel isn't good:

- With most fish. While a white Zin may succeed, as would a Riesling, with many seafood preparations, the red stuff just isn't as happy. The fuller-bodied the wine, the more difficult the match.
- With fiery hot food. This combination can actually be painful in the mouth, given the tannic and alcoholic content of most Zinfandels. If you must drink Zin with these dishes, the off-dry white versions can take the edge off moderate heat. But even white Zin is too hot (alcoholic) for almost any seriously spicy food.
- With most delicate food. It's simply not fair to the food to be overshadowed by such a bold personality.
- When it's too old. This is a matter of opinion, but, for most people, Zin has the most charm when it's flavor-packed, young, and explosive. An aged Zin will react very differently with food, more like an aged Merlot or Cabernet.

SEARED TUNA WITH ROSEMARY, GARLIC, AND HOT PEPPER

SERVES 4

4 6-ounce slices sashimi-grade tuna (preferably ahi), ¾ to 1 inch thick

Salt and freshly ground black pepper

¼ cup olive oil

1 cup dry red wine

1 cup fish stock

2 tablespoons chopped fresh rosemary

1 tablespoon finely minced garlic

1 tablespoon red pepper flakes, or more to taste

Sprinkle the fish fillets with salt and pepper.

In a heavy sauté pan, heat the olive oil over medium-high heat. Sear the tuna slices quickly until browned, turning once, 6 to 8 minutes total. Transfer to a plate and tent with foil to keep warm.

Add the wine, stock, rosemary, garlic, and 1 tablespoon red pepper flakes to the sauté pan and cook over high heat until the liquids are reduced by half, 5 to 8 minutes. Season to taste with salt, pepper, and additional red pepper flakes. Return the fish to the pan and simmer to coat with the sauce, about 1 minute. Serve immediately.

The rich, meaty quality of tuna stands up well to a powerful mixture of flavors: bitter rosemary and gar-lic, hot chiles, and tart wine. You can treat tuna as if it were steak, so for moistness and a buttery tex-ture, don't overcook: it's best to cook it rare to medium. The tuna pairs nicely with an assertive vegetable, such as broccoli, cauliflower, Brussels sprouts, Swiss chard, or eggplant, but potatoes are a safer bet for pairing with Zinfandel. —Joyce

Here's a fish dish that works with Zin, but you need a wine whose fruit is Hawaiian punch–like, with soft, easy tannins. This sauce, which is also lovely with chicken and a number of other dishes, works with the wine by bringing out the wine's fruit flavors through its inherent sweetness and jazzing things up with the hot pepper flakes. For me, the rosemary really makes this dish. You may want to place half of it in the sauce and half directly on the fish before serving for a bit more impact. Choose a Zinfandel rel-atively low in alcohol—about 12 percent—for a successful match, and chill the wine slightly for maxi-mum pleasure. —Evan

RECOMMENDED PRODUCERS
Easy-Drinking, Fruit-Forward Zinfandels

EVERYDAY	PREMIUM
A. Mano (Apulia, Italy)	Cline (Sonoma County, California)
Calatrasi (Apulia, Italy)	Dashe (Napa Valley, California)
Rancho Zabaco (Sonoma County, California)	Seghesio (Sonoma County, California)

PASTA WITH ARTICHOKES, PANCETTA, MUSHROOMS, AND PEAS

SERVES 4

1 lemon, halved

4 large artichokes

13 tablespoons olive oil

½ cup water, or more as needed

Salt and freshly ground black pepper

2 cups sliced mushrooms (any combination of button,
cremini, chanterelles, or fresh porcini)

⅔ pound pancetta sliced ¼ inch thick,
unrolled and cut crosswise into ¼-inch strips

2 cups sliced red onions

1 tablespoon very finely minced garlic

1 cup peas, blanched

2 teaspoons chopped fresh thyme (optional)

1 pound dried garganelli or fresh fettuccine

¼ cup freshly grated Parmesan cheese

¼ cup chopped fresh flat-leaf parsley

Fill a large bowl with cold water. Squeeze most of the juice from the lemon halves into the bowl, reserving a little juice for later. Remove the leaves of each artichoke until you reach the heart. (You can keep some of the tender green inside leaves if you like.) Pare away all of the dark green around the outside of the heart. Using a sharp spoon, remove the fuzzy choke. Cut the artichoke hearts into ¼-inch slices and drop them into the prepared acidulated water.

Heat 4 tablespoons of the olive oil in a sauté pan or skillet over medium heat. Drain the artichokes and add to the pan. Squeeze a little of the reserved lemon juice over the artichokes and drizzle them with ½ cup water. Cook, stirring occasionally and adding additional water as needed, until the artichokes are tender but not too soft, about 10 minutes. Season to taste with salt and pepper. (Artichokes can be prepared up to 8 hours in advance. Cover and refrigerate until ready to use.)

In a large, heavy sauté pan, heat 3 tablespoons oil over high heat. Add the mushrooms and sauté until just softened, about 3 minutes. Remove with a slotted spoon and set aside.

Add 2 tablespoons olive oil to the sauté pan and warm over medium heat. Add the pancetta and cook, stirring often, until cooked through and just starting to brown, 5 to 8 minutes. Using a slotted spoon, transfer the pancetta to the bowl with the mushrooms, leaving any fat in the pan.

Bring a large pot of salted water to a boil for the pasta.

Add 4 tablespoons olive oil to the pancetta drippings. Add the onions and cook over medium heat until tender, about 8 minutes. Add the artichokes, mushrooms, pancetta, garlic, peas, and thyme, if using. Cook until heated through. Season the vegetables to taste with salt and pepper.

Meanwhile, cook the pasta in the boiling water until tender if using fresh pasta or al dente if using dried. Drain the pasta and add to the vegetable mixture in the sauté pan. Toss well over low heat for a minute or two. Transfer to a serving bowl or to individual bowls. Sprinkle with Parmesan and parsley. Serve hot.

· · · · ·

I first ate this delicious pasta at a little Roman trattoria called Alfredo alla Chiesa Nuova. The restaurant faced the Chiesa Nuova and looked out onto a piazza with the most outrageous fountain, which resembled a giant soup tureen. When spring vegetables were just starting to come into season, they did a fabulous version of this classic pasta. Oh, those little sweet peas! If you can't wait for peas or can't find any really good ones, use asparagus. Or add both. Alas, a sad footnote: in the name of progress, this charming neighborhood restaurant has been demolished—for a bank. Fortunately, nothing can erase my memories or my passion for this recipe.

Garganelli are a quill-shaped dried egg pasta. They resemble penne rigate, but are more delicate in texture. —Joyce

Many wine drinkers are convinced that artichokes and wine never work. That's true if the artichoke is the focal point. Artichokes can distort white wines (making them taste sweet and flat) and red wines (twisting tannins and taking the middle palate out of the wine, making it taste thin). But when they are sautéed and treated as an added ingredient, they contribute nuttiness and complexity. This pasta recipe includes several Zin-friendly ingredients: mushrooms, noodles (which provide texture and match the wine weight), and pancetta. The combination is an appetizing tapestry of flavors that sets off the stylish, spicy interpretations of this varietal. —Evan

RECOMMENDED PRODUCERS

Rich, Elegant Zinfandels

EVERYDAY	PREMIUM	SPLURGE
Bogle (multiple appellations, California)	Renwood (Sierra Foothills, California)	Biale (Napa Valley, California)
Peachy Canyon (Southern Central Coast, California)	Alderbrook (Sonoma County, California)	Paraduxx (Napa Valley, California)
Ravenswood (multiple appellations, California)	Quivira (Sonoma County, California)	Ridge (Northern Central Coast, California)

BRAZILIAN FEIJOADA

SERVES 8

1 pound (about 2½ cups) dried black beans
4 tablespoons olive oil, bacon fat, or lard
2 large onions, chopped
2 green bell peppers, seeded and chopped
5 cloves garlic, minced
Salt and freshly ground black pepper
2 pounds pork shoulder, cut into 1½-inch cubes
1 pound chorizo (see note below)
1 to 1½ pounds linguiça or polish sausage
½ cup fresh orange juice
1 cup dry red wine
1 small jar dried beef, cut into ½-inch strips (optional)

Place the beans in a large pot. Add enough cold water to cover the beans by 4 inches. Soak the beans overnight. Drain.

In a Dutch oven, heat 2 tablespoons of the oil over medium heat. Add the onions and bell peppers and sauté until soft, about 8 minutes. Add the garlic and sauté for 2 minutes longer. Season the vegetables to taste with salt and pepper. Add the beans and water to cover by 1½ inches. Bring to a gentle boil, reduce the heat to low, and cover the pan. Simmer until the beans are tender but not mushy, 30 to 40 minutes. Drain any excess liquid. Puree 1 to 2 cups of beans (but not too much) and add the puree back to the beans in the Dutch oven. You don't want this to be soupy. Set aside.

Preheat the oven to 350 degrees.

In a large sauté pan, heat the remaining 2 tablespoons oil over high heat. Add the pork and sauté in batches until golden brown, about 8 minutes per batch. Using a slotted spoon, transfer the pork to the beans in the Dutch oven.

Add the chorizo and linguiça to the pork drippings in the sauté pan and sauté over high heat until the sausages are lightly colored, 5 to 7 minutes. Using a slotted spoon, transfer the sausages to a cutting board. Cut into large pieces and add to the bean mixture.

Deglaze the sauté pan with the orange juice and wine. Add the pan juices to the meat and beans along with the dried beef, if desired. Mix well. Cover and bake until the pork is tender, about 1 hour.

VARIATION The stew can be cooked on the stovetop instead of baked. Cover and simmer on low until the pork is tender, about 1 hour.

NOTE Brands of chorizo differ widely. Some are very soft and come packed in plastic wrap, some are soft and come enclosed in sausage casings, and some are firm. If the chorizo is soft, remove the casing, form a small piece into a little meatball, and sauté it until firm and lightly colored. If it browns well, continue making and sautéing meatballs with the remaining chorizo. If it doesn't firm up, and starts to scorch or stick, add the rest of the sausage meat directly to the bean mixture. It will break down completely and melt into the beans with no distinct shape. A firm sausage can be sautéed a bit and then sliced, as described in the recipe.

· · · · ·

In Brazil, feijoada is served on Saturday so everyone can take a nap or take it easy after such a filling meal. Serve this with orange slices, rice, and cooked greens, dressed lightly with a sauce made of lemon juice, chiles, and garlic. This dish is easy to assemble ahead and reheat at serving time. It's a party! —Joyce

The traditional beverages to accompany the Brazilian national dish are a crisp pilsner beer and some lethal cocktail that includes cachaça, Brazil's rum. To me, feijoada's bold, rib-sticking personality demands a red wine of ample body and character. The black beans, sausage, pork, and beef create a thick and rich stew, and a classic, chewy Zinfandel is one of the few wines that can hold its own while adding yet another layer of flavor complexity. If you can track down a big, jammy Zinfandel that's coarse and peppery, you'll be especially pleased, though any full-bodied bottle will suffice. —Evan

RECOMMENDED PRODUCERS
Classic, Ample, Powerful (Monster) Zinfandels

EVERYDAY	PREMIUM	SPLURGE
Cantina Due Palme (Apulia, Italy)	Rosenblum (multiple appellations, California)	Turley (Napa Valley, California)
Boeger (Sierra Foothills, California)	St. Francis (Sonoma County, California)	Martinelli (Sonoma County, California)
Lake Sonoma Winery (Sonoma County, California)	Edmeades (Mendocino County, California)	Carlisle (Sonoma County, California)

BARBECUED CHICKEN SANDWICHES

SERVES 6

BASIC BARBECUE SAUCE (MAKES ABOUT 2½ CUPS)
1 tablespoon dry mustard powder
3 tablespoons chili powder (such as Grandma's or Gebhardt's)
1 teaspoon ground ginger
½ cup apple cider vinegar
1½ cups canned tomato puree
2 tablespoons Worcestershire sauce
½ cup (packed) brown sugar
½ cup fresh orange juice, or ¼ cup fresh lemon juice (optional)
1 tablespoon freshly ground black pepper, or more to taste
Cayenne pepper or hot sauce to taste
Salt to taste

6 bone-in or boneless chicken breast halves
Sandwich rolls

For the sauce: In a small bowl, combine the mustard powder, chili powder, and ginger. Add some of the vinegar and whisk into a paste. When the mixture is smooth and lump-free, whisk in the rest of the vinegar. Pour the spice mixture into a medium saucepan. Whisk in the tomato puree, Worcestershire sauce, brown sugar, orange juice (if desired), and 1 tablespoon black pepper.

Bring the sauce to a boil over medium heat and simmer for 5 minutes. If it is too thick, add a bit of water. Season to taste with additional black pepper, cayenne pepper, and a little salt. Cover and refrigerate until ready to use. (The barbecue sauce can be refrigerated for up to 2 months.) Rewarm the sauce in a small saucepan over medium heat before continuing.

For the chicken: Preheat the broiler. Pour ½ cup sauce into a small bowl to use for basting. Reserve 1 cup sauce to serve alongside the finished sandwiches, and refrigerate the remaining sauce for another meal. Broil the chicken breasts, brushing occasionally with the basting sauce and turning once, until the juices are clear, about 5 minutes per side (3 minutes per side if boneless).

Transfer the chicken to a cutting board. If you used bone-in breasts, remove the meat from the bones and shred. Boneless chicken may be shredded or cut into ¼-inch slices. Dip the chicken in the reserved barbecue sauce and place on rolls. Serve the remaining warm sauce alongside.

VARIATION For barbecued pork sandwiches, use 1½ pounds of pork tenderloin, trimmed of silver skin. Season with salt and pepper and roast in a 350-degree oven, basting occasionally with ½ cup barbecue sauce, until an instant-read thermometer registers 140 degrees, about 30 minutes. Let stand 10 minutes before slicing. Or broil pork tenderloins, turning a few times, until an instant-read thermometer registers 140 degrees, about 10 minutes per side, basting with ¼ cup sauce during the last 5 minutes. Slice thin and dip the meat in extra sauce before placing it in the sandwiches.

. . . . .

These juicy, spicy sandwiches are casual fare. Supply lots of napkins and plenty of barbecue-friendly Zinfandel, white or a light-bodied red. The sweet, tangy, and spicy barbecue sauce can be made days ahead of time. Chicken is a great sandwich choice, but pork tenderloin works well, too. Provide buns that are substantial enough to absorb the sauce. Pass additional sauce for dipping. And don't forget the potato salad and coleslaw. —Joyce

This simple but tasty sandwich is a wonderful twist on barbecued chicken. Even if you'd never dream of serving white Zin, humor me on this one. What really makes this pairing ring true is the citrus juice, which, through its acidity, brings out the watermelon-like fruit of this fun pink wine. The match is sublime, with the sweet, spicy tastes of the wine and food mirroring each other, while the cool, crisp qualities of the wine refresh the palate. To enjoy the full package, serve these sandwiches warm and toast the bread for a moment right before serving. A great pairing for a picnic. —Evan

RECOMMENDED PRODUCERS
White Zinfandels

EVERYDAY
Baron Herzog (Sonoma County, California)
Beringer (multiple appellations, California)
Buehler (Napa Valley, California)

part four

A DESSERT WINE JOURNEY

DESSERT WINES

For years I've noted sadly that, with a few exceptions (mostly avid sommelier types and pastry chefs), people don't give dessert wines much thought. It's their loss. Admittedly, many diners are sated by the time they reach the end of the meal, but those who always pass on dessert wines are missing out on many of the wine world's greatest and most delectable offerings.

STYLES OF WINE AND WINE-GROWING AREAS

While styles of dessert wines differ by grape, from country to country, and regionally, virtually all wine-growing areas make and adore their sticky wines! Style makes for an easier breakdown than geography or varietal, so in this last wine journey I cut loose from the template.

Almost all the great dessert wines are products of accident. Nobody, at the time most of these wines were born, made a conscious effort to define or produce distinguished sweet wines. They just happened.

LATE-HARVEST WINES

The best-known category of stickies is late-harvest wines. As the descriptor implies, the grapes are picked late in the season. Wine producers of the past, farmers who simply grew grapes and made their own wine, did not have access to all the equipment, charts, and tools we utilize to-day to judge when to pick the grapes. As a result, some grapes were picked later than intended, and they were made into wines mostly so as not to waste the fruit. Late-harvested grapes—some of them left so long that they have begun to shrivel and turn to raisins on the vine—have higher levels of sugar. During fermentation, the yeast dies when the alcohol level in the wine reaches 18 to 19 percent. Simply stated, then, with very sweet grapes, fermentation stops before all the sugar has been consumed, and the residual sugar results in a sweet wine.

In the past, though initially delicious, many of these sweet wines would spoil rapidly or even re-ferment. Today, once a dessert wine is made, it is stabilized to enhance its keeping qualities:

this process most often involves filtration, to remove all remaining yeast, and the addition of very small amounts of sulfur to inhibit microbial activity. Consequently, today's dessert wines are clean, scrumptious, and often long-lived. Indeed, because sugar acts as a natural preservative, sweet wines have been known to age much longer than dry wines.

Some late-harvest grapes are simply allowed to dehydrate on the vine (or after harvesting), a process that concentrates their sugar and flavors. However, the desiccation doesn't always preserve the grape's internal flavor balance, which can be overpowered by pure sweetness. Raisins, the ultimate product of grape dehydration, have lost their acidity and are fundamentally just fruit sugar. Another accidental discovery in the vineyard can produce exceptional balance in late-harvest wines: *Botrytis cinerea,* also known as the "noble rot." *Botrytis* is a mold that can occur in vineyards when warm and wet weather patterns alternate while the grapes are ripening. *Botrytis* mold settles on the skins of the grapes and punctures small holes in them, allowing water to escape without affecting the fruit's flavors or inherent acidity.

As you can imagine, the original discoverers of *Botrytis,* said to be German small-business owners in the late eighteenth century, were initially not happy to encounter fields of moldy grapes. However, they weren't simply going to toss out their crop. Once again, thrift led to a happy discovery. Though prized, *Botrytis* does not occur on all late-harvested grapes, which is why it's frequently mentioned on the labels of affected wines. (It is occasionally induced, as in the grapes that go into Beringer's Nightingale dessert wine.) You'll always recognize *Botrytis,* even if the wine is not labeled as such, by its distinct honey character layered over other complex fruit nuances. Examples of classic botrytized wines include France's Sauternes, Germany's *Beerenauslese* and *Trockenbeerenauslese,* and Hungary's Tokaji Aszú.

Late-harvest wines are made in many parts of the world but are most commonly associated with Europe. In France, late-harvest wines go hand in hand with the effects of *Botrytis cinerea.* Bordeaux and the surrounding regions of southwestern France are the home of some great dessert wines, among them Sauternes, Barsac, Cérons, Ste. Croix-du-Mont, and Cadillac. Here the wines are made from a blend of white grapes (as is typical for late-harvest wines): lush and succulent Semillon, structured and complex Sauvignon Blanc, and exotic and pungent Muscadelle. This magic trio, which makes great dry wines, too, has been the model for other areas around the world, including Australia and California.

In France's Loire Valley, Chenin Blanc is harvested late in Anjou's Chaume and Quartes de Chaume, among other appellations. Chenin Blanc's innate, puckery acidity makes it a great candidate for dessert wines, which can be cloying if not balanced with tartness. Powerful aromas of candied apple, dried orange, and quince are accented by vanilla-scented oak, and the wines can age for decades.

To the north, in Alsace, late-harvest *(vendange tardive)* wines are made from Riesling, Pinot Gris, Gewürztraminer, and Muscat. Here most interpretations are less sweet, and they can be intriguing when paired with savory foods. The other style, known as *sélection des grains nobles,* can be very sweet, and good examples are sublime with both cheeses and desserts.

In Italy, the most exciting late-harvest wines are crafted from white grapes. Wines made from the best late-harvested clusters are often labeled as *recioto.* Other Italian terms for sweet wines include *passito* (the literal translation of "dried-grape wines"), *dolce* (Italian for sweet), *amabile* (a synonym for *dolce*), and *abboccato* (less sweet than *dolce*). Many of the finest Italian sweet wines are made in the north, especially the Veneto, home to both the unctuous and complex Recioto di Soave and Torcolato, the amazing honeyed wine of the vintner Fausto Maculan. The latter is another accidental success story: it is a wine blended of local Venetian grapes (the most noteworthy being Vespaiolo) patterned after the French Sauternes. Returning from a trip to France, Maculan found a vineyard still unpicked and applied the late-harvest techniques he had learned from the French.

More examples from northern Italy are made from the local Picolit grape in Friuli–Venezia Giulia and Moscato in Trentino–Alto Adige. Intriguingly, a *passito*-style red dessert wine, Recioto della Valpolicella, is also made in the Veneto and is marked by its powerful dark-raisin, licorice, and bitter-chocolate notes. Tuscany offers us Vin Santo, a *passito* wine made from raisined grapes that have been left to dry further on straw mats before being fermented and aged in barrels. Pungent with the flavors of candied orange, brown sugar, and golden raisins, these bottles offer a lovely change of pace. A trip farther south, to the islands off Sicily, is highlighted by the *passito* wines made locally of the Malvasia and Muscat grapes, which display flavors of sweet flowers, marmalade, and chamomile.

Moving northeast, Germany is, for many wine aficionados, the home of many of the finest of all dessert wines (and some of the most tongue-twisting names for them). *Auslese* simply refers to selected late-harvest wines. *Beerenauslese* refers to a grape-selected (literally, "berry-selected") late harvest (that is, wines for which the winemaker selects individual grapes or clusters); the name is often abbreviated as BA and usually designates wine from grapes infected with *Botrytis. Trockenbeerenauslese* (TBA) is a richer late-harvest wine, again infected with *Botrytis,* for which the grapes have been left on the vine to desiccate. These amazing wines, 100 percent varietal and most often made from Riesling, are nectar-like and explode with aromas and flavors of sweet apricot, ripe, juicy peach, and candied pear. In neighboring Austria, similar styles of wine are made and given similar names, with the addition of the local *Ausbruch,* which falls between a BA and a TBA in sweetness. Austrian dessert wines are generally similar in sweetness to their German counterparts.

A quick stop in Hungary brings us to Tokaji (pronounced tok-*eye*-ee), the celebrated wines of Tokaj-Hegyalja, made from local grapes (most notably Furmint). These are rated by the traditional measure of *puttonyos,* referring to a bucket *(puttony)* of sweet crushed-grape paste added to the wine, which determines its ultimate sugariness. The wines range from the sweet classification of three *puttonyos* through the super-sweet six *puttonyos*. Even sweeter than a six-*puttonyos* Tokaji Aszú is the extremely rare and expensive elixir Tokaji Eszencia.

In the New World, delectable late-harvest wines are made in Australia (especially good are those made from Semillon and Muscat), the United States (particularly in California and Washington), New Zealand, and South Africa.

EISWEIN

From the world of late-harvest wines comes one other special style: *Eiswein*, or ice wine. Again, it's a creation of pure happenstance: grapes left out on the vine during a late harvest in Germany succumbed to frost. The grapes were rushed back to the winery to crush immediately, whereupon it was found that the water (in the form of ice crystals) could be removed and the sticky-sweet essence of the grape allowed to ooze into a barrel (or, later, a tank). This liquid, when very slowly fermented, produced the amazing nectar *Eiswein*. This style of wine (which is often *Botrytis*-affected) is produced in the coolest of cool climates, including regions of Austria, Canada's Ontario province, upstate New York, and occasionally northern Michigan. It is a process that can be mimicked artificially by picking late-harvested grapes, placing them on trays, and then freezing and crushing them, though the resulting wines rarely measure up to the real McCoy.

FORTIFIED WINES

I always chuckle to think back to a snooty customer back in my restaurant days who insisted that fortified wines were higher in vitamins and minerals! That's for cornflakes: fortified wines are something different.

Fortified wines are so named because extra alcohol is added. The resulting wines are fuller-bodied and rich, running between 16 and 24 percent alcohol, as opposed to still wines, which generally top out at 14.5 or 15 percent. Fortified wines were also a product of accident: the English, always enthusiastic wine drinkers, decided, back in the eighteenth century when they weren't getting along so well with the French, to seek other suppliers. The Portuguese and Spanish were obvious choices, and so the British set about fostering diplomatic relations and trade.

The ballast on trading ships at the time was barrels of liquid. Red wine, made from local Douro grapes, was the liquid of choice, as it did double duty as cargo. In order to stabilize the wine for the long ride, distilled alcohol (think Everclear!) was added. During one hot harvest, this Douro Valley red did not complete fermentation because it contained high levels of sugar, which the yeast did not completely metabolize before the wine was shipped. It was barreled up, and—whoops!—port was created. The unexpected result was that the added alcohol effectively killed off any remaining live yeast, and the wine ended up with residual sugar as well as the kick from the additional alcohol.

Several hundred years and many improvements later (today, for example, the alcohol is added during fermentation when the wine reaches the desired level of sweetness), modern port is a very different wine, but that mishap was what opened the door. Port comes in two types: vintage and wood. Vintage ports, which also include a category called Single Quinta (referring to exceptional wines made from the crop from a single vineyard), are bottled and produced in particularly wonderful years, with dense, dark color and explosive flavors of black fruit and peppery spice. They improve over years of aging. Wood ports, which include ruby, tawny, vintage character, and late-bottled vintage, are blended across several years and cask-aged. They range from the easy-drinking ruby or vintage character, marked by red and black fruit aromas, easy tannins, and accessible fruit flavors, to the more complex ten-, twenty-, and thirty-year-old tawnies, which, after ample time in the cask, take on caramel, buttered-nut, and golden-raisin notes.

Spanish wines from Jerez (sherries) were also fortified and shipped in casks, but, as the wines were always fermented dry (that is, to the point of containing no residual sugar), no problems were encountered. But then someone decided to add "color wine" (*arrope*) and "sweet wine" to this already fortified elixir to make it suitable for drinking with dessert. Cream sherries, brown sherries, and sweeter *olorosos* belong in this category. Additionally, there are exotic and stunning Muscat dessert sherries that are worth seeking out.

Madeira came into existence by being "cooked" in its casks as ships went through the equatorial heat on their way to Asia and America—another accident that proved beneficial. Seek out the candied-citrus- and fruitcake-fragranced (Bual and Malmsey) bottlings.

Back in Italy we find several styles of fortified wines, led by Marsala. To most people, Marsala connotes the cheap stuff used to deglaze the pan to make a sauce for veal scalloppine, but the best Marsalas are sublime and range, like sherry or madeira, from dry (*secco*) to very sweet. You may find bottles labeled *vino licoroso*, which contain a sweet fortified style of wine.

A lighter style of fortified wine is VDN (*vin doux naturel* in French), in which neutral spirit or brandy is added to the grape must during the fermentation to retain sweetness while bringing the final wine up to a moderate 14 percent alcohol. As the name suggests, many great VDNs come from France, and they can be made from various grapes: Muscat (as in the Rhône's Beaumes de Venise, Roussillon's Muscat de Lunel, and Frontignan) and Grenache (as in Banyuls and Rasteau). In Spain, a VDN Muscat is made in Sitges, and in Portugal we find a great VDN Muscat from Setúbal. All are laced with flavors of raisin, candied tangerine, and exotic spice.

Finally, in Australia, we find amazing fortified wines, such as those from Rutherglen. These are usually Muscat-based and exude powerful aromas of butterscotch, golden raisins, and light mocha.

SPARKLING WINES

A fair amount of sweet sparkling wine is made. In most cases, the sweetness is determined by the *dosage*, a small amount of sugar added to wine or brandy just before corking it. The larger the *dosage*, the sweeter the wine. (See the sparkling wine journey for a grid showing degrees of sweetness and a table of wine-producing regions.) This approach is used with almost all sweet sparkling wines coming from France's Champagne as well as those from California and other areas of the globe that emulate the classic interpretations. These wines are labeled extra dry (which really means slightly sweet to sweet), demi-sec (decidedly sweet), or *doux* (ultrasweet and, I might add, quite rare). Occasionally you'll see the term *crémant* on a bottle of California sparkling wine, denoting a sweeter style of wine with slightly less fizz. (In France, the term has a different meaning: it simply refers to sparkling wines not made in Champagne.)

Sweet sparkling wines made from other grapes, such as Chenin Blanc (for instance, the Loire Valley's Vouvray Mousseux) or Muscat (Italy's Asti Spumante and the less fizzy Moscato di Asti), are made from wines which are sweet to begin with and to which bubbles are "added" by different methods. For the adventurous there is Brachetto d'Acqui, a red sparkler that's super with chocolate.

In Germany you will see bottles of *Sekt*, German bubbly, labeled as *halbtrocken* (half dry), which will be somewhere in the extra dry or demi-sec range of sweetness, depending on the producer.

And if you want something totally different, there are sparkling Shiraz wines made in Australia, which are usually off-dry and can be quite intriguing.

A table of principal wine-growing regions for dessert wines appears on pages 286–88.

VINTNER CHOICES

LATE-HARVEST WINES

Choice of fruit; desiccation of fruit; botrytized or not;
oak-aged or not; level of sweetness; frozen or not

In making late-harvest wine, the winemaker has a number of choices, depending on the style of wine to be made. First is the choice of fruit. Though most dessert wines are made from grapes, many great wines are made from other fruits. I've had stellar examples from berries, cherries, and even apples. Assuming, though, that we're dealing with grapes, different grapes lend themselves to different styles of wine. Next comes the question of whether the fruit will simply be harvested late, left out purposely to "raisin," or dry further (for Vin Santo or other *passito*-style wines), or be affected by *Botrytis*. Botrytization is almost always desired and adds a lushness of texture in addition to the signature honeyed flavor. Late-harvest wines have a dried-fruit character but still maintain an opulent level of fruit, whereas raisined fruit is always higher in alcohol (because of the level of sugar you begin with) and has a very desiccated quality. Of course, the presence of *Botrytis* and the level of sugar in the harvested fruit will often decide the type of wine made (a BA versus a TBA, for instance). Finally, if weather favors the production of one of those coveted *Eisweins,* the winemaker will want to take advantage of it.

PORT, SHERRY, MADEIRA, AND MARSALA

Vintage or wood; age of blend; degree of fortification; type, age, and size of wood

In making fortified wines, the winemaker encounters many forks in the road. With port and madeira, the quality of the fruit usually determines whether the wine will be vintage, in which case much of the aging will take place in the bottle. If not, it will spend more time in wood and be blended before bottling. The age of the blend will often determine the wine's character and how it is classified. Port, sherry, madeira, and Marsala are all blends. The older the base blend, the less overt the primary fruit flavor and the greater the influence of oak and dried-fruit and herbal flavors. Longer barrel aging softens the tannins in port, and leaches color from and adds texture to all wines. The degree of fortification will vary from producer to producer, but the higher the level of alcohol added, the longer it takes for the spirit to integrate into the wine so that it doesn't come across as hot in the mouth. If you have ever sampled a young fortified wine that tastes very alcoholic and burns your mouth, it has most likely been heavily fortified. The choice of wood is almost always oak, though, as with other wines, the age and size of the barrels are crucial. Most port is aged in larger and older oak (or chestnut) casks, except for vintage ports, for which some new oak is often used. For sherry, winemakers prefer older American oak barrels, often those previously used (and thus seasoned) by Scotch or bourbon distilleries.

VDN/OTHER

Degree of fortification; rancio *style (reds); oaked or unoaked*

Like other fortified wines, VDNs vary depending on the degree of fortification. Some, such as Beaumes de Venise, are made in a lightly fortified style, while others are simply late-harvest, nonfortified interpretations. Most VDNs are very lightly fortified so as to arrest fermentation without significantly boosting the alcohol level. Banyuls and some Muscats are allowed to become *rancio,* a process in which barrels are left outside, exposed to the elements. *Rancio* wines taste of nuts, dried fruit, and not-quite-rancid butter; they have aromas of oxidized, overripe, and desiccated fruit, those you might smell from fallen apples or pears decomposing in a field after harvest. The style of wine may or may not mandate wood aging. Oak is typically used for Banyuls and Pineau de Charentes, a VDN from Bordeaux, but not for Beaumes de Venise.

SPARKLING

Level of dosage *(extra dry, demi-sec, or doux); sweetness; amount of effervescence*

With sparkling wines, the level of *dosage* is critical, as the style classifications are based on total sugar content by volume. If you prefer your dessert bubbly sweeter, opt for a demi-sec; if you like a somewhat drier option, an extra dry will suffice. In bubblies made from a sweet still wine, such as Asti Spumante, the level of sweetness is determined by the final blend of the cuvée. Some dessert wines are made with less effervescence: these include *crémant* wines from the United States and Moscato d'Asti, which is less fizzy than Asti Spumante.

FLAVORS

LATE-HARVEST WINES

Fruit: Apricot, peach, nectarine, yellow apple, pear, fruit salad, sultana (golden raisin), kumquat, loquat, custard apple, quince, pineapple, mango, banana, marmalade, fig, citrus peel, prune, lychee, guava, candied citrus

Floral: Acacia, fresh herbs, verbena, saffron

Earth: Mineral, stone

Wood (oak): Toffee, caramel, flan, butterscotch, vanilla, cinnamon, cardamom, nutmeg, clove, chocolate, *rancio*

Other: Almond, nut, *Botrytis* (honey), marzipan, fruitcake, beeswax, lanolin

FORTIFIED WINES

Fruit and vegetable: Blackberry, black or red cherry, black currant, plum, prune, dark or golden raisin, fig (dried or fresh), citrus peel, tangerine, Mandarin orange, lychee, squash, rhubarb

Floral: Anise, herbal, mint, menthol, violets, lavender, straw, rose petal

Earth: Dust, truffle

Wood (oak): Chocolate, coffee, mocha, burnt sugar, molasses, maple syrup, coconut, vanilla, cinnamon, clove, nutmeg, pie spice

Other: Nougat, marzipan, walnut, pecan, malt, *rancio,* honey

SPARKLING WINES

Fruit: Apple, pear, lemon, lime, grapefruit, melon (green- or orange-fleshed), strawberry, passion fruit, pineapple, lychee, apricot, guava, fruit salad, peach, quince, raisin, marmalade, lemon curd, watermelon

Floral: Grass, lavender, citrus blossom, honeysuckle, gardenia, freesia, straw

Earth: Mineral, chalk, dust, flint

Wood (oak): n/a (in most cases)

Other: Honey, lanolin, yeast, dough, nut, butter, toffee, brioche, perfume, custard

When you're serving wine with a dessert, the wine's sweetness must be equal to or greater than that of the dessert, or the wine will taste very sour and unappealing. This is the one hard-and-fast rule in this otherwise relaxed exploration of wine and food. If you follow it, you'll be happier and your matches will always be fundamentally sound.

INGREDIENTS AND STYLES

When pairing desserts with late-harvest wines, it's best to play off the implied fruit character in the wine. Desserts incorporating stone fruits (such as peaches, nectarines, and apricots), tree fruits (apples and pears), and sweeter citrus (orange and tangerine) are safe bets. The sweeter the fruit, the more playful you can be (keeping in mind the above rule, of course). Tarts, pies, and other desserts celebrating fruit are great platforms for late-harvest wines. If your wine is less sweet, you can opt for tart citrus (lemon and lime) or sharp tropical fruit such as passion fruit, star fruit, or less-ripe pineapple. Preparing sweeter desserts based on those tart fruit flavors would, of course, work well for sweeter examples of dessert wines, too.

If the wine has oak flavors, recipes that pick up on those vanilla, caramel, or sweet spice flavors are good—dishes featuring butterscotch, caramel, toffee, or crème brûlée. Custard, pastry cream, and crème anglaise nicely complement a wine's round texture. Reconstituted dried fruit is always welcome alongside late-harvest wines that have intrinsic desiccated-fruit characteristics, and any use of honey in a dish will pick up on the presence of *Botrytis* in a wine and echo its sexy flavor nuances.

If you are a chocoholic, late-harvest Muscat wines (especially those based on black and orange Muscat) and wines made from other fruits (such as cherry and berry) can be marvelous with chocolate. However, late-harvest wines are generally not ideal partners with chocolate: don't serve a chocolate torte to show off a great Sauternes or a German TBA. The same is true of sweet sparkling wines (except for the Italian Brachetto d'Acqui and a few examples of sparkling Shiraz), as I can attest from many winemakers' dinners at the hands of chefs who insist on pairing sparkling wine with chocolate. However, white chocolate isn't really chocolate; maybe that's why it can pair well with sweet sparkling wines.

Chocolate, mocha, and similar flavors are best with fortified wines, especially port and the French Grenache-based Banyuls. These wines echo the dessert's bittersweet nature, and the black-fruit character of the wines contributes complexity to the match. Incorporating fruit into a chocolate dessert is a great trick for showcasing dessert wines. A filling of berry jam between layers of a chocolate cake or a cherry sauce drizzled over a chocolate pot de crème can be sublime. Nonfortified wines that can be lovely with chocolate (especially when accompanied by dark stone fruit) include the Italian Brachetto d'Acqui, a sweet red sparkling wine, and Recioto della Valpolicella, a *passito*-style red.

Cream or brown sherries, tawny ports, and Bual and Malmsey madeiras are delectable with nuts, caramel, coffee, and some chocolate-based sweets. These wines are also delicious with traditional holiday fare: pumpkin, mincemeat, and pecan pies, and the assortments of candies and cookies that generally accompany them.

Summer's bounty of fruit is at its best when prepared simply. Placed on a shortcake or phyllo base, succulent berries, apricots, or peaches don't require much to highlight their flavor. Such desserts are the perfect stage for sweet sparkling wines. Indeed, these fizzy wines frame fruit well and shouldn't be squashed by desserts that are too heavy. A light custard is OK; a rich buttercream is not.

PAIRING POINTERS

With the vast range of styles in dessert wines, it's difficult to take cooking methods into consideration. Because most desserts are really distinguished more by their combinations of ingredients and textures than by the manner in which they are prepared, I have grouped them by main ingredients and made recommendations on that basis.

CITRUS AND TROPICAL FRUIT DESSERTS

These desserts go well with sweet sparkling wines and late-harvest wines.

- Candied fruit and dried citrus show off botrytized wines well.
- A touch of vanilla helps these fruits pair well with wood-aged wines and *passito*-style wines, as does any subtle use of caramel, caramelized sugar, or sweet spice (such as cinnamon or nutmeg).
- These desserts don't pair well with fortified wines, with the exception of madeiras, which possess an inherent lemony character.

BERRY DESSERTS

These desserts go well with sweet sparkling wines and some late-harvest and fortified wines.

- Berries served alone or as the focal point of the dessert are best with sparkling wines, less dramatic late-harvest styles (including Black Muscat), and wines made from cherries or berries.
- When berries are used as an accent, pairings can be more flexible. For example, berries served in a tuile with custard are fine for a late-harvest wine; with zabaglione or a mousse, they can accompany a botrytized wine; served with a chocolate dessert or as a sauce (coulis), they pair well with port.
- Berries alone are not at their best with most fortified wines, though they can be fun with some of the Muscat-based examples.

TREE- AND STONE-FRUIT DESSERTS

These desserts go well with late-harvest wines, botrytized wines, and some fortified wines and sweet sparkling wines.

- Apples and pears match well with late-harvest Semillons, Chenin Blancs, and blends based on Semillon and Sauvignon Blanc. If the wine is botrytized, the dessert can include honey, vanilla, and more texture (such as custard or pastry cream).
- Peaches, apricots, and nectarines set off Riesling, Muscat, and Semillon and Sauvignon blends well. Again, if *Botrytis* is a factor, the dessert can include honey, vanilla, and more texture.
- Simple preparations of tree or stone fruit (such as poached fruit), served with or without a light sauce, are delightful with sweet sparkling wines.
- Recipes based on reconstituted dried fruit (think dried apricots poached in wine or a compote of dried apricots, pears, and prunes) pair well with fortified wines such as sherry, madeira, and tawny port. If the dish is a simple compote, a sweet sparkler is a nice choice, too.
- If these fruits are used as an accent alongside or in chocolate, you can play around with a variety of wines, but if the chocolate is what drives the dessert, stick to fortified wines.

CREAMY AND CUSTARD DESSERTS

These dishes go well with almost every style of dessert wine, including Eiswein.

- Custards are a neutral canvas, and your wine selection will be driven by what, if anything, accompanies them. Vanilla and sweet spices pair well with oak-aged wines. Caramel or a caramelized crust (as in crème brûlée) can mirror the flavors of aged wines. A chocolate custard is great for port, while an orange custard is a super stage for a late-harvested wine. (For desserts including fruit, refer to the pairing suggestions for fruit-based desserts.)
- The rich texture of a custard or mousse can handle richer wines, including wood-aged examples, and fortified styles.
- A lighter mousse or yogurt-based dessert can pair well with sweet sparklers, especially if the dessert includes fresh fruit.

NUT AND DRIED-FRUIT DESSERTS

*These dishes go well with fortified wines (especially tawny ports and cream sherries) and some late-harvest wines (*passito *styles and nonbotrytized late-harvest examples).*

- Nut-based desserts are great for showing off older oak-aged wines (including Vin Santo and Tokaji) and those that are nutty in their flavor profile (tawny ports and cream and brown sherries) or more desiccated (nonbotrytized late-harvest wines).
- Dried fall fruits (apples, pears, and prunes), especially in desserts incorporating honey, are wonderful with botrytized wines. A dollop of crème fraîche allows you to serve slightly richer styles.
- Dried summer fruits (apricots, peaches, and nectarines) are great with Rieslings and sublime with Muscats, especially rich examples (Australian Muscat ports are a favorite of mine).

CHOCOLATE, COFFEE, AND CARAMEL DESSERTS

These desserts go well with port and other "dark" dessert wines (port and port styles, Banyuls).

- Coffee and caramel together work well with virtually all fortified wines, as does chocolate with nuts and caramel.
- More oxidated styles of fortified wines (those aged in wood for an extended period, such as sherries and tawny ports) are particularly good with caramel, toffee, butterscotch, and nougat.
- Coffee and chocolate (or mocha) can pair with berry- or cherry-based wines and orange- or citrus-scented VDN wines (especially Muscat) if there's a strong fruit accent to the dessert. Think marmalade in a torte, a berry sauce served alongside a cake, or brandied cherries accompanying chocolate pots de crème.
- Fruit-forward wines (such as Riesling and Sauternes) have a very hard time with chocolate. Incorporating some fruit with the chocolate can help, but it's still tough on the wine and usually flattens it.
- Avoid *Eisweins,* young late-harvest wines, and sparkling wines (except Brachetto d'Acqui and sparkling Shiraz).

HAZELNUT TORTE WITH COFFEE BUTTERCREAM

SERVES 12

1 to 2 tablespoons butter, as needed

2 cups hazelnuts

1¼ cups sugar

8 egg whites

Pinch of salt

12 egg yolks

1 teaspoon vanilla extract

¼ cup all-purpose flour

Coffee Buttercream (see recipes below)

12 whole hazelnuts (optional)

Preheat the oven to 350 degrees. Butter two 9-inch round cake pans. Line with baker's parchment and butter the parchment.

Spread 2 cups hazelnuts on a baking sheet and toast until they are fragrant and have deepened in color, 10 to 15 minutes. Transfer the warm nuts to a rough-textured kitchen towel and rub them briskly between your towel-lined palms to loosen and remove the skins. (Do not worry if a little skin remains.) Place the nuts in a food processor. Add ¼ cup sugar and grind finely. Set aside.

Using an electric mixer, beat the egg whites with salt until soft peaks form. Gradually beat in the remaining 1 cup sugar, 1 tablespoon at a time, until the egg whites are stiff and glossy.

In a separate bowl, beat the egg yolks until foamy and light. Beat in the vanilla and then stir in ¼ of the beaten whites. Sprinkle the egg yolks with the nut mixture and flour, and fold in. Fold in the remaining beaten egg whites.

Pour the batter into the prepared pans. Bake until the cakes are springy to the touch, 30 to 40 minutes. Cool 10 minutes and then turn the cakes out onto racks. Peel off the parchment. Cool completely.

To assemble: Place 1 layer on a cake plate. Spread the top with about ¾ cup buttercream. Top with the second layer and then cover the top and sides with the remaining buttercream. Decorate with the whole hazelnuts, if desired. Refrigerate until serving.

COFFEE BUTTERCREAM WITH EGG WHITES

1 cup sugar
½ cup water
1 tablespoon corn syrup
6 egg whites
¾ pound (3 sticks) unsalted butter, room temperature, cut into small pieces
4 tablespoons very strong coffee,
or 2 or 3 tablespoons instant espresso dissolved in 2 tablespoons hot water

In a small saucepan, combine the sugar, ½ cup water, and corn syrup. Place over high heat and stir until the sugar is dissolved. Bring to a boil without stirring, brushing any sugar crystals down with a wet pastry brush. Cook to the soft ball stage (238 degrees on a candy thermometer). Immediately pour the syrup into a glass measuring cup (do not scrape the saucepan).

In the bowl of an electric mixer, using the whisk attachment, beat the egg whites until the mixture is foamy. Turn the mixer off, and slowly add about ⅓ of the hot sugar syrup. (Do not allow the syrup to spin on the sides of the bowl.) Beat briefly on low speed, just until incorporated. Add another ⅓ of the syrup. Beat again briefly, just until incorporated, then stop and add the remaining syrup. Turn the mixer on high speed and beat until the whites are satiny, hold stiff peaks, and have cooled completely. Slowly add the butter, 1 piece at a time. Keep beating until smooth. Then beat in the coffee. If the buttercream breaks, chill for 15 minutes and then re-beat. Chill until thick enough to spread.

COFFEE BUTTERCREAM WITH EGG YOLKS

1 cup sugar
⅓ cup water
¼ teaspoon cream of tartar
5 egg yolks
¾ pound (3 sticks) unsalted butter, room temperature, cut into small pieces
4 tablespoons very strong coffee,
or 2 or 3 tablespoons instant espresso dissolved in 2 tablespoons hot water

Combine the sugar, water, and cream of tartar in a small saucepan and bring to a boil. Boil until the mixture spins a thread and registers 236 to 238 degrees on a candy thermometer. Immediately pour into a glass measuring cup (do not scrape the saucepan).

Using an electric mixer with a whisk attachment, beat the yolks until fluffy. Turn the mixer off, and slowly add ⅓ of the hot sugar syrup. (Do not allow the syrup to spin on the sides of the bowl.) Beat briefly on low speed, just until incorporated. Add another $\frac{1}{3}$ of the syrup. Beat briefly, just until incorporated, then stop and add the remaining syrup. Turn the mixer on high speed and beat until the yolks are thick and pale. Continue beating until the yolks are cool and thick. Gradually beat in the butter 1 piece at a time. Then beat in the coffee. Chill until thick enough to spread.

· · · · ·

This hazelnut torte with coffee buttercream is rich but, surprisingly, not heavy. I have given two methods for making buttercream, one based on egg whites, the other on egg yolks. The nut and coffee flavors harmonize well with an aged, fortified dessert wine. —Joyce

Nuttiness is the foundation of the oxidated flavor profile, so nuts are a natural for a dessert to complement these wines. The richness of the torte pairs especially well with a fortified, oxidized wine. Even if you're intimidated by baking, as I am, take your time and give this one a try: it's well worth the effort and really shows off the wine. The coffee buttercream adds a delicious accent and, again, echoes the flavor profile of many aged fortified wines, including most sherries and tawny ports. Hazelnuts, in general, are the most flexible of nuts, followed by almonds and walnuts. —Evan

RECOMMENDED PRODUCERS
Sherries and Sherry-Like Dessert Wines

EVERYDAY	PREMIUM	SPLURGE
Harvey's (Jerez, Spain)	Lustau (Jerez, Spain)	Domecq (Jerez, Spain)
Ramos Pinto (Porto, Portugal)	Niepoort (Porto, Portugal)	Cockburn's (Porto, Portugal)
Benjamin (Victoria, Australia)	Sandeman (Porto, Portugal)	Blandy's (Madeira, Portugal)

CITRUS MARMALADE TART

SERVES 8

PASTRY FOR CRUST AND LATTICE
2½ cups all-purpose flour
6 tablespoons sugar
Pinch of salt
12 tablespoons (1½ sticks) chilled unsalted butter, diced
5 tablespoons ice water, or as needed

MARMALADE
3 to 4 large navel oranges, or 6 blood oranges,
or 4 blood oranges and 4 Meyer lemons
½ cup sugar
Juice of 1 lemon
½ cup water

FILLING
1 cup sugar
3 tablespoons cornstarch
4 tablespoons (½ stick) unsalted butter, room temperature
3 eggs
3 tablespoons Grand Marnier or other orange liqueur

TOPPING
1 cup whipping cream
2 tablespoons sugar
2 tablespoons Grand Marnier or other orange liqueur

For the pastry: Blend the flour, sugar, and salt in a food processor to combine. Add the butter and pulse until the mixture resembles cornmeal. Gradually mix in the ice water by tablespoon-fuls until the dough comes together. Turn the dough out onto a floured work surface and form into two flattened discs, one slightly larger than the other. Wrap in plastic and chill for at least 1 hour. (The dough can be made up to 2 days ahead of time. Keep refrigerated.)

For the marmalade: Wash and dry the oranges. With a sharp peeler, carefully remove all of the zest from all of the fruit and finely chop enough zest to measure about 1 cup. Cut away any white pith from the fruit. Separate the fruit into segments and peel off the outer membrane from enough segments to measure 3 cups of citrus pulp. In a medium saucepan, combine the pulp, chopped zest, sugar, lemon juice, and water. Bring to a boil and simmer until thick, stirring occasionally, about 20 minutes. Let the mixture cool to room temperature. (The marmalade can be made 1 day ahead of time and left at room temperature.)

Roll out the larger dough disc between 2 sheets of very lightly floured baker's parchment to form a 13-inch-diameter circle. Remove the top piece of parchment and carefully ease the crust into a 9-inch pie plate or 10-inch tart pan with a removable bottom. Chill the crust while making the filling.

Preheat the oven to 450 degrees.

For the filling: In a large bowl, whisk the sugar with the cornstarch. Using an electric mixer, beat in the softened butter until smooth and fluffy. Beat in the eggs, 1 at a time. Fold in the cooled marmalade and 3 tablespoons Grand Marnier.

Roll out the remaining pastry between lightly floured sheets of baker's parchment into a 12 × 9–inch rectangle. Remove the top piece of parchment and use a pastry wheel to cut the dough lengthwise into 1-inch-wide strips. Pour the filling into the chilled crust. Moisten the edge of the crust with a bit of water and then arrange the strips in a lattice pattern on top of the filling. Cut off any overhanging strips. Pinch to seal.

Bake the tart 10 minutes, then reduce the oven temperature to 350 degrees and continue baking the tart until the filling is set and the crust is slightly colored, about 25 minutes longer.

For the topping: Just before serving, prepare the whipped cream. Using an electric mixer, beat the cream to soft peaks. Add the 2 tablespoons sugar and 2 tablespoons Grand Marnier and beat until thick.

Serve the tart warm or at room temperature accompanied by the Grand Marnier–flavored whipped cream.

· · · · ·

Jam-filled lattice-topped tarts are popular all over Italy. This recipe takes homemade orange marmalade and binds it with eggs and cornstarch. Blood oranges add a special perfume and color to the tart. I love a combination of the bittersweet blood orange and sweet-tart Meyer lemon, but if you cannot find these winter citrus fruits, use regular navel oranges. —Joyce

Yum. That's really all I need to say here. The marmalade picks up on the candied- and dried-fruit character of the wine, while the lemon or orange base really frames the wine's core flavors. However, it's actually the tempering of the fruit and wine with the scrumptious and flaky crust that makes this pairing work. And do absolutely serve it with the Grand Marnier–flavored whipped cream for added texture and resonance of flavor. —Evan

RECOMMENDED PRODUCERS
Raisin-Accented, Concentrated Dessert Wines

EVERYDAY	PREMIUM	SPLURGE
Campbells (Victoria, Australia)	Maculan (Veneto, Italy)	Alois Kracher (Burgenland, Austria)
Oremus (Tokaj-Hegyalja, Hungary)	J. M. Fonseca (Setúbal, Portugal)	Disznókő (Tokaj-Hegyalja, Hungary)
Yalumba (multiple appellations, South Australia)	Isole e Olena (Tuscany, Italy)	Klein Constantia (Coastal Region, South Africa)

LEMONY RICOTTA SOUFFLÉ CAKE
WITH RASPBERRY SAUCE

SERVES 6 TO 8

2 tablespoons unsalted butter, room temperature

½ cup fine dry breadcrumbs, or as needed

½ cup sugar

5 eggs, separated

1 pound (2 cups) fresh ricotta cheese

2 tablespoons all-purpose flour

2 tablespoons whipping cream or sour cream

1 teaspoon vanilla extract

Grated zest of 2 lemons

¼ cup toasted pine nuts (optional)

Raspberry Sauce (see recipe below)

Preheat the oven to 325 degrees. Butter the bottom and sides of a 9-inch springform pan. Sprinkle with breadcrumbs and tap out the excess.

Using an electric mixer, beat together the sugar and egg yolks until very thick and pale. On low speed, beat in the ricotta, flour, cream, vanilla, and lemon zest. Mix gently until well combined. Stir in the pine nuts, if desired.

Using an electric mixer with a clean bowl, beat the egg whites until stiff peaks form. Stir ¼ of the beaten egg whites into the cheese mixture to lighten it, and then fold in the remaining whites just until no white streaks remain. Spoon the mixture into the prepared pan. (Leave an inch of space at the top, as the pudding will rise.) Bake until set but still a little wiggly, about 50 minutes. Let cool in the oven with the door ajar for about 1 hour (to prevent too much cracking or sinking), or remove from the oven and cool on a rack.

To serve, run a knife along the sides of the cake to loosen it from the pan, and then remove the sides of the springform pan. Cut the cake into wedges and serve with raspberry sauce.

RASPBERRY SAUCE

1 12-ounce package frozen whole raspberries (not in syrup), thawed
Framboise to taste (optional)

In a blender or food processor, puree the raspberries. Using a fine mesh strainer, strain the raspberry puree over a bowl to remove the seeds. Whisk in Framboise to taste, if desired. (Can be prepared up to 2 days ahead of time. Cover and refrigerate until ready to use.)

· · · · ·

Not all cheesecakes have a pastry or graham cracker crust. Some—like this one—have a simple coating of toasted breadcrumbs. In other words, they are more like a baked cheese pudding. While fresh sheep's milk ricotta is ideal for this dessert, cow's milk ricotta works well, too. Toasted pine nuts may be added to the basic cheesecake mixture just before you fold in the egg whites. —Joyce

When you are serving a sweet bubbly, it is very important not to overwhelm it. Even when amplified by the sugar, the core flavors are very delicate. This cheesecake is both subtle and flavorful and has just the proper balance of texture and implicit sweetness to highlight the wine without dominating it. Most bubblies, if based on Pinot Noir, have a core of sweet citrus, ripe tree fruit (apples and pears), and nuances of red fruit. The lemon in this dessert frames the wine's flavors, while the raspberry sauce makes a delicious match. Berry and citrus combinations are great with virtually all off-dry to sweet sparkling wines. —Evan

RECOMMENDED PRODUCERS
Sparkling Dessert Wines

EVERYDAY	PREMIUM	SPLURGE
Cinzano (Piedmont, Italy)	G. H. Mumm (Champagne, France)	Domaine Huët (Loire Valley, France)
Mumm Napa (Napa Valley, California)	La Spinetta (Piedmont, Italy)	Veuve Clicquot (Champagne, France)
Domaine Chandon (Napa Valley, California)	Schramsberg (Napa Valley, California)	Piper-Heidsieck (Champagne, France)

CARAMEL-COATED CREAM PUFFS

MAKES ABOUT 18 SMALL OR 12 MEDIUM PUFFS

CREAM PUFF DOUGH
½ cup water
½ cup milk
7 tablespoons unsalted butter, cut into pieces
¼ teaspoon salt
1 cup flour
1 tablespoon sugar
5 large eggs
½ cup chopped toasted almonds

PASTRY CREAM
2 cups milk
3 eggs
⅔ cup sugar
⅔ cup sifted flour
2 teaspoons vanilla extract

SIMPLE CARAMEL
2 cups sugar
½ cup orange juice
¼ cup water

Preheat the oven to 400 degrees. Line 2 baking sheets with baker's parchment.

For the cream puff dough: In a medium saucepan, combine the water, milk, butter, and salt and bring to a boil over high heat. Add the flour and sugar all at once. Stir until the mixture is dry and pulls away from the sides of the pan. Transfer the warm dough to the bowl of an electric mixer. Beat in the eggs, 1 at a time, until each is incorporated. (The mixture should be smooth and glossy after each addition.) Drop by tablespoonfuls or use a pastry bag to pipe 1-inch mounds onto the prepared baking sheets. Sprinkle with toasted almonds. Bake 15 minutes, then lower the temperature to 350 degrees and bake until golden, about 10 minutes longer. Turn off the oven, leave the door ajar, and let the puffs stay in the oven to cool and dry.

For the pastry cream: In a saucepan, scald the milk. In a large bowl, beat the eggs with the sugar until lemon-colored and thick. Sprinkle the sifted flour over the mixture and whisk well. Gradually add the hot milk, whisking constantly. Return the custard to the saucepan and use a wooden spoon to stir constantly over medium heat until it comes to a boil and thickens, about 5 minutes. Remove from the heat and stir in the vanilla. Transfer to a bowl and set in an ice-water bath to cool.

Cut a small hole in each puff and pipe in the pastry cream using a pastry bag or plastic ziplock storage bag with the end snipped off. (If you're using the Creamy Caramel Sauce, below, you may simply cut the puffs in half and fill with the pastry cream.)

For the caramel: In a small, heavy saucepan over medium-high heat, combine the sugar, orange juice, and water. Stir until the sugar is dissolved. Bring to a simmer and cook, swirling the pan occasionally and brushing down the sides of the pan with a wet pastry brush, until the sugar is caramelized and golden brown (not dark brown). Immediately remove from the heat.

With tongs, carefully dip the top of each puff in the hot caramel. Cool the puffs on a rack until the caramel is cool and crisp, about 10 minutes. Serve immediately or refrigerate until serving time. The caramel will stay crisp for up to 6 hours.

CREAMY CARAMEL SAUCE

1 cup whipping cream
2 cups sugar
Juice of ½ orange
8 tablespoons (1 stick) unsalted butter
2 tablespoons Grand Marnier (optional)

In a small saucepan, heat the cream to barely simmering and keep warm.

Place the sugar and orange juice in a small, heavy saucepan and stir until the sugar is moistened. Cook over high heat, swirling the pan occasionally and brushing down the sides of the pan with a wet pastry brush, until the sugar caramelizes to a golden (not dark) brown. Gradually pour in the hot cream, stirring constantly. (The mixture will bubble up vigorously.) Heat to boiling, stirring constantly. Remove from the heat and whisk in the butter and Grand Marnier, if desired. Serve warm.

The sauce can be prepared up to 1 week ahead of time. Cover and refrigerate. Reheat in a double boiler, or heat in the microwave for about 1 minute, until creamy.

. . . . .

I love the special Christmas dessert called croquembouche, *with its crunchy caramel-coated cream puffs stacked in a dramatic pyramid. However, for the average dinner, it's easier to serve a deconstructed version of the dessert, with no intricate architectural work required. The crunch of the cream puff (or* choux *pastry) and caramel coating is a fabulous contrast to the custard filling.*

I've also given a creamy caramel sauce that can be spooned over custard- or ice-cream-filled puffs. It does not develop the crunchy exterior of the simple caramel. It is, however, easier to prepare, as the puffs don't need to be dipped in the hot syrup. The results are excellent but different. —Joyce

Custard, caramel, honey, and vanilla are the classic pairings for botrytized dessert wines, and I suppose you could go for the grand slam by using honey as the sweetener in this dessert. In this dessert, the caramel and vanilla complement the wine's barrel-aged elements (many of these wines are aged in oak), while the custard's rich texture is splendid against these more unctuous wines. The flavors of botrytized white fruit are honey, pears, peaches, and apricots, which can be highlighted by adding Grand Marnier to the creamy caramel sauce. While this is a playful accent, it's not obligatory, as the wine's fruit will also pair nicely against the creamy flavor and consistency of the pastry cream. —Evan

RECOMMENDED PRODUCERS
Botrytized Dessert Wines

EVERYDAY	PREMIUM	SPLURGE
Hogue (Greater Columbia Valley, Washington)	Château Doisy-Daëne (Sauternes, France)	Dr. Bürklin-Wolf (Pfalz, Germany)
Domaine de la Motte (Loire Valley, France)	Beringer (Napa Valley, California)	Château Rieussec (Sauternes/Barsac, France)
Kiona (Yakima Valley, Washington)	Domaine de Baumard (Loire Valley, France)	Domaine Weinbach (Alsace, France)

COCONUT PANNA COTTA WITH MANGO SAUCE

SERVES 5 TO 6

2 tablespoons cold water
2 teaspoons unflavored gelatin
1½ cups canned coconut milk
1 cup whipping cream
¼ cup sugar
Pinch of salt
½ teaspoon vanilla extract
Mango Puree (see recipe below)

Pour the water into a small bowl and sprinkle the gelatin on top. Let the gelatin soften for about 10 minutes.

Place a pitcher in the refrigerator to chill.

In a large, heavy saucepan, whisk together the coconut milk, cream, sugar, and salt. Bring to a boil, stirring frequently. Remove from the heat. Add the gelatin mixture and stir until dissolved. Stir in the vanilla.

Transfer the mixture to the chilled pitcher and place in a bowl of ice water. Let stand until cooled and a little thicker than heavy cream, stirring occasionally, 15 to 20 minutes. Pour the mixture into five or six 4-ounce custard cups. Chill until set, at least 4 hours or up to 2 days.

To serve, run a knife around the edge of each cup and turn the panna cotta out onto dessert plates. Spoon some of the mango puree around the base of each panna cotta and serve.

MANGO PUREE

2 very ripe large mangos
3 tablespoons (or more) orange blossom honey
Pinch of salt

Peel the mangos and cut the flesh into small pieces. Puree in a food processor. Add 3 tablespoons honey and a pinch of salt and process again. Add additional honey to taste, if desired, and process. (Can be prepared up to 1 day ahead of time. Transfer to a small bowl or pitcher, cover, and refrigerate. Bring to room temperature before serving.)

This panna cotta is cool, creamy, and not too sweet—a perfect dessert for a warm day. It will transport you (culinarily, of course) to the tropics. The mango is a sweet-tart counterpoint to the lush coconut cream. —Joyce

This dessert is simple and so friendly to late-harvest wines. The overt sweetness of the wine is mitigated by the sumptuous consistency and milder flavors of the coconut. The mango sauce is critical to this dish but can easily dominate even these densely flavor-packed wines, so scoop it up with the coconut mousse as a deft accent and not a primary spoonful of flavor. Wines based on Muscat, Semillon, or Chenin Blanc are my preferences here. —Evan

RECOMMENDED PRODUCERS
Late-Harvest Dessert Wines

EVERYDAY	PREMIUM	SPLURGE
Selaks (Marlborough, New Zealand)	Bonny Doon (Northern Central Coast, California)	Iniskillen (Ontario, Canada)
Silver Lake (Greater Columbia Valley, Washington)	Quady (Sierra Foothills, California)	Dolce (Napa Valley, California)
Val d'Orbieu (Southwest France)	P. Jaboulet (Southern Rhône Valley, France)	Gunderloch (Rheinhessen, Germany)

TARTUFO BUDINO

SERVES 6

1 tablespoon unsalted butter, melted

12 tablespoons sugar

24 *amarene* cherries soaked in kirsch or brandy (sour cherries)

6 ounces bittersweet chocolate, chopped

14 tablespoons (1¾ sticks) unsalted butter

1 teaspoon vanilla extract

Pinch of salt

3 large eggs, separated

Whipped cream (for garnish)

Brush six 5-ounce ramekins with 1 tablespoon melted butter and sprinkle with 1 tablespoon of the sugar. Place 4 cherries on the bottom of each dish.

In the top of a double boiler, melt the chocolate and 14 tablespoons butter over medium heat. Stir in 8 tablespoons (½ cup) sugar, the vanilla, and salt. In a small bowl, whisk the egg yolks to blend. Gradually add a bit of the chocolate mixture to the yolks to warm them, whisking constantly, and then add the yolk mixture to the chocolate, whisking well.

Preheat the oven to 375 degrees.

Using an electric mixer with a wire whisk attachment, beat the egg whites with 2 tablespoons sugar until medium peaks are formed. Fold the whites into the chocolate mixture. Spoon or pour the batter into ramekins. (Can be prepared up to 5 hours ahead of time. Cover and refrigerate until ready to bake.)

Sprinkle the desserts with the remaining 1 tablespoon of sugar. Place the ramekins in a baking pan and pour hot water to the depth of 1 inch (the water should come halfway up the sides of the dishes). Bake in the center of the oven until the budinos are puffed and form a crackly crust but still remain creamy on the inside (they should wiggle a bit when shaken), 20 to 30 minutes. Serve warm, with a dollop of whipped cream.

VARIATION You can also tuck the cherries into the center of the chocolate mixture instead of placing them on the bottom.

. . . . .

In Rome, tartufo, or truffle, is a fabulous frozen chocolate ice-cream ball filled with brandied cherries, topped with chocolate shavings, and accompanied by a dollop of whipped cream. It gives you another reason, besides reveling in the beauty of the Bernini fountains, to visit the Piazza Navona, because tartufo is a specialty of the Tre Scalini café in this renowned square. Here is a warm interpretation of that dessert treat. The chocolate budino is a comforting and sensual chocolate pudding for grown-ups. You can assemble this dessert 2 to 3 hours ahead of time and reheat gently, or you can make the batter, spoon it into custard cups, and refrigerate for up to 5 hours before baking. Serve topped with a dollop of whipped cream. Amarene, or sour cherries in syrup, can be found in Italian markets or Middle Eastern stores. Drain the syrup and macerate the cherries briefly in a bit of kirsch or brandy, if you like. —Joyce

Chocolate and port (or port-style wines) are a time-honored and memorable combination, and with good reason. Chocolate is at once bitter and sweet (bitter from the cacao base and sweet from the additions of milk, cream, and sugar). Port and similar wines are also both bitter (from the skins and tannins of the red grapes) and sweet (from the residual sugar). The wine and the chocolate reflect one another's flavors in a synergistic way—a rare combination. The cherries echo similar fruit accents in the port. —Evan

RECOMMENDED PRODUCERS
Ports and Port-Like Dessert Wines

EVERYDAY	PREMIUM	SPLURGE
Dow's (Porto, Portugal)	Domaine du Mas Blanc (Languedoc, France)	Cockburn's (Porto, Portugal)
Quady (Sierra Foothills, California)	Quinta do Crasto (Porto, Portugal)	Graham's (Porto, Portugal)
Chapoutier (Rhône Valley, France)	Fonseca (Porto and Douro, Portugal)	Taylor's (Porto, Portugal)

PAIRING AT HOME: TIPS AND MENUS

Here's a short checklist of points that will enhance your wine and food experiences at home. While some are gathered from the text, others are either common sense or lessons learned from my own experience.

Decide your priority. If it's wine, select the wine or wines you intend to serve, either from your cellar or your local wine shop, and then plan the menu. If you have a special recipe you want to serve, or a specific cuisine or ingredient you want to highlight, be aware that these will, in part, dictate your wine selection(s). Think ahead about what wine will best complement your menu; don't play Russian roulette or leave things to total chance!

Make sure your wines are in optimum condition. When serving an older red wine, stand it up (if possible the day before) and let the sediment settle before decanting. When serving a young red wine, open it and let it breathe (and open up)—a good twenty to forty-five minutes before you plan to eat. For white wines or bubblies, ensure that they are chilled but not cold and, if necessary, pull them out of the refrigerator and let them warm up so you don't lose the flavor nuances.

When grocery shopping, choose the best ingredients. Buy seasonally, and buy what's best. Don't set your heart on fresh tomatoes in early spring or winter squash in the middle of summer. I usually start by choosing my fruit and vegetables and then visit the butcher or fishmonger once I've thought about what role the produce will play in the meal.

Less is more. Let a few stellar seasonal ingredients lead the meal; don't force it full of complex and possibly conflicting tastes.

Always have a nice selection of breads and cheeses. If Pinot Meunier is a winemaker's spackle, bread and cheese are the culinary equivalents, helping to fill any gaps of flavor and texture in a menu.

Prepare as much in advance as you can. I have spent many an evening in the kitchen instead of with my guests because I waited till the last minute or simply planned a menu that was too complex. Try to get the table set early and have lots of noshing foods so you can appease the hungry! Remember, it's ultimately just wine and food; enjoying time with friends and family should take precedence.

Offer options, if you can. I like to serve more than one wine. Having a choice lets people pick favorites, stimulates conversation, and prevents your guests from feeling uncomfortable if they don't like the wine that's on offer. Often you'll find the wine you thought would be best isn't the favorite.

Make things easy and fun. Shoot for basic matches of wine and food, and don't get hung up on creating an epiphany. Not everyone may be as into the art of pairing as you! The pairings should work so that if they come up in conversation, people notice, but don't make a big production out of them.

When in doubt, choose wine and food that are natural neighbors. If you are uncertain about a wine and food match, serve the cuisine of a particular region with the local wine (assuming the region has a wine and food tradition). Nine times out of ten it works splendidly—and even if it doesn't, you're a champ for trying!

Accept that it's not always going to work. Better to try new things and have them not be perfect than play it safe all the time. You'll win points for going for it! If you are going to be daring, though, you may want to ensure that your audience is equally prepared to walk on the wild side.

As I was going over the recipes with friends, the same question kept coming up: how should I mix and match these dishes? Good question. In consultation with Joyce (Mom), I have come up with the following menus that I know will be both fun and delicious.

· · · · ·

SPRING MENU
Pasta with Greens, Chickpeas, Toasted Breadcrumbs, and Pecorino (page 72)

Salmon with Soy, Ginger, and Sake (page 172)
or Moroccan Lamb Barbecue (page 195)

Lemony Ricotta Soufflé Cake with Raspberry Sauce (page 238)

SUMMER MENU
Baked Ricotta with Toast (page 64)

Ginger and Orange Fried Chicken (page 124)
or Rustic Paella (page 187)

Coconut Panna Cotta with Mango Sauce (page 243)

FALL MENU

Crab Salad in Endive Leaves (page 40)

Roast Lobster with Tarragon-Lemon Butter (page 60)
or Stuffed Roasted Squab (page 170)

Hazelnut Torte with Coffee Buttercream (page 232)

WINTER MENU

Polenta with Smoked Fish and Crème Fraîche (page 62)

Italian Meatball and Vegetable Soup (page 181)
or Duck with Sausage and Lentils (page 197)

Citrus Marmalade Tart (page 235)

FESTIVE HOLIDAY MENU

Caviar and Cream Cheese Roll (page 42)
Tuna with Rosemary and Citrus Tapenade (page 155)
Coffee- and Pepper-Rubbed Rib Roast (page 146)
Tartufo Budino (page 245)

WINE-TASTING BUFFET PARTY

Tandoori-Style Shrimp (page 89)
Scallop Ceviche with Grapefruit and Avocado (page 99)
Savory Meat Strudel (page 113)
Catalan Bean and Sausage Stew with Mint (page 157)
Lamb Shish Kebabs (page 174)
Barbecued Chicken Sandwiches (page 216)
Caramel-Coated Cream Puffs (page 240)

PAIRING WHEN DINING OUT

Dealing with the wine and food dynamic in restaurants can be trickier than at home, as things are not completely under your control. As a grizzled veteran of the hospitality world, I have definite opinions on how to maximize pleasure for restaurant guests. And, of course, I've also eaten my fair share of restaurant meals and gleaned additional information from the diner's perspective. Many people may be perfectly content to let others, in this case the team of a restaurant, do all the heavy lifting and simply enjoy the results. Some people, however, especially very serious wine lovers, tremble when the details are left to others and take comfort if they can help steer the service. Either way, the following should help.

Decide the priority. If there are specific dishes you want to order, a chef's special you are aching to try, or a dish that comes with a marvelous description from the waiter, realize that the food has taken priority. Then choose your wine(s) carefully around the dishes. If you have a savvy sommelier or are going to one of those wine-shrine restaurants, you may prefer to select your wines and work from there. Above all, don't close your eyes and point. And don't hesitate to ask for help in choosing either the wine or the food. After all, the staff works there and should know their wares!

Ask if the restaurant is known for specific dishes. If it is, and the choices suit your fancy, go with those, and then select your wines accordingly.

If you bring your own wines, help to ensure they are handled properly. Where this practice is legal (it varies by state), this means bringing the wines to the restaurant at the correct temperature, stood up if they are older reds. Tell the server anything about the wine that he or she may need to know. If it feels right, share a taste with your waiter or sommelier; you may save yourself a corkage fee, make a new friend, and become privy to insider information—for instance, about special wines that don't appear on the wine list.

Set things up the way you'd like. If you have ordered multiple wines or want wines served in a specific order or at a specific time, ask your server to accommodate you. For example, do multiple wines need different glasses? Will certain wines need to be decanted or opened ahead of time for breathing? Are the whites at the right temperature? Politely take charge if it's apparent that you are better suited to make these judgments than the service staff.

Choose multiple wines. Especially if you have a large group that's into the fun of matching wine and food, try to provide a choice of wines with as many courses as you can. It's great for conversation and for your gastronomic education! (Keep in mind, though, that with this approach it's essential to pace yourself and your dining companions. If your guests are not seasoned wine drinkers or aren't expecting a series of wines, they may get a bit tipsy. My rule of thumb is to consume a glass of water for each glass of wine that you enjoy. It may mean an extra trip to the restroom, but you'll appreciate the wine and food more, and you'll all be safer on the way home.)

When in doubt, choose wine and food that are natural neighbors. This course of action works as well in a restaurant as it does in your own dining room.

Relax, you aren't at home! No screaming kids, no dishes to do! Allow yourself to enjoy the moment and perhaps be a bit more adventuresome.

THE HALL OF FAME

Once a week, without fail, somebody asks me for a list of my favorite producers. This judgment is, of course, subjective, and my answers depend on the specific query: for example, best value, specific varietals (the best Pinot Noir), or food compatibility.

In the wine journeys, I have identified wineries that excel at producing specific varietals. In the table titled "Hall of Fame Wines," I provide a list for those of you who want to have a few names of other reliable producers at hand when you are unable to find a specific producer that I have recommended. The wineries listed here meet the following criteria: their wines are generally available nationwide, they have a proven track record, they make wines that are inherently food-friendly across the board, and they achieve success with virtually all the wines they produce.

This list is by no means exhaustive, but I've included wineries, areas, and varietals that are not included elsewhere in the book (for example, Spain's Rioja for Tempranillo and Italy's Piedmont for Nebbiolo). I've noted where the wineries are based, produce their wines, or focus their production, and what kinds of wines they are best known for. Wineries specifically known for producing good value (that is, reliable wines under $15) are designated with a V.

But first, some knowledge of importers and import companies is very helpful when you are selecting imported wines. While there are literally hundreds of importers, a small number demonstrate an ability to select great producers and the best wines, and so they can save you a lot of grunt work in narrowing down the options. I've provided a list of recommended importers in the table on page 253. If you are unfamiliar with a foreign producer, one of these importers' names on the label, while not a guarantee of quality, will guide you toward wines that are more than calculated risks.

RECOMMENDED IMPORTERS BY GEOGRAPHIC SPECIALTY

ALL-AROUND

Broadbent Selections
Clicquot, Inc.
Dreyfus Ashby
Frederick Wildman
Kobrand
Kysela Père et Fils

Michael Skurnick
Paterno
Robert Chadderdon
Vineyard Brands
Wilson Daniels
W. J. Deutsch

ITALY

Domaine Select
Empson Selections
Marco di Grazia

Vinifera
Winebow

AUSTRALIA

Australian Premium Wine Collection
Grateful Palate
Negociants USA

Old Bridge Wine Cellars
Southern Starz

FRANCE

Alain Juguenet
Bobby Kacher
Boisset America
Diageo Chateau & Estates
Kermit Lynch

Maison Marques et Domaines
Martine Saunier
Neil Rosenthal
North Berkeley Imports

GERMANY AND AUSTRIA

International Wine Cellars (Rudi Weist)
Terry Thiese

Vackenberg
Vin Divino

SPAIN

Classical Wines of Spain (Steve Metzler)
Eric Solomon

Fine Estates from Spain (Jorge Ordoñez)

NEW ZEALAND

Negociants USA

Via Pacifica

SOUTH AFRICA

Cape Classics

SOUTH AMERICA

Billington Imports

HALL OF FAME WINES

PRODUCER	COUNTRY	LOCATION	VALUE FACTOR	KNOWN FOR
AMERICAS				
Adelsheim	United States	California (multiple appellations)		reds, whites
Argyle	United States	Oregon (Willamette Valley)	V	reds, sparkling
Arrowood	United States	California (Sonoma County)		reds, whites
Au Bon Climat	United States	California (Southern Central Coast)		reds, whites
Babcock	United States	California (Southern Central Coast)		whites, reds
Bedell	United States	New York (Long Island)		reds
Bethel Heights	United States	Oregon (Willamette Valley)		reds, whites
Bogle	United States	California (multiple appellations)	V	reds, whites
Bonny Doon	United States	California (Northern Central Coast)		reds, whites, dessert
B. R. Cohn	United States	California (Sonoma County)		reds
Byron	United States	California (Southern Central Coast)		reds
Cakebread Cellars	United States	California (Napa Valley)		whites, reds
Calera	United States	California (Northern Central Coast)		reds
Casa Lapostolle	Chile	Rapel Valley		reds, whites
Catena Zapata	Argentina	Mendoza		reds, whites
Cave Spring	Canada	Ontario (Niagara)		whites
Chateau Montelena	United States	California (Napa Valley)		reds, whites
Chateau Souverain	United States	California (Sonoma County)		reds, whites
Chateau Ste. Michelle	United States	Washington (Greater Columbia Valley)	V	reds, whites
Chateau St. Jean	United States	California (Sonoma County)		reds, whites
Cline	United States	California (Sonoma County)	V	reds
Clos du Bois	United States	California (Sonoma County)	V	reds, whites
Columbia Crest	United States	Washington (multiple appellations)	V	reds, whites
Concha y Toro	Chile	Central Valley	V	reds, whites
Cristom	United States	Oregon (Willamette Valley)		reds, whites
Cuvaison	United States	California (Napa Valley)		reds, whites
Delicato	United States	California (multiple appellations)	V	reds

PRODUCER	COUNTRY	LOCATION	VALUE FACTOR	KNOWN FOR
AMERICAS				
Domaine Drouhin	United States	Oregon (Willamette Valley)		reds
Dr. Konstantin Frank	United States	New York (Finger Lakes)		whites, reds
Duckhorn	United States	California (Napa Valley)		reds
Elk Cove	United States	Oregon (Willamette Valley)		reds
Estancia	United States	California (Sonoma/Central Coast)	V	whites, reds
Etude	United States	California (Napa Valley)		reds, whites
Fisher	United States	California (Sonoma County)		reds, whites
Frog's Leap	United States	California (Napa Valley)		reds, whites
Gallo of Sonoma	United States	California (Sonoma County)		reds, whites
Gary Farrell	United States	California (Sonoma County)		reds, whites
Geyser Peak	United States	California (Sonoma County)	V	reds, whites
Grgich Hills	United States	California (Napa Valley)		reds, whites
Hanna	United States	California (Sonoma County)		reds, whites
Hedges	United States	Washington (multiple appellations)	V	reds, whites
Hess Collection	United States	California (Napa Valley)		reds, whites
Hogue	United States	Washington (Greater Columbia Valley)	V	reds, whites
Iron Horse	United States	California (Sonoma County)		sparkling, whites, reds
J. Rochioli	United States	California (Sonoma County)		reds, whites
Joseph Phelps	United States	California (Napa Valley)		reds, whites
Kendall Jackson	United States	California (multiple appellations)		whites, reds
Kenwood	United States	California (Sonoma County)		reds, whites
King Estate	United States	Oregon (Willamette Valley)		reds, whites
Kunde	United States	California (Sonoma County)		whites
Laurel Glen	United States	California (Sonoma County)		whites, reds
L'Ecole No. 41	United States	Washington (Walla Walla Valley)		reds, whites
Matanzas Creek	United States	California (Sonoma County)		reds, whites
Merryvale	United States	California (Napa Valley)		reds

PRODUCER	COUNTRY	LOCATION	VALUE FACTOR	KNOWN FOR
AMERICAS				
Morgan	United States	California (Northern Central Coast)		reds, whites
Mumm Napa	United States	California (Napa Valley)		sparkling
Navarro	United States	California (Mendocino County)		reds, whites
Oak Knoll	United States	Oregon (Willamette Valley)		reds, whites
Patz & Hall	United States	California (Napa Valley)		reds, whites
Ponzi	United States	Oregon (Willamette Valley)		reds, whites
Pride Mountain	United States	California (Napa Valley)		reds
Provenance	United States	California (Napa Valley)		reds
Qupé	United States	California (Southern Central Coast)		reds, whites
Rancho Zabaco	United States	California (Sonoma County)	V	reds
Ravenswood	United States	California (multiple appellations)		reds
Renwood	United States	California (Sierra Foothills)		reds
Rex Hill	United States	Oregon (Willamette Valley)		reds
Ridge	United States	California (Northern Central Coast)		reds
Roederer Estate	United States	California (Mendocino County)		sparkling
Rosenblum	United States	California (multiple appellations)		reds
Saintsbury	United States	California (Napa Valley)		reds, whites
Sanford	United States	California (Southern Central Coast)		whites
Schramsberg	United States	California (Napa Valley)		sparkling
Sebastiani	United States	California (Sonoma County)	V	reds, whites
Sequoia Grove	United States	California (Napa Valley)		reds
Shafer	United States	California (Napa Valley)		whites, reds
Silverado	United States	California (Napa Valley)		reds, whites
St. Francis	United States	California (Sonoma County)		reds
St. Supéry	United States	California (Napa Valley)		reds, whites
Talley	United States	California (Southern Central Coast)		reds
Valentín Bianchi	Argentina	Mendoza		reds, whites
Viña Carmen	Chile	Rapel Valley		reds, whites

▶

PRODUCER	COUNTRY	LOCATION	VALUE FACTOR	KNOWN FOR
AMERICAS				
Viña Montes	Chile	Rapel Valley		reds, whites
Viña Santa Rita	Chile	Maipo Valley	V	reds, whites
Wild Horse	United States	California (Southern Central Coast)		reds
Willakenzie	United States	Oregon (Willamette Valley)		reds, whites
Wölffer	United States	New York (Long Island)		reds
Woodward Canyon	United States	Washington (Greater Columbia Valley)		reds
EUROPE				
Alejándro Fernández	Spain	Ribera del Duero		reds
Alois Kracher	Austria	Burgenland		whites
Alois Lageder	Italy	Trentino–Alto Adige		whites
Anselmi	Italy	Veneto		whites
Antinori	Italy	Tuscany	V (some)	reds, whites
Avignonesi	Italy	Tuscany		reds, sweet
Bollinger	France	Champagne		sparkling
Bonneau du Martray	France	Burgundy		whites
Bründlmayer	Austria	Lower Austria		whites
Ceretto	Italy	Piedmont		reds
Chapoutier	France	Rhône		reds
Charles Ellner	France	Champagne	V	sparkling
Château Angélus	France	Bordeaux (Saint-Emilion)		reds
Château Cos d'Estournel	France	Bordeaux (Saint-Estèphe)		reds
Château Coutet	France	Bordeaux (Sauternes)		sweet
Château de Beaucastel	France	Rhône		reds
Château Duhart-Milon	France	Bordeaux (Pauillac)		reds
Château Figeac	France	Bordeaux (Saint-Emilion)		reds
Château Giscours	France	Bordeaux (Margaux)		reds
Château Gruaud-Larose	France	Bordeaux (Saint-Julien)		reds
Château Guiraud	France	Bordeaux (Sauternes)		sweet

▶

PRODUCER	COUNTRY	LOCATION	VALUE FACTOR	KNOWN FOR
EUROPE				
Château La Louvière	France	Bordeaux (Graves)		reds, whites
Château Léoville–Las Cases	France	Bordeaux		reds
Château Lynch-Bages	France	Bordeaux (Pauillac)		reds
Château Pichon-Lalande	France	Bordeaux (Pauillac)		reds
Château Rieussec	France	Bordeaux (Sauternes)		sweet
Château Sociando-Mallet	France	Bordeaux (Haut-Médoc)		reds
Château Talbot	France	Bordeaux (Saint-Julien)		reds
Cockburn's	Portugal	Porto		fortified
Comtes Lafon	France	Burgundy (Côte de Beaune)		whites
Corvo	Italy	Sicily		reds, whites
Delas Frères	France	Rhône		reds
Disznókő	Hungary	Tokaj-Hegyalja		sweet
Domaine Dujac	France	Burgundy		reds
Domaine Jean Grivot	France	Burgundy		reds
Domaine Olivier Leflaive	France	Burgundy		whites
Domaine Roumier	France	Burgundy		reds
Domaine Weinbach	France	Alsace		whites
Domecq	Spain	Jerez		fortified
Dr. Bürklin-Wolf	Germany	Pfalz		whites
Dr. Loosen	Germany	Mosel-Saar-Ruwer		whites
E. Guigal	France	Rhône		reds
Egon Müller	Germany	Mosel-Saar-Ruwer		whites
Emilio Moro	Spain	Castilla-León (Ribera del Duero)		reds
Fonseca	Portugal	Porto and Douro		fortified
Fontodi	Italy	Tuscany (Chianti)		reds
Franz Künstler	Germany	Rheingau		whites
G. H. Mumm	France	Champagne		sparkling

▶

PRODUCER	COUNTRY	LOCATION	VALUE FACTOR	KNOWN FOR
EUROPE				
Gaja	Italy	Piedmont (Barbaresco)		reds
Georges Du Boeuf	France	Burgundy (Beaujolais)	V	reds
Henri Bourgeois	France	Loire Valley (Sancerre)		whites
Hugel	France	Alsace		whites
J. J. Prum	Germany	Mosel-Saar-Ruwer		whites
Jean-Marc Boillot	France	Burgundy (Côte de Beaune)		whites
Jermann	Italy	Friuli		whites
Joseph Drouhin	France	Burgundy (multiple appellations)		reds
Ladoucette	France	Loire Valley		whites
La Rioja Alta	Spain	Rioja		reds
Lingenfelder	Germany	Pfalz		whites, reds
Louis Jadot	France	Burgundy		reds, whites
Louis Latour	France	Burgundy		whites
Louis Roederer	France	Champagne		sparkling
Lusco do Miño	Spain	Rías Baixas		whites
Lustau	Spain	Jerez		fortified
Maculan	Italy	Veneto		reds, whites
Marqués de Arienzo	Spain	Rioja		reds
Marqués de Riscal	Spain	Rueda		whites
Martín Códax	Spain	Galicia (Rías Baixas)		whites
Masi	Italy	Veneto		reds
Monsanto	Italy	Tuscany (Chianti)		reds
Muga	Spain	Rioja		reds
P. Jaboulet	France	Rhône	V (some)	reds
Pio Cesare	Italy	Piedmont		reds
Pol Roger	France	Champagne		sparkling
Querceto	Italy	Tuscany		reds
Robert Weil	Germany	Rheingau		whites

PRODUCER	COUNTRY	LOCATION	VALUE FACTOR	KNOWN FOR
EUROPE				
Royal Tokaji Wine Co.	Hungary	Tokaj-Hegyalja		sweet
Sauvion et Fils	France	Loire Valley		whites
Segura Viudas	Spain	Catalonia (Penedès, Cava)		sparkling
Taittinger	France	Champagne		sparkling
Taurino	Italy	Apulia		reds
Taylor's	Portugal	Porto		fortified
Torres	Spain	Catalonia (Penedès)		reds, whites
Trimbach	France	Alsace		whites
Val d'Orbieu	France	Languedoc		reds, whites
Vietti	Italy	Piedmont (Barolo)		reds
William Fèvre	France	Burgundy (Chablis)		whites
AUSTRALIA, NEW ZEALAND, SOUTH AFRICA				
Allan Scott	New Zealand	Marlborough	V	whites
Babich	New Zealand	Marlborough		whites
Boekenhoutskloof	South Africa	Coastal Region		reds, whites
Brancott	New Zealand	Multiple appellations	V	reds, whites
Cape Indaba	South Africa	Coastal Region (Stellenbosch)	V	reds
Cloudy Bay	New Zealand	Marlborough		whites
Coldstream Hills	Australia	Victoria		reds, whites
Cullen	Australia	Western Australia		reds, whites
d'Arenberg	Australia	South Australia	V (some)	reds, whites
De Trafford	South Africa	Coastal Region (Stellenbosch)		reds, whites
Elderton	Australia	South Australia		reds, whites
Fairview	South Africa	Coastal Region		reds, whites
Glen Carlou	South Africa	Coastal Region		whites
Goldwater	New Zealand	Marlborough		whites, reds
Hamilton-Russell	South Africa	Coastal Region		whites
Hardys	Australia	South Australia	V	reds, whites

PRODUCER	COUNTRY	LOCATION	VALUE FACTOR	KNOWN FOR
AUSTRALIA, NEW ZEALAND, SOUTH AFRICA				
Huia	New Zealand	Marlborough		reds, whites
Isabel	New Zealand	Marlborough		whites
Kanonkop	South Africa	Coastal Region		reds
Kim Crawford	New Zealand	Marlborough		whites
Kirralaa	Australia	South Australia		reds, whites
Klein Constantia	South Africa	Coastal Region		reds, whites, sweet
Kumeu River	New Zealand	Auckland		whites
Leasingham	Australia	South Australia		reds, whites
Leeuwin	Australia	Western Australia		whites, reds
Lindauer	New Zealand	Multiple appellations	V	sparkling
Mitchelton	Australia	Victoria		reds
Mount Langi	Australia	Victoria		reds
Mulderbosch	South Africa	Coastal Region		reds, whites
Neil Ellis	South Africa	Multiple appellations	V	reds, whites
Omaka Springs	New Zealand	Marlborough		whites
Penfolds	Australia	South Australia	V	reds, whites
Penley	Australia	South Australia		reds
Petaluma	Australia	South Australia		reds, whites
Peter Lehmann	Australia	South Australia		reds, sweet
Plantagenet	Australia	Western Australia		reds, whites
Rosemount	Australia	Multiple appellations	V	reds, whites
Rustenberg	South Africa	Coastal Region		reds
Rust en Vrede	South Africa	Coastal Region		reds
St. Hallett	Australia	South Australia		reds
Te Kairanga	New Zealand	Wairarapa (Martinborough)		reds, whites
The Crossings	New Zealand	Marlborough		whites
Thelema	South Africa	Coastal Region		reds

▶

PRODUCER	COUNTRY	LOCATION	VALUE FACTOR	KNOWN FOR
AUSTRALIA, NEW ZEALAND, SOUTH AFRICA				
Vasse Felix	Australia	Western Australia		reds
Villa Maria	New Zealand	Multiple appellations	V	reds, whites
Wolf Blass	Australia	Multiple appellations	V	reds, whites
Yalumba	Australia	South Australia		whites, sweet
Yangarra Park	Australia	South Australia	V	reds, whites
Yarra Yering	Australia	Victoria		reds

PRINCIPAL WINE-GROWING REGIONS

The twelve core grapes discussed in this book are grown in dozens of regions and appellations in countries throughout the world. And that doesn't include the sparkling and dessert wines. The following tables show where the featured grapes come from and the specific areas where they thrive.

SPARKLING WINES

REGION OR STATE	APPELLATIONS	SUBAPPELLATIONS
UNITED STATES		
California	Napa Valley	Carneros, Yountville
	Sonoma County	Alexander Valley, Carneros, Russian River Valley (including Green Valley), Sonoma Coast
	Mendocino County	Anderson Valley
Oregon	Willamette Valley	
Washington	Greater Columbia Valley	
New York	Finger Lakes	
	Long Island	North Fork
Michigan	Leelanau Peninsula	
New Mexico		
Arizona		
FRANCE		
Champagne	Côte des Blancs	
	Montagne de Reims	
	Vallé de la Marne	
	Aube	
	Côte de Sézanne	

REGION OR STATE	APPELLATIONS	SUBAPPELLATIONS
FRANCE		
Loire Valley	Anjou	Saumur
	Touraine	Vouvray
Alsace	Die	
Rhône		
Southwest	Gaillac	
Languedoc	Limoux	
Bordeaux		
Burgundy	Mâconnais	
	Côte Chalonnaise	Rully
ITALY		
Lombardy	Franciacorta	
Piedmont	Asti	
Veneto	Prosecco	
GERMANY		
Mittelrhein		
Rheingau		
SPAIN		
Catalonia	Penedès	Cava
SOUTH AFRICA		
Franschhoek		
AUSTRALIA		
Tasmania		
South Australia		
NEW ZEALAND		
South Island	Marlborough	
CHILE		
Aconcagua	Casablanca Valley	
OTHER COUNTRIES		
Portugal, India, Argentina		

CHARDONNAY

REGION OR STATE	APPELLATIONS	SUBAPPELLATIONS
UNITED STATES		
California	Napa Valley	Carneros, Mount Veeder, Spring Mountain, Yountville
	Sonoma County	Alexander Valley, Carneros, Chalk Hill, Russian River Valley (including Green Valley), Sonoma Coast
	Mendocino County	Anderson Valley
	Northern Central Coast	Arroyo Seco, Chalone, Monterey, Santa Clara Valley, Santa Cruz Mountains
	Southern Central Coast	Arroyo Grande, Edna Valley, Santa Barbara, Santa Maria, Santa Ynez (Santa Rita Hills)
	San Francisco Bay	Livermore Valley, Santa Clara Valley
Washington	Yakima Valley	
	Greater Columbia Valley	
Oregon	Willamette Valley	
Virginia		
New York	Long Island	North Fork
Texas		
FRANCE		
Champagne	Côte des Blancs	
	Vallé de la Marne	
	Aube	
Burgundy	Chablis	
	Côte de Beaune	Aloxe-Corton, Beaune, Chassagne-Montrachet, Meursault, Montrachet, Puligny-Montrachet
	Côte Chalonnaise	Bouzeron, Montagny, Rully
	Mâconnais	Pouilly-Fuissé, Saint-Véran, Viré-Clessé
Loire Valley	Anjou	
	Touraine	
Ardèche		
Languedoc		

▶ CHARDONNAY

REGION OR STATE	APPELLATIONS	SUBAPPELLATIONS
ITALY		
Trentino–Alto Adige		
Tuscany		
Friuli–Venezia Giulia	Grave del Friuli	
	Collio	
Veneto		
Umbria		
Piedmont		
SPAIN		
North-Central	Navarra	
Catalonia	Penedès	Cava
AUSTRIA		
Styria		
GERMANY		
Pfalz		
OTHER EUROPEAN COUNTRIES		
Bulgaria, Hungary, Moldova, Romania		
SOUTH AFRICA		
Coastal Region	Paarl	
	Stellenbosch	
	Constantia	
Overberg		
Breede River		
Western Cape		
CHILE		
Central Valley	Rapel Valley	Cachapoal Valley
Aconcagua	Casablanca Valley	
ARGENTINA		
Mendoza	Luján de Cuyo	
	Uco Valley	
San Juan	Pedernal Valley	

▶

▶ CHARDONNAY

REGION OR STATE	APPELLATIONS	SUBAPPELLATIONS
CANADA		
British Columbia	Okanagan Valley	
AUSTRALIA		
New South Wales	Hunter Valley	
Victoria	Bendigo	
	Goulburn Valley	
	Yarra Valley	
South Australia	Adelaide Hills	
	Barossa Valley	
	Clare Valley	
	Eden Valley	
	McLaren Vale	
Western Australia	Margaret River	
Tasmania	Piper's Brook	
NEW ZEALAND		
North Island	Hawkes Bay	
	Gisborne	
	Auckland	Kumeu-Huapai
South Island	Marlborough	

SAUVIGNON BLANC

REGION OR STATE	APPELLATIONS	SUBAPPELLATIONS
UNITED STATES		
California	Napa Valley	Calistoga, Oakville, Rutherford, Saint Helena, Yountville
	Sierra Foothills	Amador County, Shenandoah Valley
	Lake County	High Valley
	Mendocino County	Potter Valley
	Sonoma County	Alexander Valley, Bennett Valley, Chalk Hill, Dry Creek, Knights Valley
	San Francisco Bay	Livermore Valley
	Northern Central Coast	Carmel Valley, Santa Cruz Mountains
	Southern Central Coast	Santa Barbara, Santa Ynez
Washington		
Texas		
Oregon		
FRANCE		
Bordeaux	Graves	Pessac-Léognan
	Médoc	
	Southern Bordeaux	Barsac, Cérons, Sauternes
	Entre-Deux-Mers	
Loire Valley	Central vineyards	Menetou-Salon, Pouilly-Fumé, Quincy, Reuilly, Sancerre
	Touraine	Haut-Poitou
Burgundy	Chablis	Saint-Bris
Southwest	Bergerac	
	Buzet	
	Montravel	
	Pacherenc du Vic-Bilh	
ITALY		
Friuli–Venezia Giulia	Collio	

▶ SAUVIGNON BLANC

REGION OR STATE	APPELLATIONS	SUBAPPELLATIONS
SPAIN		
North-Central	Navarra	
Castilla-León	Rueda	
OTHER EUROPEAN COUNTRIES		
Austria, Bulgaria, Moldova, Romania, Serbia, Slovenia		
SOUTH AFRICA		
Coastal Region	Stellenbosch	
	Paarl	
Overberg	Elgin	
	Mossel Bay	
CHILE		
Central Valley	Curicó	
Aconcagua	Casablanca Valley	
OTHER SOUTH AMERICAN COUNTRIES		
Argentina, Brazil, Uruguay		
AUSTRALIA		
New South Wales		
Victoria		
South Australia		
Western Australia		
NEW ZEALAND		
North Island	Hawkes Bay	
South Island	Marlborough	Awatere Valley, Brancott Valley, Cloudy Bay
ISRAEL		
Golan Heights		
Galilee		

RIESLING

REGION OR STATE	APPELLATIONS	SUBAPPELLATIONS
UNITED STATES		
California	Napa Valley	
	Sonoma County	
	Mendocino County	Anderson Valley
	Northern Central Coast	Monterey
	Southern Central Coast	Edna Valley, Santa Barbara
Oregon	Willamette Valley	
Washington	Greater Columbia Valley	
	Yakima Valley	
Michigan	Old Mission Peninsula	
	Leelanau Peninsula	
New York	Finger Lakes, Niagara	
Virginia		
FRANCE		
Alsace		
GERMANY		
Rheingau		
Mosel-Saar-Ruwer		
Nahe		
Franken		
Rheinhessen		
Pfalz		
ITALY		
Friuli–Venezia Giulia		
Trentino–Alto Adige		
AUSTRIA		
Lower Austria	Wachau	
	Weinviertel	
	Kamptal-Donauland	

▶ RIESLING

REGION OR STATE	APPELLATIONS	SUBAPPELLATIONS
OTHER EUROPEAN COUNTRIES		
Bulgaria, Hungary, Moldova, Slovenia		
ARGENTINA		
Mendoza		
AUSTRALIA		
Tasmania	Coal River Valley	
South Australia	Clare Valley	
	Eden Valley	
	Adelaide Hills	
Victoria	Geelong	
	Goulburn Valley	
NEW ZEALAND		
South Island	Marlborough	
	Central Otago	
CANADA		
British Columbia	Okanagan Valley	
Ontario	Niagara	

PINOT GRIS

REGION OR STATE	APPELLATIONS	SUBAPPELLATIONS
UNITED STATES		
California	Napa Valley	Carneros
	Sonoma County	Carneros, Russian River Valley, Sonoma Coast
	Mendocino County	Anderson Valley
	Northern Central Coast	Monterey, San Benito, Santa Lucia Highlands
	Southern Central Coast	Edna Valley, Santa Barbara
Oregon	Willamette Valley	Dundee Hills, McMinnville, Yamhill-Carlton
Washington	Greater Columbia Valley	
	Columbia Gorge	
FRANCE		
Alsace		
Loire Valley		
ITALY		
Trentino–Alto Adige		
Friuli–Venezia Giulia		
Tuscany		
GERMANY		
Baden		
Pfalz		
AUSTRIA		
Lower Austria	Weinviertel	
Styria		
OTHER EUROPEAN COUNTRIES		
Switzerland, Slovenia, Romania, Hungary		
NEW ZEALAND		
South Island		
CANADA		
British Columbia	Okanagan Valley	

GEWÜRZTRAMINER

REGION OR STATE	APPELLATIONS	SUBAPPELLATIONS
UNITED STATES		
California	Napa Valley	
	Mendocino County	Anderson Valley
	Northern Central Coast	Monterey, San Benito
	Southern Central Coast	Edna Valley
Washington	Greater Columbia Valley	
Oregon	Rogue River Valley	
New York	Finger Lakes	
FRANCE		
Alsace		
ITALY		
Trentino–Alto Adige		
GERMANY		
Baden		
Pfalz		
AUSTRIA		
Styria		
CHILE		
Bío-Bío Valley		
CANADA		
British Columbia	Okanagan Valley	
SOUTH AFRICA		
Breede River (Robertson)		
Coastal Region	Durbanville	
AUSTRALIA		
Tasmania		
South Australia		
NEW ZEALAND		
North Island	Gisborne	
South Island	Marlborough	

VIOGNIER

REGION OR STATE	APPELLATIONS	SUBAPPELLATIONS
UNITED STATES		
California	Napa Valley	Mount Veeder, Oakville
	Mendocino County	Anderson Valley, McDowell Valley
	Sierra Foothills	Amador County, Shenandoah Valley
	Sonoma County	Alexander Valley, Carneros, Russian River Valley, Sonoma Valley
	Northern Central Valley	Clarksburg, Lodi
	Northern Central Coast	Mount Harlan, Santa Lucia Highlands
	Southern Central Coast	Edna Valley, Paso Robles, Santa Barbara, Santa Ynez
Washington	Yakima Valley	
	Walla Walla Valley	
	Greater Columbia Valley	
Oregon	Willamette Valley	
	Rogue River Valley	
Virginia	Orange County	
FRANCE		
Rhône	Northern Rhône Valley	Château Grillet, Condrieu, Côte Rôtie
Languedoc		
Ardèche		
AUSTRALIA		
South Australia		
SOUTH AFRICA		
Coastal Region	Paarl	
	Stellenbosch	
CHILE		
Aconcagua	Casablanca Valley	
ARGENTINA		
Mendoza		
NEW ZEALAND		
North Island	Hawkes Bay	
South Island	Marlborough	

CABERNET SAUVIGNON

REGION OR STATE	APPELLATIONS	SUBAPPELLATIONS
UNITED STATES		
California	Napa Valley	Diamond Mountain, Howell Mountain, Mount Veeder, Oakville, Pritchard Hill, Rutherford, Saint Helena, Spring Mountain, Stags Leap District, Wild Horse Valley
	Sonoma County	Alexander Valley, Knights Valley, Sonoma Mountain, Sonoma Valley
	Northern Central Coast	Carmel Valley, Santa Cruz Mountains
	Southern Central Coast	Paso Robles
Washington	Yakima Valley	
	Walla Walla Valley	
	Greater Columbia Valley	Horse Heaven Hills, Rattlesnake Hills, Red Mountain, Wahluke Slope
Oregon	Columbia Valley	
	Rogue River Valley	
New York	Long Island	North Fork
Texas	Hill Country	
FRANCE		
Bordeaux	Médoc	Haut-Médoc, Listrac, Margaux, Moulis, Pauillac, Saint-Estèphe, Saint-Julien
	Graves	Pessac-Léognan
	"Right bank"	Pomerol, Saint-Emilion
	Satellite areas	Blaye, Bourg, Libourne
	Entre-Deux-Mers	
Loire Valley	Anjou	
	Touraine	
Southwest	Bergerac	
	Buzet	
Languedoc		

▶

► CABERNET SAUVIGNON

REGION OR STATE	APPELLATIONS	SUBAPPELLATIONS
ITALY		
Piedmont		
Tuscany		
Friuli–Venezia Giulia		
Veneto		
SPAIN		
Castilla-León	Ribera del Duero	
Catalonia	Penedès	
OTHER EUROPEAN COUNTRIES		
Austria, Bulgaria, Hungary, Moldova, Romania		
SOUTH AFRICA		
Coastal Region	Paarl	
	Stellenbosch	
	Constantia	
CHILE		
Central Valley	Rapel Valley	Cachapoal Valley, Colchagua Valley
	Maipo Valley	
	Maule Valley	
	Curicó	Lontué Valley, Santiago
ARGENTINA		
Mendoza	Luján de Cuyo	
	Uco Valley	La Consulta, Tupungato
Salta		
San Juan	Pedernal Valley	
OTHER LATIN AMERICAN COUNTRIES		
Brazil, Mexico, Uruguay		

REGION OR STATE	APPELLATIONS	SUBAPPELLATIONS
AUSTRALIA		
New South Wales	Mudgee	
Victoria	Bendigo	
	Goulburn Valley	
	Yarra Valley	
South Australia	Adelaide Hills	
	Barossa Valley	
	Clare Valley	
	Limestone Coast	Coonawarra
	McLaren Vale	
	Eden Valley	
Western Australia	Margaret River	
	Mount Barker	
NEW ZEALAND		
North Island	Hawkes Bay	Gimblett Gravels, Havelock North
	Waiheke Island	
LEBANON		
Bekaa Valley		
ISRAEL		
Golan Heights		
Galilee		

MERLOT

REGION OR STATE	APPELLATIONS	SUBAPPELLATIONS
UNITED STATES		
California	Napa Valley	Carneros, Howell Mountain, Mount Veeder, Oakville, Rutherford, Saint Helena, Spring Mountain, Stags Leap District, Wild Horse Valley
	Sonoma County	Alexander Valley, Carneros, Dry Creek Valley, Knights Valley, Sonoma Mountain, Sonoma Valley
	Northern Central Coast	Monterey, Santa Cruz Mountains
Washington	Yakima Valley	
	Walla Walla Valley	
	Greater Columbia Valley	Horse Heaven Hills, Rattlesnake Hills, Red Mountain
Oregon	Rogue River Valley	
New York	Long Island	North Fork
Virginia	Shenandoah Valley	
FRANCE		
Bordeaux	Médoc	Haut-Médoc, Listrac, Margaux, Moulis, Pauillac, Saint-Estèphe, Saint-Julien
	Graves	Pessac-Léognan
	"Right bank"	Pomerol, Saint-Emilion
	Satellite areas	Blaye, Bourg, Libourne
	Entre-Deux-Mers	
Southwest	Bergerac	
	Buzet	
Languedoc		
ITALY		
Piedmont		
Tuscany		
Veneto		
Trentino–Alto Adige		
Friuli–Venezia Giulia		

▶

▶ **MERLOT**

REGION OR STATE	APPELLATIONS	SUBAPPELLATIONS
SPAIN		
Castilla-León	Ribera del Duero	
SOUTH AFRICA		
Coastal Region	Paarl	
	Stellenbosch	
CHILE		
Central Valley	Rapel Valley	Cachapoal Valley, Colchagua Valley
	Maipo Valley	
	Maule Valley	
	Curicó	
Aconcagua	Casablanca Valley	
ARGENTINA		
Mendoza	Uco Valley	
San Juan	Pedernal Valley	
AUSTRALIA		
Victoria		
South Australia	Barossa Valley	
	McLaren Vale	
Western Australia	Margaret River	
NEW ZEALAND		
North Island	Hawkes Bay	Gimblett Gravels, Red Metal Triangle, Te Mata
	Waiheke Island	
ISRAEL		
Galilee		

PINOT NOIR

REGION OR STATE	APPELLATIONS	SUBAPPELLATIONS
UNITED STATES		
California	Napa Valley	Carneros, Yountville
	Sonoma County	Carneros, Russian River Valley (including Green Valley), Sonoma Coast
	Mendocino County	Anderson Valley
	Northern Central Coast	Arroyo Seco, Chalone, Santa Cruz Mountains, Santa Lucia Highlands
	Southern Central Coast	Arroyo Grande, Edna Valley, Santa Barbara, Santa Maria, Santa Ynez (Santa Rita Hills)
Oregon	Willamette Valley	Dundee Hills, Eola Hills, McMinnville, Polk County, Red Hill, Ribbon Ridge, Yamhill-Carlton
	Umpqua Valley	
FRANCE		
Champagne	Montagne de Reims	
	Vallé de la Marne	
	Aube	
Burgundy	Côte de Nuits	Chambolle-Musigny, Gevrey-Chambertin, Morey-Saint-Denis, Nuits-Saint-Georges, Vosne-Romanée, Vougeot
	Côte de Beaune	Beaune, Pommard, Volnay
	Côte Chalonnaise	Givry, Mercurey, Rully
	Mâconnais	
Alsace		
Loire Valley	Central vineyards	Sancerre
ITALY		
Lombardy	Franciacorta	
Trentino–Alto Adige		
Veneto	Breganze	
GERMANY		
Pfalz		
Baden		

▶ PINOT NOIR

REGION OR STATE	APPELLATIONS	SUBAPPELLATIONS
SPAIN		
Catalonia		
AUSTRIA		
Styria		
SWITZERLAND		
Valais		
Neuchâtel		
OTHER EUROPEAN COUNTRIES		
Bulgaria, Croatia, Hungary, Moldova, Romania		
SOUTH AFRICA		
Coastal Region	Paarl	
	Stellenbosch	
	Constantia	
Overberg	Walker Bay	
	Mossel Bay	
Breede River		
CHILE		
Aconcagua	Casablanca Valley	
CANADA		
British Columbia		
AUSTRALIA		
Tasmania	Coal River Valley	
	Piper's Brook	
Victoria	Yarra Valley	
	Mornington Peninsula	
South Australia	Adelaide Hills	
NEW ZEALAND		
South Island	Marlborough	Awatere Valley, Brancott Valley
	Central Otago	Cromwell Basin, Gibbston Valley
	Canterbury	Waipara
North Island	Wairarapa	Martinborough

SANGIOVESE

REGION OR STATE	APPELLATIONS	SUBAPPELLATIONS
UNITED STATES		
California	Napa Valley	Atlas Peak
	Sonoma County	Dry Creek Valley, Sonoma Valley
	Sierra Foothills	Amador County
	Southern Central Coast	San Luis Obispo
ITALY		
Tuscany	Chianti	Classico, Colli Aretini, Colli Fiorentini, Colline Pisane, Colli Senesi, Montalbano, Rufina
	Carmignano	
	Bolgheri	
	Montalcino	
	Montepulciano	
Marche		
Umbria	Torgiano	
Emilia-Romagna		
Abruzzo		
ARGENTINA		
Mendoza		
San Juan		

SYRAH

REGION OR STATE	APPELLATIONS	SUBAPPELLATIONS
UNITED STATES		
California	Napa Valley	Carneros, Mount Veeder, Oakville, Saint Helena
	Mendocino County	Anderson Valley, McDowell Valley
	Sonoma County	Carneros, Knights Valley, Russian River Valley, Sonoma Valley
	Sierra Foothills	El Dorado
	Northern Central Coast	Santa Lucia Highlands
	Southern Central Coast	Edna Valley, Paso Robles, Santa Barbara, Santa Ynez
Washington	Yakima Valley	
	Walla Walla Valley	
	Greater Columbia Valley	Horse Heaven Hills, Red Mountain
FRANCE		
Rhône	Northern Rhône Valley	Cornas, Côte Rôtie, Crozes-Hermitage, Hermitage, Saint-Joseph
	Southern Rhône Valley	Châteauneuf du Pape, Côtes du Rhône, Gigondas, Vacqueyras
Savoie		
Provence		
Languedoc		
Ardèche		
Corsica		
ITALY		
Tuscany		
SPAIN		
Catalonia		
SWITZERLAND		
Valais		
SOUTH AFRICA		
Coastal Region	Paarl	
	Stellenbosch	
	Swartland	

▶ **SYRAH**

REGION OR STATE	APPELLATIONS	SUBAPPELLATIONS
CHILE		
Central Valley	Rapel Valley	Colchagua Valley
	Maipo Valley	
Aconcagua		
ARGENTINA		
Mendoza	Uco Valley	Tupungato
	Luján de Cuyo	
Salta		
San Juan		
AUSTRALIA		
New South Wales	Mudgee	
	Hunter Valley	
Victoria	Bendigo	
	Goulburn Valley	
	Yarra Valley	
South Australia	Adelaide Hills	
	Barossa Valley	
	Limestone Coast	Padthaway
	Clare Valley	
	McLaren Vale	
	Eden Valley	
Western Australia	Margaret River	
NEW ZEALAND		
North Island	Hawkes Bay	
South Island	Marlborough	

ZINFANDEL

REGION OR STATE	APPELLATIONS	SUBAPPELLATIONS
UNITED STATES		
California	Napa Valley	Calistoga, Howell Mountain, Mount Veeder, Oakville, Rutherford, Saint Helena, Spring Mountain
	Sonoma County	Alexander Valley, Dry Creek Valley, Rockpile, Russian River Valley, Sonoma Valley
	Mendocino County	Mendocino Ridge, Redwood Valley
	Sierra Foothills	Amador County, Shenandoah Valley
	San Francisco Bay	Contra Costa County
	Northern Central Valley	Lodi, Oakley
	Northern Central Coast	Carmel Valley, Santa Cruz Mountains
	Southern Central Coast	Paso Robles
Washington	Greater Columbia Valley	Red Mountain
ITALY		
Apulia	Manduria	
Calabria		
Basilicata		
CROATIA		
Dalmatian Coast		
LATIN AMERICAN COUNTRIES		
Mexico, Brazil		
AUSTRALIA		
Western Australia	Margaret River	

Although all the wines listed in this table are late harvest and/or botrytized, many styles are sold under geographically unique names, which are noted in the first column. See the table on pages 263–64 for wine-growing areas for sparkling wines.

DESSERT WINES Late-Harvest and Botrytized Wines

STYLE OR NAME OF WINE	REGION OR STATE	APPELLATION	MAIN VARIETALS
UNITED STATES			
Late harvest, botrytized, *Eiswein*	California	Various	Semillon–Sauvignon Blanc, Riesling, Chenin Blanc, Black, White, and Orange Muscat
	Oregon	Willamette Valley	Pinot Gris
	Washington	Greater Columbia Valley	Riesling, Semillon, other fruit (e.g., blueberry, blackberry, cherry)
	New York	Finger Lakes	Riesling, American varietals (e.g., Vidal Blanc, Seyval Blanc)
	Michigan	Leelanau Peninsula, Old Mission Peninsula	Riesling, other fruit (e.g., cherry, apple, berry)
FRANCE			
Vendange tardive (VT), *sélection des grains nobles* (SGN)	Alsace		Riesling, Gewürztraminer, Muscat, Pinot Gris
Late harvest, botrytized	Loire Valley	Coteaux du Layon, Bonnezeaux, Chaume, Quarts de Chaume, Vouvray	Chenin Blanc
	Southwest	Jurançon, Monbazillac	Gros and Petit Manseng, Semillon–Sauvignon Blanc
	Bordeaux	Cérons, Cadillac, Loupiac, Ste.-Croix-du-Mont	Semillon–Sauvignon Blanc, Muscadelle
Sauternes		Sauternes, Barsac	Semillon–Sauvignon Blanc, Muscadelle

▶ **DESSERT WINES** Late-Harvest and Botrytized Wines

STYLE OR NAME OF WINE	REGION OR STATE	APPELLATION	MAIN VARIETALS
ITALY			
Late harvest, botrytized	Trentino–Alto Adige		Golden Muscat, Picolit, Verduzzo
Recioto	Veneto	Soave, Valpolicella	Garganega, Corvina-Rodinella
Torcolato	Veneto	Breganze	Vespaiolo
Vin Santo	Tuscany		Trebbiano, Malvasia
	Emilia-Romagna		Albana
	Islands		Albana
Passito	Islands	Lipare, Pantelleria	Malvasia, Moscato
GERMANY			
Auslese, Beerenauslese, Eiswein, Trockenbeerenauslese	Mosel-Saar-Ruwer, Rheingau, Rheinhessen, Pfalz		Riesling, Scheurebe, Ortega
AUSTRIA			
Ausbruch, Auslese, Beerenauslese, Eiswein, Trockenbeerenauslese	Lower Austria, Burgenland		Riesling, Grüner Veltliner
HUNGARY			
Tokaji Aszú (3–6 *puttonyos*), Eszencia	Tokaj-Hegyalja		Furmint, Hárslevelű
AUSTRALIA			
Late harvest, botrytized	New South Wales	Murrumbidgee Irrigation Area	Semillon, Riesling
	South Australia	Barossa Valley	Semillon, Riesling
NEW ZEALAND			
Late harvest, botrytized	North Island	Hawkes Bay	Semillon–Sauvignon Blanc, Riesling
	South Island	Marlborough	Semillon–Sauvignon Blanc, Riesling
SOUTH AFRICA			
Late harvest, botrytized	Coastal Region	Constantia	Muscat
CANADA			
Eiswein	Ontario	Niagara	Riesling, Seyval Blanc

STYLE OR NAME OF WINE	REGION OR STATE	APPELLATION	MAIN VARIETALS
UNITED STATES			
Ports and sherries	California	Madera County, Amador County	Various
PORTUGAL			
Port	Porto, Douro	Douro Superior, Cima Corgo	Touriga Nacional, Touriga Francesca, Tinta Cão, Tinta Roriz
Madeira (Bual, Malmsey)	Madeira	Madeira	Bual, Malmsey (Malvasia)
Vin doux naturel (VDN)	Setúbal		Muscat
FRANCE			
VDN	Roussillon	Banyuls	Grenache
		Rivesaltes	Grenache, Muscat
		Maury	Grenache, Muscat
	Languedoc	Frontignan	Muscat
		Saint-Jean de Minervois	Muscat
	Rhône	Beaumes de Venise	Muscat
		Rasteau	Grenache
ITALY			
Vino licoroso	Apulia	Manduria	Primitivo, Aleatico
Marsala (amber, gold, ruby; dry to sweet)	Sicily	Marsala	Inzolia, Grillo, Catarratto, Nero d'Avola, Nerello Mascalese
VDN	Islands	Pantelleria	Moscato
AUSTRALIA			
Liqueur Muscat	Victoria	Rutherglen	Muscat
Tokay	Victoria	Rutherglen	Muscat
SOUTH AFRICA			
Hanepoot		Various	Muscat of Alexandria (Hanepoot)
SPAIN			
Sherry (cream, brown, Muscat, *oloroso*)	Jerez		Palomino, Pedro Ximénez (PX), Muscat
	Málaga, Montilla-Moriles		PX, Muscat
VDN	Sitges		Muscat

GLOSSARY

Acidity The level of acid in the wine. A wine's acidity is reflected by the perception of tartness or sharpness in the wine. It's critical to the wine's structure and balance and to the wine's ability to pair with food. Acidity is the ultimate contrast to foods that are fatty, rich, salty, greasy or mildly spicy. Additionally, it brings out the taste of quality ingredients, acting as a vinous highlighter pen.

Appellation The geographical area or regions from which a wine comes, which is usually identified on the label, such as the Napa Valley or Champagne. In countries where the labeling of appellations is legally restricted, a wine using the name may have to contain a certain minimum percentage of a particular varietal, be made from grapes grown within a specific area, or conform to other requirements.

Astringency The puckery sensation in the mouth often associated with the tannins in red wines. *Bitterness* suggests the same flavor sensation but without the puckering, mouth-drying effects.

Auslese (*aus*-lay-zeh) Literally "select picking," the German category of sweet wines made from selected, very ripe bunches. *Auslese* made in both classic and dry (*trocken*) styles generally have alcohol levels of 10 to 12 percent and are exquisite with food. See also *Qualitätswein mit Prädikat*.

Austerity A term often used to describe wines which are lean and sharp in nature. Although sometimes unpleasant to drink solo, austere wines can be remarkable with food and often provide a needed contrast to a rich dish.

Balance What all winemakers strive for—the sense that all the components are in place and equal: acidity, tannin, flavor, and sweetness. If one characteristic seems to dominate the rest, the wine may be described as being out of balance. Balance can be achieved not only in the wine itself but also by judicious pairings of wine and food.

Barrel fermentation Alcoholic fermentation of wine that takes place inside an oak barrel. Using barrels rather than stainless-steel tanks for this process adds different flavors and textures: typically a toastiness, butterscotch or toffee flavor, and rounder, creamier consistency. Although barrel fermentation is most often associated with white wines, many reds today are also barrel-fermented.

Barrique The French term for "barrel," used globally to describe the small coopered barrels (holding about sixty gallons) universally employed by the wine industry. The classic choice of wood is French oak. However, to address increasing demand and price increases resulting from fluctuating exchange rates, producers have started to use barrels of similar size and style, and produced with French coopering techniques, made out of oak from other regions, including the United States and Eastern Europe.

Beerenauslese (BA) (*bare*-en-*aus*-lay-zeh) Literally "select picking of berries," the German and Austrian category of wines made from the harvest of individually selected, overripe (botrytized) berries. These are produced only in exceptional years, when conditions allow. See also *Qualitätswein mit Prädikat.*

Bleeding This term is used in winemaking as a translation of the French *saigné*. Bleeding is the process of removing some of the fermenting must (pulp, juice, and skins) in red wines partway through alcoholic fermentation to concentrate the remaining wine-to-be. Often this "bled" wine, pinkish in hue, is fermented dry and made into a rosé wine called *vin gris* (gray wine).

Body The weight and texture of the wine as it appears in the glass (the viscosity as you swirl it) and as it tastes and feels in your mouth. Body is directly related to the alcohol content of the wine and is described as ranging from light to full.

Botrytized Refers to grapes that have been affected by the "noble rot," *Botrytis cinerea,* which affects grapes in conditions of alternating warm and wet weather. It attacks the grapes and dehydrates them without spoiling the natural balance of the fruit, thus intensifying flavor.

Bouquet The spectrum of scents associated with a wine as it ages and develops. Younger, fruity smells are often described as aroma rather than bouquet.

Clarity The absence of any debris in a wine. A clean-looking wine is a well-made wine, although the flavor may or may not be to your liking and the degree of clarity has no effect on wine and food pairings.

Clone A selected, isolated, heat-treated, and disease-free selection of a specific grape varietal which has gone through the rigorous cataloguing, segregation, and testing required to be deemed worthy of carrying a unique name or code. Char-

donnay clones, for example, include UC Davis 05, 06, and 07 and the French clones 124, 131, and 133. *Clone* is often used interchangeably with *selection* (see below), but they are not synonymous.

Cold soaking The macerating of the unfermented grape must (pulp, juice, and skins) before alcoholic fermentation to extract more fruit flavors and create deeper color. Chilling the must prevents fermentation, because yeasts are not active at lower temperatures; once the maceration period is over, the temperature is raised to allow fermentation to proceed. This process is most commonly used for Pinot Noir.

Color The hue of the wine as determined first by the grapes (red or white) and then by the beholder. One person's ruby is another's purple, so descriptors are highly subjective. Color gives some indication of age: red wines lighten as they mature, whereas white wines and rosés gain color.

Complexity The presence of multiple layers of flavor and aroma. The more tastes you can perceive in the wine or food, the more complex it is said to be. While complex wines can be fabulous with food, they are often best savored on their own, as their subtleties can be lost behind complicated recipes.

Cuvée The blending (or, in French, *assemblage*) of many wines, from different years, different varietals, or different vineyards.

Dryness A measure of the sweetness in a wine. Dryness is not the same as fruitiness, the level of fruit presence in a wine. Although ripe-fruit aromas may suggest sweetness, the wine may still be dry to the taste.

Earthiness Flavors suggesting the earth—dust, earth, mineral, slate, gravel, forest floor, humus, and even barnyard. Many wines, especially those from Western Europe, exhibit earthiness.

Eiswein Ice wine: that is, a wine made from grapes that are harvested and pressed while frozen. While the best of these are made from grapes naturally frozen by cold weather, they can be replicated by freezing grapes artificially and crushing them while frozen (a process called cryovacking). In Germany, *Eiswein* is of at least *Beerenauslese* intensity. See also *Qualitätswein mit Prädikat*.

Filtration The final step in producing most wines. Very fine, flavor-neutral cellulose filters are used. Filtration removes any bacteria that might spoil the wine as it ages. Contrary to the opinion of many, it does not remove flavor, as flavor molecules are so much smaller than bacteria that they pass easily through the filter.

Fining A process by which the wine is purified of small solids and particulates by the addition of a fining agent that attracts these particles, chemically binds with them, and can then be removed from the wine. Fining agents include gelatin, isinglass (a fish by-product), egg whites, bentonite (clay), and casein (a milk product). While the main purpose of fining is to clarify the wine, it also provides some stabilizing effects by eliminating any remaining active yeasts.

Finish Also referred to as *persistence* or *length*, this is a measure of how long the taste of the wine can be detected after you have swallowed it. The longer the finish, the better the wine—assuming you like the flavor!

Flabby A term for wine that has ample weight and not enough acidity or tartness to balance it. A dessert wine that doesn't have adequate sharpness to foil the sugar will be at once flabby and cloying.

Fruity The term for a wine that is abundant in its suggestion of fruit flavors other than grape. A Chardonnay may suggest citrus or tropical fruit flavors in its aroma. A Zinfandel may exhibit a strong aroma of blackberries or black raspberries. The younger the wine, the fruitier it's likely to be. *Fruity* is not synonymous with *sweet*.

Grassy An all-encompassing term for many of the "green" flavors associated with wine. It may refer to the varietal character of a Sauvignon Blanc or the underripe nature of a Chardonnay or even a Merlot.

Kabinett A category of German wines encompassing light wines (between 7 and 11 percent alcohol), made from fully ripe grapes and geared toward easy drinking with meals. *Kabinett*s range between dry and off-dry. See also *Qualitätswein mit Prädikat*.

Late harvest(ed) A term for wine made from grapes picked late in the year and at higher levels of sugar, so that they are left with some residual sugar after fermentation. Most such wines are dessert wines.

Lees The spent (dead) yeast residues that fall to the bottom of the fermentation vessel once alcoholic fermentation has been completed and all the sugar from the grapes metabolized. In making white wines, these lees are often stirred back into the wine to add additional flavor and texture. Lees stirring (also called *batonnage*) is most commonly associated with Chardonnay.

Legs The rivulets of wine that run down the sides of the glass when the wine is swirled. Also referred to as *tears*. In general, the slower the tearing, the higher the alcohol (or sugar) content.

Length See *Finish*.

Malolactic fermentation Often referred to by the abbreviation ML, this process can be controlled to transform some percentage of the sharp malic acid (such as that found in green apples) to a softer lactic acid (such as that in yogurt or sour cream). Additionally, a by-product called diacetyl is released that adds a strong buttery or buttered-popcorn flavor. ML decreases the perception of tartness in a wine, adds a rounder, softer texture, and can make it more microbially stable.

Must The combination of grape juice, pulp, and skins that is ultimately fermented into wine. In making white wines, the skins, if present in the must at all, are removed after a short period of macerating with the pulp and juice.

Oak The wood of choice for the production of wine barrels. The age and size of the oak barrels affects the wine: younger oak expresses itself much more than older, previously used oak. Using larger oak barrels, which results in a smaller surface area of wine in contact with the wood, results in less oak flavor. Too much oak on a wine makes it both unbalanced and harder to match with food.

Off-dry A term for wines that have some sweetness but are not as sweet as dessert wines; more commonly used among wine professionals than *semi-sweet*.

Overcropping The practice of allowing too much fruit to ripen on a vine. Although it increases yield, it dilutes the fruit's flavors. Removing some of the fruit during the growing season, a practice called *green harvesting,* results in greater flavor concentration in the remaining grapes.

Oxidation (1) The process by which wines ultimately age and lose character and flavor. As a wine develops, it oxidizes (or maderizes) as minute amounts of oxygen in the bottle are incorporated into the wine and react with the chemical compounds in it. (2) The natural incorporation of air into wine as it sits in the glass, which makes the aromas and flavors more apparent. (3) In winemaking, the natural process of oxygen coming into contact with the wine in the tank or barrel.

Qualitätswein mit Prädikat A term from the German wine law meaning "quality wines with attributes." The terms for these attributes, used to designate different categories of wines, represent increasing levels of ripeness: *Kabinett, Spätlese, Auslese, Beerenauslese* (BA), and *Trockenbeerenauslese* (TBA). See the individual glossary entries for these.

Recioto An Italian term that originally referred to the "ears," or the fattest and ripest clusters of grapes on a vine. Today the term has come to mean a selection of high-quality fruit that has been made into dried-grape wines that are usually, though not always, sweet.

Reserve A term frequently understood to imply high quality but which, in the United States, has no legal meaning. At its best, it refers to wines that are produced from the finest lots and the best vineyard plots and treated with extra care, resulting in superb wines. At its worst, it's co-opted by disingenuous wineries who prey on the consumer's thinking that *reserve* must mean better. The European terms *reserva* (Spanish) and *riserva* (Italian) are, however, legally binding and have to do with aging requirements in the barrel and bottle.

Residual sugar The amount of sugar that is left in a wine after alcoholic fermentation is completed.

Selection A cutting from an existing vine selected for propagation in new or other vineyards to produce varietal fruit with the desired character. The term *selection* is often used interchangeably with *clone* (see above), but they are not synonymous.

Semi-sweet See *Off-dry*.

Skin contact The process of fermenting grapes in the presence of their skins. In red wines this is critical, for all of the flavor, color, and tannins are in the skins themselves. The juice may also be left in contact with the skins either before or after alcoholic fermentation.

Soft A term suggesting an approachable wine. In the positive sense, *soft* suggests a gentle elegance that can match splendidly with food. In the negative sense, it implies that the wine is lacking in character and apt to be easily dominated by a dish.

Spätlese (*schpate*-lay-zeh) Literally "late harvest," the German term for a category of wines that are intense in flavor and concentration and are slightly sweeter and richer than most *Kabinetts*. See also *Qualitätswein mit Prädikat*.

Spiciness The suggestion of spice aromas in a wine. They can be inherent to the grape type (as pepper is to Syrah and cardamom to Gewürztraminer), but more often they come from extended oak aging. Sweet spices (such as cinnamon, nutmeg, clove, and allspice) are easily detected in many oak-aged wines.

Structure The overall sense of weight and tactile sensation; a direct function of the levels of alcohol, tannin, acidity, and other essential characteristics of the wine.

Super Tuscan A popular term for wines made in Italy's Tuscany region that are proprietary blends of the local Sangiovese and other grapes, mainly Cabernet Sauvignon and Merlot, aged in small French oak barrels. The resulting combination can produce world-class red wines. Many Cabernet-based blends, some of them almost 100 percent Cabernet, now dominate this category.

Sweetness Quite literally, the amount of sugar perceived. In the case of wines, sugar can range from nonexistent or not perceptible (as in dry wines) to slightly sweet (off-dry or semi-sweet) to very sweet (as in dessert wines).

Tannins Naturally occurring compounds in wine which are extracted from the skins, stems, and seeds of the grapes. Although tannins are most often associated with red wines, which ferment on their skins and extract tannins as well as color and flavor, white wines can be tannic if fermented in contact with the grape skins. Wines that spend time in oak may also pick up tannins from the barrels. Tannins enable a wine to age well (in the case

of reds) and must be taken into account in wine and food matching.

Taste The perception in the mouth of the basic components of a food or wine. Basic components of flavor—salt, sweet, tart, and bitter—can be measured; the aromas and bouquet suggested by olfactory perception cannot.

Thin A term applied to both foods and wines that lack some aspect of character or flavor. A thin wine may come off as dilute or simply vapid. Thin (light, uninteresting) foods can be very difficult to match with wine because they are so easily dominated.

***Trockenbeerenauslese* (TBA)** (*troh*-ken-bare-en-*aus*-lay-zeh) Literally "select picking of dried berries," the German category of rare wines produced from individually selected, botrytized berries which are overripe and shriveled on the vine almost to raisins. See also *Qualitätswein mit Prädikat*.

Varietal The fancy term for a type of grape; also used to designate types of wine. Zinfandel and Chardonnay are both varietals. When a wine tastes very much of the specific grape it is made from, it is said to exhibit strong varietal character. Whereas many American wines are labeled according to varietal, most European wines are labeled according to geographic region of origin.

Vintage The year that the grapes were harvested and the resultant wine made, a significant determinant of flavor and quality. Vintages vary around the globe: a good year in California may not equate to a good year in Bordeaux. *Vintage* can also be used to describe the actual grape harvest. Wines labeled as vintage must contain at least 95 percent wine from the stated year.

RECOMMENDED READING

LEARNING MORE ABOUT WINE

Clarke, Oz. *Sainsbury's Encyclopedia of Wine: An A–Z Guide to Wines of the World*. London: Webster's Wine Price Guide, 1993.

Johnson, Hugh, and Jancis Robinson. *The World Atlas of Wine*. 5th ed. London: Mitchell Beazley, 2001.

Julyan, Bryan. *Sales and Service for the Wine Professional*. 2nd ed. New York: Continuum, 2003.

MacNeil, Karen. *The Wine Bible*. New York: Workman, 2001.

Robinson, Jancis, ed. *The Oxford Companion to Wine*. New York: Oxford University Press, 1994.

Stevenson, Tom. *The Sotheby's Wine Encyclopedia*: *The Classic Reference to the Wines of the World*. 4th ed. New York: DK, 2005.

Wine Spectator Online. www.winespectator.com.

Zraly, Kevin. *Windows on the World Complete Wine Course, 2006 Edition*. New York: Sterling, 2006.

PAIRING WINE AND FOOD

Goldstein, Sid. *The Wine Lover's Cookbook: Great Recipes for the Perfect Glass of Wine*. San Francisco: Chronicle Books, 1999.

Immer, Andrea. *Great Tastes Made Simple: Extraordinary Food and Wine Pairing for Every Palate*. New York: Broadway Books, 2002.

Rosengarten, David, and Joshua Wesson. *Red Wine with Fish: The New Art of Matching Wine with Food*. New York: Simon & Schuster, 1989.

GENERAL INDEX

Names of wine producers are flagged with an asterisk.
Page numbers in italics refer to tables and boxed text.

dosage, 37, 224–25, 226–27
Douro, 223, *288*
Douro Superior, *288*
Dow's*, *246*
Dr. Bürklin-Wolf*, *88, 242*
Dr. H. Thanisch*, *90*
Dr. Konstantin Frank*, *92*
Dr. Loosen*, *90*
Dr. Pauly-Bergweiler*, *90*
dryness, defined, *290*
duck, pairing with, 82, 83, 109, 110,
    122, 138, 167
    See also holiday foods
Duckhorn*, *161*
Durbanville, 108, 173
Dureza grape, 190
Duriff grape, 191

E
E. Guigal*, *131, 196*
E & M Tement*, *77*
earthiness (*terroir*), 7–8, *290*
Eberle*, *202*
Echéeaux, 162
Echelon*, *129*
Eden Valley
    Cabernet Sauvignon, *277*
    Chardonnay, *267*
    Riesling, 81, *271*
    Syrah, *198, 284*
    Viognier, 120
Edmeades*, *215*
Edna Valley*, *175*
egg dishes, pairing with, 39, 83, 109
eggplant, pairing with, 26, 69, 138,
    139, 151, 161, 193
Eiswein (ice wine), 80, 81, 223, 225,
    230, *287, 290*–91
Elgin, 67, *269*
Elk Cove*, *175*
Emilia-Romagna, *282, 287*
Emmenthaler, pairing with, 56, 96
endive, pairing with, 18, 26, 139
en tirage (on its yeast), 37
Entre-Deux-Mers
    Cabernet Sauvignon, *275*
    Merlot, *278*
    Sauvignon Blanc, 66, *268*
Eroica*, *92*

escarole, pairing with, 73, 138,
    139
Estancia*, *143, 173*
Etude*, *175*
Evans & Tate*, *65*

F
Fairview*, *129*
Falesco*, *186*
Fattoria del Felsina*, *189*
Fattoria le Pupille*, *184*
Felton Road*, *169*
fennel, pairing with, 77, 112, 151,
    167, 179
fermentation. *See* barrel fermenta-
    tion; malolactic fermentation;
    secondary fermentation
Ferrari*, *45*
Ferrari-Carano*, *79, 186*
feta, pairing with, 22, 39, 69
filtration
    of Cabernet Sauvignon, 137
    defined, *291*
    of late-harvest wines, 221
    of Pinot Noir, 164
    of sparkling wine, 34
Finger Lakes
    dessert wines, *286*
    Gewürztraminer, *273*
    Riesling, 81, 92, *270*
    sparkling wines, *263*
fining process, 137, 164, *291*
finish, 9, 34, *291*
Firesteed*, *102, 169*
fish and shellfish, pairing with
    milder fish, 54
    oily or strong, 15, 38
    raw, 38, 39, 83, 96
    smoked, 63, 83
    stew, 106, 193
    with tomato-based sauces, 179
    See also individual fish and shellfish
flabby, defined, *291*
flavors
    from barrel fermentation, 19, 52–
        53, 68
    contrasted with taste, 14, 15
    from cooking methods, 21, 23
    from cooking with wine, 24–25

from marinating and macerating,
    25
    See also oaky flavor
Fleur du Cap*, *156*
Foley*, *173*
Fonseca*, *246*
Fontanafredda*, *47*
Fonterutoli*, *186*
Fontodi*, *182*
Forefathers*, *145*
Foris*, *98, 112*
fortified wines
    alcohol content, 223
    flavors, 227
    origins, 223
    pairing with, 228–29, 230, 231, 234
    production decisions, 226
    recommended producers, *234*
    styles, 224
    wine-growing regions, *288*
Fortius*, *184*
fowl, pairing with, 54, 82, 83, 109,
    110, 138, 166, 193
Franciacorta, 33, 35, 163, *264, 280*
Franciscan*, *154*
François Cotat*, *79*
Franken, *270*
Franschhoek, *264*
Franz Künstler*, *88*
Frescobaldi*, *182*
fritto misto, pairing with, 39
Friuli-Venezia Giulia
    Cabernet Sauvignon, *276*
    Chardonnay, 51, *266*
    late-harvest wines, *222*
    Merlot, *156, 278*
    Pinot Gris, 93, *100, 106, 272*
    Prosecco, 33, 35
    Riesling, *270*
    Sauvignon Blanc, *268*
Frog's Leap*, *77*
Frontignan, 224, *288*
fruit, pairing with
    citrus, 228, 229, 236, 239
    dried, 17, 26, 114, 122, 131, 230
    tart-flavored, 38, 179, 200
    tropical, 47, 83, 110, 228, 229
    See also individual fruits
fruity aroma, 7, *291*

Malmsey, 224, 229, *288*
malolactic fermentation (ML), 53,
    54, 94, 109, 120, 291
Malvasia, 222, *287*, *288*
Manduria, *285*, *288*
mangos, pairing with, 17, 47, 244
Marcel Deiss*, *86*, *98*
Marche, *282*
Margaret River
    Cabernet Sauvignon, 277
    Chardonnay, 51, *61*, *65*, *267*
    Merlot, *279*
    Syrah, *284*
    Zinfandel, *285*
marinades, pairing with, 83, 151
    See also sauces; *individual flavor*
        ingredients
Markham*, *79*, *154*
Marlborough
    Chardonnay, *267*
    dessert wines, 244, *287*
    Gewürztraminer, *114*, *273*
    Pinot Noir, 163, *169*, *281*
    Riesling, 81, *92*, *271*
    Sauvignon Blanc, 67, 77, *269*
    sparkling wines, *41*, *264*
    Syrah, *284*
    Viognier, *274*
Marsala, 224, 226, *288*
Martinelli*, *215*
Martine's Wines*, *129*
Mason*, *73*
Maule Valley, 135, *276*, *279*
Maury, *288*
Mauzac grape, *35*
Mayacamas*, *65*
McDowell*, *202*
McLaren Vale
    Cabernet Sauvignon, 277
    Chardonnay, *267*
    Merlot, *279*
    Syrah, 191, 200, *284*
meat. *See* beef; lamb; pork; veal
Médoc
    Cabernet Sauvignon, 134, *275*
    Merlot, 148, *278*
    Sauvignon Blanc, *268*
Mendocino County
    Chardonnay, 51, *265*

Gewürztraminer, 108, *112*, *273*
Pinot Gris, *272*
Pinot Noir, 163–64, *169*, *280*
Riesling, 81, *88*, *270*
Sauvignon Blanc, 67, *79*, *268*
sparkling wines, *41*, *263*
Syrah, *283*
Viognier, *274*
Zinfandel, 205, *215*, *285*
Mendoza
    Cabernet Sauvignon, 135, *145*,
        276
    Chardonnay, 52, *61*, *266*
    Merlot, 149, *156*, *279*
    Riesling, *271*
    Sangiovese, 177, *189*, *282*
    Syrah, 191, 200, *284*
    Viognier, *127*
menus, 248–49
Méo-Camuzet*, *171*
Meredith, Carole, 190, 203
Meridian*, *118*, *175*
Merlot
    bridge ingredients to, 22
    flavors, 150
    grape, in Sangiovese blends, 179
    origins, 148
    pairing with, 20, 151–52, 154, 156,
        158, 161
    recommended producers, *154*, *156*,
        158, *161*
    serving temperature, 10–11
    styles, 150
    wine-growing regions, 148–49,
        278–79
Merryvale*, *79*
méthode champenoise, 32, 34, 35, 37
méthode traditionnelle, 33, 34, 35
methoxypyrozines, 66
Michaud*, *65*
Michel Chapoutier*, *202*
    See also Chapoutier
Michele Chiarlo*, *47*
Michel Lynch*, *75*
Michigan
    dessert wines, 223, *286*
    Riesling, 81, *270*
    sparkling wines, *263*
micro-oxygenation, 137, 150

Middle Eastern cuisine, pairing
    with, 39, 69, 169
Miguel Torres*, *161*
Miner Family*, *63*, *143*
mint, pairing with, 14, 75, 100
Mionetto*, *45*
Mitchelton*, *147*
Mittelrhein, *264*
ML (malolactic fermentation), 53,
    54, 94, 109, 120, 291
Möet et Chandon*, 36, *47*
Moldova, 67, 149
Monbazillac, *286*
Mondeuse Blanche grape, 190
Monmousseau*, *43*
Monsanto*, *182*
Montagne de Reims, *263*, *280*
Montalcino, 176–77, 179, *282*
Monte Antico*, *182*
Montepulciano, 176–77, *282*
Montravel, *268*
Morgan*, *175*
Mornington Peninsula, *281*
Moroccan cuisine, pairing with,
    101, 121, 131, 196
Moscato d'Asti, 25, 33, 225, 227
Moscato grape
    in fortified wine, *288*
    in late-harvest wine, 222, *286*
Mosel-Saar-Ruwer, 80, *88*, *90*, *270*,
    287
Mossel Bay, 163, *269*, *281*
Mount Barker, 277
Mourvedre grape, 5
mouthfeel, 9, 53, 137
mozzarella, pairing with, 16, 45, 70,
    95, 138
Mudgee, 277, *284*
Mulderbosch*, *73*
Müller-Thurgau grape, *35*
Mumm Napa*, *41*, 47, *239*
Muré*, *116*
Murrumbidgee Irrigation Area, *287*
Muscadelle de Bordelais grape, *35*
Muscadelle grape, 66, 221, *286*
Muscat de Lunel, 224
Muscat grape
    in late-harvest wine, 221–22, 223,
        287

Muscat grape *(continued)*
   pairing with late-harvest styles,
      228, 229, 230
   in sparkling wine, 33, 35, 225
   in VDN *(vin doux naturel)*, 224,
      226, 231, 288
Muscat of Alexandria grape, 288
mushrooms, pairing with, 55, 151, 212
   bridge effects of, 22
   wild or dark, 138, 139, 167, 180, 186
mussels, pairing with, 55, 96, 188
must, 52, 291–92
mustard, pairing with, 141, 169, 192

N
Nahe, 270
Napa Valley
   Cabernet Sauvignon, 134, 135, *143,
      145, 147*, 275
   Chardonnay, 51, *59, 61, 63, 65*, 265
   dessert wines, 239, 242, 244
   Gewürztraminer, 273
   Merlot, 149, *154, 161*, 278
   Pinot Gris, 106, 272
   Pinot Noir, 163, 169, 175, 280
   Riesling, 92, 270
   Sangiovese, 177, *182, 184*, 282
   Sauvignon Blanc, 67, *73, 75, 77, 79*,
      268
   sparkling wines, 41, 47, 263
   Syrah, 202, 283
   Viognier, 125, 274
   Zinfandel, 204, *205*, 210, *213, 215,
      217*, 285
Navarra, 51, 135, 266, 269
Navarro*, 88, 112*, 169
nectarines, 228, 230
Neil Ellis*, 73
Nerello Mascalese grape, 288
Nero d'Avola grape, 288
Neuchâtel, 281
New Mexico, 35, 263
New South Wales
   Cabernet Sauvignon, 277
   Chardonnay, 267
   dessert wines, 287
   Sauvignon Blanc, 269
   Syrah, *284*
Newton*, 125

New York State
   Cabernet Sauvignon, 136, 275
   Chardonnay, 265
   dessert wines, 223, 286
   Gewürztraminer, 273
   Merlot, 149, 278
   Riesling, 81, 92, 270
   sparkling wines, 35, 263
Niagara, 81, *271*, 287
Niepoort*, 234
noodles. *See* pasta
North African cuisine, pairing with,
      26, 71, 131, 196, 207
North-Central (Spain), 266, 269
Northern Central Coast (California)
   Cabernet Sauvignon, *145*, 275
   Chardonnay, 63, 65, 265
   Gewürztraminer, *112*
   late-harvest wines, 244
   Merlot, 149, 278
   Pinot Gris, 272
   Pinot Noir, 164, *175*, 280
   Riesling, 270
   Syrah, 283
   Viognier, 127, *129*, 274
   Zinfandel, 204, *213*, 285
Northern Central Valley (Califor-
      nia), 285
North Island (New Zealand)
   Cabernet Sauvignon, 277
   Chardonnay, 267
   dessert wines, 287
   Gewürztraminer, 273
   Merlot, 279
   Pinot Noir, 163, *281*
   Sauvignon Blanc, 269
   Syrah, *284*
   Viognier, 274
Northstar*, 158
Nuevo Latino cuisine, pairing with,
      26, 54, 83
nuts, pairing with, 38, 55, 69, 79
   almonds, 22, 234
   bridge effects of, 22
   cashews, 55, 121
   in desserts, 207, 229, 230, 234
   hazelnuts, 234
   macadamia, 55, 121
   pine, 114, 116

   raw, 54
   toasted or roasted, 139
   walnuts, 22, 79, 98, 234

O
oak barrels. *See* barrel fermentation; barrels
Oak Knoll*, 102
oaky flavor
   from barrel fermentation, 52–53,
      68
   bridge ingredients to, 22
   food-pairing guidelines, 19–20,
      26, 138
   from inner staving, 136
   in wine used for cooking, 25
off-dry wines
   cooking with, 25
   defined, 292
   Gewürztraminer, 107, 108,
      109–10, *114*
   pairing with, 5, 15, 17, 18, 26, 27
   Pinot Gris, 94
   Riesling, 80, 82–83, 90, 92
   serving temperature, 5
   sparkling wines, 47
   style and *dosage*, 37
   Viognier, 121
Okanagan Valley
   Chardonnay, 52, 267
   Gewürztraminer, 273
   Pinot Gris, 94, 272
   Pinot Noir, 164
   Riesling, 81, *271*
Old Mission Peninsula, 81, 270, 286
olives, pairing with, 69, 70, 151, 154,
      156, 184
   bridge effects of, 22
   oloroso sherry, 224
onions, pairing with, 55, 151
   bridge effects of, 22
   caramelized, 63, 86, 116
Ontario
   dessert wines, 223, 244, 287
   Riesling, 81, *271*
Orange County, 274
oranges, pairing with, 25, 118, 127,
      169, 184
   in desserts, 83, 228, 230, 236

RECIPE INDEX